NVQ INTERMEDIATE
LEVEL 3 DIPLOMA FOR
ACCOUNTING TECHNICIANS (QCF)

COURSE **COMPANION** Unit 5

Maintaining Financial Records and Preparing Accounts

Ninth edition May 2009
First edition 2001

ISBN 9780 7517 6701 8 (previous edition 9780 7517 4623 5)

British Library Cataloguing-in-Publication Data
A catalogue record for this book is available from the British Library

Published by

BPP Learning Media Ltd
BPP House
Aldine Place
London
W12 8AA

www.bpp.com/learningmedia

Printed in the United Kingdom

Your learning materials, published by BPP Learning Media Ltd, are printed on paper sourced from sustainable, managed forests.

CONTENTS

INTRODUCTION

BPP Learning Media's highly popular Companions range of AAT materials is ideal for students who like to get to grips with the essentials and study on the move.

The range comprises:

- **Course Companions**, covering all the knowledge and understanding and performance criteria specified by the Standards of Competence and needed by students, with numerous illustrations, practical examples and activities for students to use to consolidate their learning.

- **Revision Companions**, ideal for classroom courses, which contain an additional range of graded activities for each chapter of the Course Companion, plus specially written practice assessments and answers for the Unit, the AAT's own specimen assessment and the assessment set in December 2008. Full answers to all activities and assessments, prepared by BPP Learning Media Ltd, are included.

- **Tutor Companions**, providing a further bank of questions, answers and practice assessments for classroom use, available separately only to lecturers whose colleges adopt the Companions for the relevant Unit.

This Course Companion for Unit 5, Maintaining Financial Records and Accounts, has been written specifically to ensure comprehensive yet concise coverage of the Standards of Competence and performance criteria. It is fully up to date as at May 2009 and reflects both the Revised Standards of Competence and the exams set so far.

Each chapter contains:

- clear, step by step explanation of the topic
- logical progression and linking from one chapter to the next
- numerous illustrations and practical examples
- interactive activities within the text of the chapter itself, with answers at the back of the book
- a bank of questions of varying complexity, again with answers supplied at the back of the book

The emphasis in all activities and questions is on the practical application of the skills acquired.

If you have any comments about this book, please e-mail helendarch@bpp.com or write to Helen Darch, AAT Range Manager, BPP Learning Media Ltd, BPP House, Aldine Place, London W12 8AA.

VAT

You will find examples and questions throughout this companion which need you to calculate or be aware of a rate of VAT. This is stated at 17½% in these examples and questions. Please use this rate when you are tackling these questions and not the temporary rate of 15% that applies at present.

Diploma Pathway

This Course Companion is the ideal learning aid for Unit 5, directly relevant to both the NVQ and AAT Diploma Pathway.

UNIT 5 STANDARDS OF COMPETENCE

Introduction

This document should be read in conjunction with the 2003 standards for the unit.

This unit relates to the maintenance of accounts from the preparation of an initial trial balance through to the production of a set of final accounts. The unit requires students to extract and manipulate information to prepare trial balances, extended trial balances, profit and loss accounts and balance sheets of sole traders and partnerships. As part of the processes, it may be necessary to make adjustments and corrections to information and carry out reconciliations to ensure accuracy in the maintenance of the records. The knowledge and understanding refers to restructuring accounts from incomplete evidence, and this will be used in the exam as a means of testing a number of the performance criteria.

At all stages, it is necessary to follow the organisation's policies and procedures and to ensure that discrepancies, unusual features or queries are identified and either resolved or referred to the appropriate person. Communicating in an appropriate and understandable manner, whilst at the same time maintaining confidentiality, is essential in carrying out tasks, handling queries and making suggestions for improvement in the record keeping of the organisation.

Terminology

Throughout the unit, ledgers will be referred to as main ledger, sales ledger and purchases ledger. This is consistent with the Level 2 standards. Candidates will be expected to understand these terms.

'Profit and loss account' should be taken to read 'Trading and Profit and Loss Account' where appropriate.

The International Accounting Standards (IAS) will not be tested in this unit but candidates will not be penalised for referring to them or using IAS terminology.

Guidance on knowledge and understanding

All three elements contain the following under the heading of knowledge and understanding.

SSAPs and FRSs

SSAP 5

Students should have a knowledge and understanding of the treatment of VAT within an accounting system. Their knowledge and understanding should include in particular the following:

- the nature of VAT input tax and output tax and how to account for them
- how the balance on the VAT control account in the main ledger is generated and what it means.

SSAP 9

Students should have knowledge and understanding of how SSAP 9 affects the valuation of stock for the final accounts of a business. They should expect to be assessed on:

- the principle of valuation of stock - lower of cost and net realisable value
- how to calculate net realisable value
- methods of stock valuation that is LIFO, FIFO and average cost.

SSAP 13 and SSAP 21 is no longer assessed.

FRS 15

Candidates should have knowledge and understanding of the term depreciation as set out in FRS 15. They should be able to apply their knowledge and understanding by doing the following:

- explaining the purpose of depreciation and how it is an application of the accruals concept
- calculating depreciation using the straight line method and explaining why a particular accounting policy might be adopted, including an explanation of the factors, which affect depreciation
- explaining under what circumstances depreciation rates and/or methods can be changed.

The statement of principles and FRS 18

Students should be able to apply the concepts of going concern and accruals (FRS 18), and show understanding of the objectives used in selecting accounting policies - relevance, reliability, comparability and understandability, as defined in the statement of principles. They should understand and be able to explain that if information is not material, then it cannot be useful or have any of the four qualitative characteristics. They should understand and be able to briefly and simply explain theoretical basis for accounting adjustments such as doubtful debt provision, depreciation provision, accruals and prepayments. This could be tested by practical application in a numeric task or by requiring the student to explain its application in a written task. It is very likely that a written explanation will be linked to a preceding practical task, and students who understand and use that link will be more successful in demonstrating their competence in the examination. This tests both the underpinning knowledge and understanding and communication skills.

The importance of maintaining the confidentiality of business transactions

Students should understand the need for care when communicating on business matters. They should appreciate the need to consider at all times the confidentiality of the data and the appropriate level of information to which employees or external agents should have access.

Principles of double entry accounting

Although many of the principles of double entry are assessed at the Foundation Level, students need to appreciate that a sound knowledge and understanding of all the principles underpin a substantial number of the performance criteria at Intermediate Level. Students must expect to be assessed on double entry in both skills tests and examinations. This aspect of the unit is particularly important for students who have not taken the Foundation Level but will be expected to be familiar with all double entry principles.

The way the accounting systems of an organisation are affected by its organisational structure, its administrative systems, procedures and the nature of its business transactions. Students need to appreciate that accounting systems are not exactly the same in all organisations. For example, differences will exist between a retail organisation and a service organisation. This unit will examine differences in accounting systems from one type of organisation to another by presenting students with different scenarios within and between exams and skills tests.

Unit 5: Maintaining financial records and preparing accounts

Guidance on element 5.1 – maintaining records relating to capital acquisition and disposal

The following notes are intended to provide clarification, where this is likely to be required, and should be read in conjunction with the performance criteria, range statement, and knowledge and understanding.

Element 5.1 is concerned with maintaining records relating to capital acquisition and disposal. The range statement refers to:

- asset registers
- books of original entry
- ledgers.

Whenever an asset is purchased, sold, scrapped or otherwise disposed of, authorisation should take place and the correct amounts involved should be identified and entered into the records together with appropriate details of the asset.

In order that a purchase can take place, appropriate funding is required. Students require a knowledge and understanding of methods of funding, which should include:

- borrowing
- part exchange.

Having created fixed asset registers, it becomes necessary to set up and maintain systems of control.

These should include:

- reconciliations with actual fixed assets
- reconciliations with the main ledger.

Depreciation features prominently within the standards and will always be tested in the exam. Students should be able to explain the purpose of depreciation (see FRS 15 above) as well as be in a position to make:

- calculations using straight line and reducing balance methods
- calculations for depreciation for assets acquired or disposed of during the accounting period in accordance with the policies of the organisation
- entries into provision for depreciation account, asset register, asset disposals account and profit and loss calculations.

When a fixed asset is disposed of, students should be able to calculate depreciation to the date of disposal of an asset, transfer the necessary amounts into an asset disposal account and calculate the final profit or loss on disposal.

Additionally students should appreciate:

- the distinction between capital and revenue expenditure and the implications of that distinction

- the differences between fixed assets and current assets, and tangible assets and intangible fixed assets (namely, goodwill).

In the exam, element 5.1 will be assessed as an integral part of the section 1 or the section 2 scenario.

Guidance on element 5.2 – collecting and collating information for the preparation of final accounts

The following notes are intended to provide clarification, where this is likely to be required, and should be read in conjunction with the performance criteria, range statement, and knowledge and understanding.

Element 5.2 is concerned with dealing with accounting information ready for the preparation of final accounts from a trial balance or extended trial balance. This includes ensuring that information is accurate and complete by the use of checks and controls.

Reconciliations

Students must be able to reconcile lists of balances from the subsidiary ledgers to the control accounts in the main ledger (sales ledger, purchases ledger and stock). They must also be able to explain why the differences might have occurred, correct the discrepancies and explain the purpose and importance of the reconciliations. Examples of differences that might arise:

- errors in either the subsidiary or the main ledger
- timing differences, for example goods in transit
- errors in period end cut off, for example stock included in valuation but subsequently dispatched and the sale included in the ledger.

Having established any differences, students should be able to correct them by use of the journal, or refer them to the appropriate person.

When they make journal entries, students will not usually be required to provide dates and narratives. If they are required to do so, this instruction will be given in the exam.

Trial Balance

Students should be:

- able to close off the revenue accounts in the ledger
- able to accurately prepare a trial balance either from a list of balances or from ledger accounts
- able to accurately prepare a trial balance from incomplete records
- aware of the types of errors detected and not detected by the trial balance
- able to open a suspense account and take the appropriate action to clear it by use of the journal if the trial balance does not balance.

Adjustments

Students should be able to make adjustments to the trial balance in accordance with the organisation's policies and procedures. Examples of adjustments required:

- depreciation
- writing off bad debts
- adjustment to doubtful debt provision or the creation of a doubtful debt provision
- adjustment to stock valuation by applying principles of SSAP 9 (see above)
- accruals and prepayments
- correction of errors.

These adjustments will often be made by use of the journal. The student may be asked to transfer these to the extended trial balance. The list of adjustments might include the correction of errors required to clear the suspense account. It might also include items that do not affect the suspense account, and students must be able to distinguish between these.

Students need to be able to explain their reasons for making adjustments by reference to the underpinning accounting legislation and regulations.

Care should be taken by students when identifying specific accounts. For example, labelling the sales ledger account and purchases ledger account "debtors" and "creditors" will not be acceptable. Systems used may also refer to day books, and students should be familiar with the purpose and use of these as books of original entry.

Students should be in a position to make appropriate entries in the accounting system of a particular organisation in accordance with that organisation's policies and procedures. For example, if the task states that insurance costs are charged to general expenses, then the general expenses account should be used to make the required adjustment. The student should not open a new insurance account. Organisations will take the form of sole traders or partnerships.

Partnerships

Students will need to understand the use of the capital and current accounts and be able to explain what each represents. They will be expected to make the following entries and adjustments:

- appropriation of profit, including salaries, interest on capital accounts and share of profit or loss
- drawings
- admission of a new partner to an existing partnership with capital injection in the form of cash paid to bank
- introduction of goodwill
- subsequent elimination of goodwill
- retirement of a partner, with settlement in the form of cash or loan
- change in profit share during the period.

Students will be expected to deal with partnerships with up to three partners. The details of the partnership agreement, in as far as they are needed in the examination, will be provided as part of the data for the tasks. Therefore, the default provisions of the Partnership Act 1890 will not need to be recalled by the students.

They will not be expected to deal with:

- more than three partners
- admission and retirement of partners in one scenario
- revaluation of fixed assets
- formation of a partnership from a sole trader
- dissolution of a partnership
- introduction of capital in any form other than cash paid to bank
- retirement of a partner with settlement in any form other than cash or loan
- Limited Liability Partnerships (LLP).

Restructuring accounts from incomplete evidence

Included under the knowledge and understanding for elements 5.2 and 5.3 is methods of restructuring accounts from incomplete evidence. In the exam, this will usually take the form of preparing control accounts and making calculations (for example mark up and margin) in a structured task that will lead the student through the logical process required. This process might follow with the production of a trial balance to test the accuracy of the balances produced and might further be followed with the production of final accounts. However, the task is unlikely to be identical, either in order or in process, to any previously set. Therefore students need to fully understand what they are doing, apply their knowledge to the new context, and not approach this area of the standards by rote learning previous exams.

Guidance on element 5.3 – preparing the final accounts of sole traders and partnerships

The following notes are intended to provide clarification, where this is likely to be required, and should be read in conjunction with the performance criteria, range statement, and knowledge and understanding.

Students should be able to prepare:

- trading and profit and loss accounts for sole traders and partnerships
- balance sheets for sole traders and partnerships
- partnership appropriation accounts (see element 5.2 for guidance on scope of partnership transactions).

Assessment strategy

For the National Vocational Qualification (NVQ) / Scottish Vocational Qualification (SVQ) Pathway, this unit is assessed by both skills test and exam.

For the Diploma Pathway, this unit is assessed by exam only.

Exam

Each exam will last for three hours (with an additional 15 minutes' reading time) and will be divided into two sections. The lengths of the two sections will not necessarily be equal (guidance on time allocation will be given) and the case studies on which they are based may be different.

Exams will contain practical tests linked to the performance criteria, and will focus on underpinning knowledge and understanding. Students should expect each exam to contain tasks taken from across a broad range of the standards.

Repetitive tasks will be avoided, as this is not an effective use of exam time. Therefore, double entry bookkeeping will not be tested by requiring students to write up all the ledger accounts of an organisation. Instead, students will be asked to complete a number of accounts. For example, the cash book, disposal account or purchases ledger account might be requested. This could be in section 1, section 2 or both. Double entry bookkeeping will also be tested by use of the journal. Students must know the difference between writing up an account and preparing a journal entry. Dates and narratives will not usually be required, in order to save time, but will probably be required in AAT simulations (see also reconciliations).

Either or both sections will contain a memo or letter style task. This will often be linked to a previous task where the student will be expected to justify an accounting entry or explain an adjustment.

The extensive use of computers in accounting is recognised, but in order to meet the requirements of the standards it will often be necessary to base the tasks on an organisation or organisations using manual systems of accounting. If a scenario using a computerised system is used, it will be based on an integrated system of ledgers, which could include an integrated stock ledger. Where records are kept, these will consist of a main ledger, where double entry takes place, a sales ledger and a purchases ledger. Students can assume (but will also be told) that the sales ledger control account and purchases ledger control account will be contained in the main ledger, forming part of the double entry. The individual accounts of debtors and creditors will be in the sales ledger and purchases ledger and will therefore be regarded as memoranda accounts.

Section 1

This section aims to cover the performance criteria, knowledge and understanding relating to element 5.2. Aspects of element 5.1 may be tested in either section. Therefore, this section will consist of a number of tasks concerned with the processing, restructuring and production of information for a sole trader or partnership, and the production of a trial balance to test the integrity and accuracy of their processes and calculations.

Sample tasks:

- produce information from data given and/or incomplete records for either a sole trader or a partnership
- provide brief explanations, calculations, accounting entries, or select from a number of given answers
- process, restructure and produce information, for example:
  - calculation of opening and/or closing capital
  - restructuring the cash and/or bank account
  - preparation of total sales ledger account and total sales ledger account to calculate, for example, sales and purchases
- use mark up and margin to calculate or check sales or purchases figures
- restructure ledger accounts, for example to calculate expenses paid accruals and prepayments, profit or loss on the sale of an asset
- draft journal entries
- produce a trial balance or extended trial balance from reconstructed accounts or information
- produce a memo, letter or notes in response to a client or supervisor.

Section 2

This section focuses on covering the performance criteria and knowledge and understanding relating to element 5.3, but aspects of element 5.2 may also be tested. Aspects of element 5.1 may be tested in either section. Therefore, this section will be concerned with taking the accounts from trial balance stage to final accounts.

Students will be given a trial balance or extended trial balance. They will then be expected to carry out tasks that lead to the production of final accounts. Adjustments may be required, and it might be appropriate for an extended trial balance to be produced or completed. Following this, students will be required to produce either the profit and loss account or the balance sheet, or both, in good form, including the correct headings. In the case of a partnership the appropriation account will be requested. The statement of recognised gains and losses will not be required.

Sample tasks:

- preparation of journal entries to clear the suspense account or make adjustments
- preparing capital accounts or journal entries for changes to partnerships (see guidance notes above)
- completion of the extended trial balance
- preparation of profit and loss account for sole trader or partnership, in good form
- preparation of appropriation account for partnerships
- preparation of current accounts for partnerships
- preparation of balance sheet for sole trader or partnership and in good form
- short questions, explanations, letters or memos concerning the underpinning knowledge relating to the tasks undertaken.

Skills test

AAT skills test will always be based on a partnership scenario. This is to ensure that all students are tested on the additional features relating to partnership accounts, which will not necessarily always be tested in the examination. As far as possible, AAT simulations will be structured in parts corresponding to separate elements for unit 5, and will be capable of being taken in two sittings.

Knowledge and understanding

To perform this unit effectively you will need to understand:

	The business environment:	**Chapter**
1	The types and characteristics of different assets and key issues relating to the acquisition and disposal of capital assets (Element 5.1)	5, 7
2	The relevant legislation and regulations (Elements 5.1, 5.2 & 5.3)	3, 5
3	The main requirements of relevant Statements of Standard Accounting Practice and Financial Reporting Standards (Elements 5.1, 5.2 & 5.3)	3, 4, 5, 6, 12
4	Legal requirements relating to the division of profits between partners (Element 5.3)	15
5	The methods of recording information for the organisational accounts of sole traders and partnerships (Elements 5.2 & 5.3)	2, 8, 9, 13, 14, 15
6	The structure of the organisational accounts of sole traders and partnerships (Elements 5.2 & 5.3)	1, 13, 14, 15
7	The need to present accounts in the correct form (Elements 5.2 & 5.3)	3, 13, 14, 15
8	The form of final accounts of sole traders and partnerships (Element 5.3)	3, 13, 14, 15
9	The importance of maintaining the confidentiality of business transactions (Elements 5.1, 5.2 & 5.3)	9, 13

Accounting techniques:		**Chapter**
10	Methods of depreciation and when to use each of them: straight line; reducing balance (Element 5.1)	6
11	The accounting treatment of capital items sold, scrapped or otherwise retired from service (Element 5.1)	7
12	How to use plant registers and similar subsidiary records (Element 5.1)	5, 6, 7
13	How to use the transfer journal (Elements 5.1 & 5.2)	5, 6, 11, 13, 15
14	The methods of funding: part exchange deals (Element 5.1)	7
15	The accounting treatment of accruals and prepayments (Elements 5.2 & 5.3)	8
16	The methods of analysing income and expenditure (Element 5.2)	8, 13, 15
17	The method of closing off revenue accounts (Element 5.2)	3
18	The methods of restructuring accounts from incomplete evidence (Elements 5.2 & 5.3)	16
19	How to identify and correct different types of error (Element 5.2)	10, 11
20	How to make and adjust provisions (Elements 5.2 & 5.3)	9
21	How to draft year end final accounts of sole traders and partnerships (Element 5.2)	13, 14, 15
Accounting principles and theory:		
22	Basic accounting concepts that play a role in the selection of accounting policies – accruals and going concern (Elements 5.1, 5.2 & 5.3)	3
23	The objectives and constraints in selecting accounting policies – relevance, reliability, comparability and ease of understanding, materiality (Elements 5.1, 5.2 & 5.3)	3
24	The principles of double entry accounting (Elements 5.1, 5.2 & 5.3)	2, 6, 8, 9, 10, 11, 16
25	The distinction between capital and revenue expenditure and what constitutes capital expenditure (Element 5.1)	5
26	The function and form of accounts for income and expenditure (Elements 5.1, 5.2 & 5.3)	2, 8
27	The function and form of a trial balance and an extended trial balance (Element 5.2)	2, 11, 13, 14, 15
28	The function and form of a profit and loss account and balance sheet for sole traders and partnerships (Element 5.3)	3, 13, 14, 15
29	The basic principles of stock valuation including those relating to cost or NRV and to what is included in cost (Elements 5.2 & 5.3)	12
30	The objectives of making provisions for depreciation and other purposes (Elements 5.2 & 5.3)	6, 9

The organisation:		**Chapter**
31	The ways the accounting systems of an organisation are affected by its organisational structure, its administrative systems and procedures and the nature of its business transactions (Elements 5.1, 5.2 & 5.3)	1

Element 5.1 Maintaining records relating to capital acquisition and disposal

Performance criteria

In order to perform this element successfully you will need to:		**Chapter**
A	record relevant details relating to capital expenditure in the appropriate records	5
B	ensure that the organisation's records agree with the physical presence of capital items	7
C	correctly identify and record all acquisition and disposal costs and revenues in the appropriate records	5, 7
D	correctly calculate and record depreciation charges and other necessary entries and adjustments in the appropriate records	6
E	ensure that the records clearly show the prior authority for capital expenditure and disposal and the approved method of funding and disposal	5, 7
F	correctly calculate and record the profit and loss on disposal in the appropriate records	7
G	ensure that the organisation's policies and procedures relating to the maintenance of capital records are adhered to	5, 6
H	identify and resolve or refer to the appropriate person any lack of agreement between physical items and records	7
I	make suggestions for improvements in the way the organisation maintains its capital records where possible to the appropriate person	7

Range statement

Performance in this element relates to the following contexts:

Records

- asset register
- books of original entry
- ledgers

Depreciation

- straight line
- reducing balance

Element 5.2 Collecting and collating information for the preparation of final accounts

Performance criteria		**Chapter**
In order to perform this element successfully you need to:		
A	correctly prepare **reconciliations** for the preparation of final accounts	10, 12
B	identify any discrepancies in the reconciliation process and either take steps to rectify them or refer them to the appropriate person	10, 12
C	accurately prepare a trial balance and open a suspense account to record any imbalance	11, 13, 14, 15
D	establish the **reasons** for any imbalance and clear the suspense account by correcting the errors, or reduce them and refer outstanding items to the appropriate person	11, 13, 14, 15
E	correctly identify, calculate and record appropriate **adjustments**	8, 9, 12, 13, 14, 15
F	make the relevant journal entries to close off the revenue accounts in preparation for the transfer of balances to the final accounts	13, 15
G	conduct investigations into business transactions with tact and courtesy	9
H	ensure that the organisation's policies, regulations, procedures and timescales relating to preparing final accounts are observed	13, 14, 15

Range statement

Performance in this element relates to the following contexts:

Reconciliations:

- purchase ledger reconciliation
- sales ledger reconciliation
- closing stock reconciliation

Adjustments:

- prepayments and accruals
- provisions for doubtful debts
- provisions for depreciation
- closing stock

Reasons for imbalance:

- incorrect double entries
- missing entries
- numerical inconsistencies and wrong calculations
- insufficient data and incomplete records have been provided
- inconsistencies within the data

Element 5.3 Preparing the final accounts of sole traders and partnerships

Performance criteria	**Chapter**
In order to perform this element successfully you need to:	
A prepare **final accounts of sole traders** in proper form, from the trial balance	13, 14
B prepare **final accounts of partnerships** in proper form and in compliance with the partnership agreement, from the trial balance	15
C observe the organisation's policies, regulations, procedures and timescales in relation to preparing final accounts of sole traders and partnerships	13, 14
D identify and resolve or refer to the appropriate person discrepancies, unusual features or queries	13, 14

Range statement

Performance in this element relates to the following contexts:

Final accounts of sole traders:

- profit and loss account
- balance sheet

Final accounts of partnerships:

- profit and loss account
- balance sheet
- partnership appropriation account
- partners' capital and current accounts

chapter 1: REVISION OF HOW ACCOUNTING SYSTEMS WORK

chapter coverage 

In this introductory chapter we will revise the way in which accounting systems operate before considering the details of double entry bookkeeping in the following chapter. This should all be fairly familiar if you have been through the AAT Foundation stage as it was covered in detail for Units 1, 2 and 3. However understanding the accounting system is so vital to the Unit 5 topics that it is worth revising. The topics that we shall cover are:

- the aims of an accounting system
- transactions of a business
- primary documents that record transactions
- primary records
- the main ledger and subsidiary ledgers
- the types of reconciliation that are carried out
- the trial balance and financial statements
- manual and computerised accounting systems

KNOWLEDGE AND UNDERSTANDING AND PERFORMANCE CRITERIA COVERAGE

knowledge and understanding

- the structure of the organisational accounts of sole traders and partnerships
- the ways the accounting systems of an organisation are affected by its organisational structure, its administrative systems and procedures and the nature of its business transactions

student notes

AIMS OF THE ACCOUNTING SYSTEM

The aims of any accounting system will be threefold:

- to ensure that all transactions are recorded in the accounting records
- to ensure that the transactions have been correctly recorded
- to gather together all the transactions for a period in order to prepare a set of financial statements

The details of the accounting systems of different organisations will differ depending upon the structure of the organisation, its administrative systems and the nature of its business. The detailed workings of the accounting system will also depend to some extent on the degree to which the accounting system is computerised (see later in the chapter).

However all accounting systems will have the following general elements which will each be considered in turn below.

THE ACCOUNTING SYSTEM

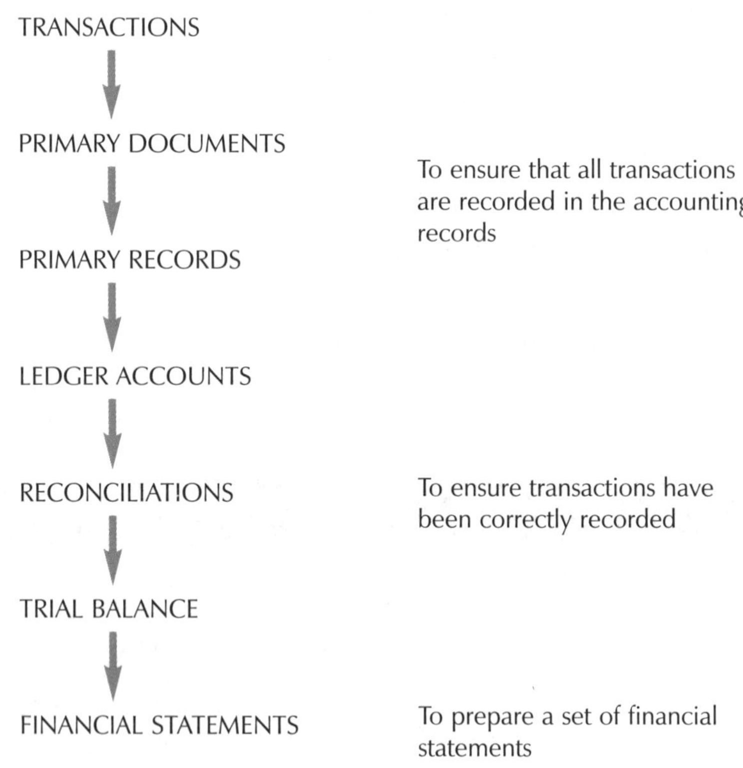

TRANSACTIONS

student notes

All organisations will have different types of transactions but the typical ones are summarised below:

Cash sales	–	a sale that is made where the goods are paid for at the time of the sale by cash, cheque, credit or debit card
Credit sales	–	a sale which is made but payment is not required for a specified period of time such as 30 days
	–	the customer then becomes a DEBTOR of the business as he now owes money to the business
Sales returns	–	where goods are returned by a customer for being faulty or not what was ordered
Receipts from credit customer	–	these will normally be in the form of cheques received in the post but can also be BANK GIRO CREDITS paid directly into your bank account
Cash purchases	–	PURCHASES, in accounting terms are the purchase of goods that are either to be used to make goods that the business will sell or goods that are due to be resold by the business
	–	cash purchases are purchases that are paid for at the time of purchase, normally by cheque
Credit purchases	–	purchases that are made from a supplier who gives a period of credit therefore payment is not due for say 30 days
	–	your business then has a CREDITOR being someone who is due to be paid by the business
Purchases returns	–	returns of goods to a credit supplier due to the goods being faulty or not what was ordered
Payments to credit supplier	–	these will normally be made in the form of cheque payments although some payments can be made directly into a supplier's bank account by a bank giro credit
Capital expenditure	–	purchase of FIXED ASSETS which are items that are to be used in the business for the long term (this will be considered in more detail in Chapter 5)

student notes

Revenue expenditure	–	payment of the general everyday expenses that a business incurs
Cash payments	–	most businesses will on occasion need to make small cash payments, for example, paying the window cleaner

Activity 1

K Jones owes your business £1,200. Is he a debtor or a creditor of your business?

PRIMARY DOCUMENTS

For each of the types of transactions considered above there will be some form of PRIMARY DOCUMENT to support and evidence that transaction.

Cash sales	–	either a receipt will be given for the monies received from the customer or the sale will be automatically recorded on the till roll
Credit sales	–	a SALES INVOICE will be issued to the customer showing the details of the goods or services sold, the amount due, the date the amount is due and any other terms such as discounts (see Chapter 2)
Sales returns	–	a CREDIT NOTE is issued to the customer showing the details of the goods returned, the total amount of the goods and the reason for the credit note
Receipts from credit customers	–	the primary document may be the actual cheque received or in some accounting systems each cheque received in a day is initially listed on a REMITTANCE LIST
Cash purchases	–	if a cheque is written for the goods then the primary document will be the CHEQUE COUNTERFOIL where the details of the amount and the payee will be recorded
Credit purchases	–	a PURCHASE INVOICE will be received from the supplier showing the details of the goods or services purchased, the amount due, the date that the amount is due and any other terms of payment

student notes

Purchases returns – a credit note will be received from the supplier showing the details of the goods returned, the amount of the credit and the reason for the return of the goods

Payments to credit suppliers – these will normally be paid for by cheque so the primary document will be the cheque counterfoil

Capital expenditure – this will normally be paid for by cheque so again the primary document will be the cheque counterfoil

Revenue expenditure – this will normally be paid for by cheque so the cheque counterfoil will give the relevant details

Automated payments – some expenses may be paid by automated bank payments systems such as standing orders or direct debits or through the BACS system – each type of automated payment will have some form of authorisation schedule which will be the primary document for the transaction

Cash payments – these will be made out of the PETTY CASH BOX, a small amount of cash kept on the premises for the purpose of making cash payments, and will only be paid if there is a valid PETTY CASH VOUCHER

Activity 2

When your business returns goods to a credit supplier what document would you expect to receive?

PRIMARY RECORDS

Each of the different types of primary document will be recorded in its own PRIMARY RECORD (also called a book of prime entry, book of original entry or day book).

Sales invoices – when sent out to customers these are all listed in the SALES DAY BOOK

Credit notes issued – these are normally listed in the SALES RETURNS DAY BOOK but in some accounting systems are shown as negative amounts in the sales day book

student notes

Purchases invoices	–	when received from suppliers these are all listed in the PURCHASE DAY BOOK
Credit notes received	–	when credit notes are received from suppliers they are normally listed in the PURCHASE RETURNS DAY BOOK although in some accounting systems they are shown as negative figures in the purchases day book
Receipts from cash sales	–	whether these are hand-written receipts or the till roll for the day they will be recorded in the CASH RECEIPTS BOOK
Cheque counterfoils	–	the details of all cheque payments taken from the cheque counterfoils will be recorded in the CASH PAYMENTS BOOK
Automated payments	–	the details will be recorded in the cash payments book
Cash payments	–	the details of the petty cash vouchers will be recorded in the PETTY CASH BOOK together with the receipts of cash into the petty cash box

Activity 3

In what primary record would invoices received from credit suppliers be listed?

LEDGER ACCOUNTS

The totals and details of each of the primary records are then transferred to the ledger accounts using the principles of double entry bookkeeping. Double entry bookkeeping will be revised in Chapter 2 but in this chapter we will consider the different ledgers that will typically exist within an organisation.

Main ledger

The MAIN LEDGER is where there is a separate ledger account for each type of transaction and asset and liability that the business has. For example there will be ledger accounts for sales, purchases, debtors, creditors, fixed assets, and expenses to name but a few.

student notes

Subsidiary ledger – the sales ledger

In the SALES LEDGER there is an account kept for each individual debtor of the business showing precisely how much is owed by that debtor and how that amount is made up.

Subsidiary ledger – the purchases ledger

In the PURCHASES LEDGER there is an account kept for each individual creditor of the business showing precisely how much is owed to that supplier and how that amount is made up.

Cash receipts and cash payments books

In some accounting systems the cash receipts book and the cash payments book are effectively treated as separate ledgers although technically they are part of the main ledger as well as being a primary record in their own right.

Petty cash book

The petty cash book is used to record both the receipts of cash into the petty cash box and the payments of petty cash vouchers. In some accounting systems this is treated effectively as a separate ledger although like the cash receipts and payments books it is technically part of the main ledger.

Activity 4

If you needed to find the details of how much your business owed to a particular supplier, which ledger would you need to consult?

RECONCILIATIONS

The balances and totals of the ledger accounts will be used eventually to prepare the financial statements of the business. Therefore it is important that these balances and totals are as accurate as possible.

Important balances can be checked by preparing a variety of reconciliations designed to detect any errors or omissions in the ledgers. The main ones are the debtors and creditors reconciliations (see Chapter 10), and a closing stock reconciliation (see Chapter 12).

student notes

TRIAL BALANCE

The TRIAL BALANCE is a list of each and every balance on the main ledger accounts which is again designed to detect any errors in the ledger accounts. The trial balance will be considered in more detail in Chapter 2.

FINANCIAL STATEMENTS

The trial balance is also used as the basis for preparing the financial statements of the business. The financial statements will be considered in outline in Chapter 3, and in more detail later in this Course Companion. The financial statements relevant to Unit 5 are the profit and loss account and the balance sheet and are also known as final accounts.

MANUAL AND COMPUTERISED ACCOUNTING SYSTEMS

In this Course Companion for Unit 5 we will be concentrating on maintaining ledger accounts and preparing trial balances and final accounts in manual accounting systems. However the same principles apply to computerised accounting systems. The same primary documents will be entered into the same primary records and then to the ledger accounts. Reconciliations will be prepared and a trial balance and financial statements produced by the computer system in the same way as in a manual system.

The benefits of a computerised system are that there is less possibility of errors being made in the accounting records and that often where in a manual system a number of entries must be made, in a computerised system often only one entry is required and the computer system will automatically make the other entries required.

CHAPTER OVERVIEW

- the aims of any accounting system are to ensure that all transactions are accurately recorded in the accounting records in order to be able to produce a set of financial statements
- each type of transaction that a business makes will be supported and evidenced by a primary document
- the main primary documents for most businesses will be receipts issued or till rolls, sales invoices and credit notes issued, cheques received from customers, purchase invoices and credit notes received, cheque counterfoils for all types of payments, automated payment authorisations and petty cash vouchers
- each type of primary document will be recorded in its own primary record (also called a book of original entry)
- sales invoices are recorded in the sales day book and credit notes issued in the sales returns day book
- purchase invoices are recorded in the purchases day book and credit notes received in the purchases returns day book
- cheque and cash receipts and cheque payments and automated payments are all recorded in the cash receipts book and cash payments book
- cash payments are recorded in the petty cash book
- the totals and details from the primary records are recorded in the ledger accounts
- the principal ledgers are the main ledger and the subsidiary ledgers, the sales ledger and the purchases ledger
- some organisations treat the cash receipts and payments books and the petty cash book as separate ledgers but technically they are part of the main ledger

KEY WORDS

Cash sales sales that are made for immediate payment by cash, cheque, credit or debit card

Credit sales sales that are made now but payment is not required for a specified period of time

Debtor someone who owes money to the business

Sales returns returns of goods from customers

Bank giro credits a method of making a payment directly into another party's bank account

Purchases purchase of either materials that are to made into goods for resale or purchase of goods that are to be resold to customers

Cash purchases purchases made where payment is required immediately

Credit purchases purchases made now where payment is not required until the end of a specified period of time

Creditor someone who is owed money by the business

Purchases returns returns of goods to suppliers

Capital expenditure payments made for fixed assets

Fixed assets assets that are to be used for the long term within the business

Revenue expenditure payments for everyday business expenses other than the purchase of fixed assets

Primary document the document that supports and evidences a business transaction

Sales invoice issued by the seller to the purchaser of goods on credit showing the details of the goods sold, the amount due and the due date of payment

Credit note a document issued to a customer who returns goods showing the details of the goods returned and their value

CHAPTER OVERVIEW cont.

- before a trial balance is prepared a number of reconciliations are carried out in order to detect any errors or omissions in the ledger accounts
- the main reconciliations for Unit 5 are the debtors and creditors reconciliations and closing stock reconciliation
- the trial balance is a list of all of the balances in the main ledger – it is used in order to detect any errors in the ledger accounts and as a basis for preparing the financial statements
- computerised accounting systems operate in a similar manner to the manual type of accounting system described in this chapter and looked at in detail in later chapters

KEY WORDS

Remittance list an internal list made of the cheques received from credit customers each day

Cheque counterfoil the part of a cheque that remains in the cheque book when the cheque is removed and sent out, recording the details of the cheque

Purchase invoice an invoice received from a credit supplier detailing the goods purchased, the amount due and the due date of payment

Automated payments payments made directly from one bank account to the bank account of another party such as standing orders, direct debits, bank giro credits and BACS payments

Petty cash box the locked box in which any amounts of cash are kept on the business premises in order to make small cash payments

Petty cash voucher the voucher that must be completed and authorised before any petty cash will be paid out

Primary records the initial record of each type of transaction – a list of each type of primary document

Sales day book a list of each of the sales invoices sent out by the business to credit customers

Sales returns day book a list of each of the credit notes issued by the business to credit customers

Purchases day book a list of the invoices received from credit suppliers

Purchases returns day book a list of the credit notes received from suppliers

Cash receipts book a record of all of the cash and cheques received by the business

Cash payments book a record of all of the cheques written out by a business and any automated payments made

Petty cash book details of all of the petty cash payments made and the receipt of cash into the petty cash box

Main ledger the ledger in which is kept a ledger account for each type of income, expense, asset and liability

Sales ledger the ledger in which is kept an account for each individual debtor

Purchases ledger the ledger in which is kept an account for each individual creditor

Trial balance a list of the balances on each of the ledger accounts in the main ledger

HOW MUCH HAVE YOU LEARNED?

1 Describe the main aims of an accounting system.

2 If your business wished to make a one-off payment to another business by transferring funds into that business's bank account, what method would be available?

3 What is the primary document for each of the following types of transaction?

   a) a sale on credit
   b) a return of goods to a supplier
   c) receipt of a cheque from a customer
   d) payment to a supplier by cheque
   e) petty cash payment

4 In which primary record would each of the following primary documents be recorded?

   a) till rolls recording cash sales
   b) credit notes received from suppliers
   c) invoices sent out to customers
   d) payments made by cheque to credit suppliers
   e) standing order payments

5 There are normally two subsidiary ledgers in an accounting system. What are they and what do they record?

chapter 2: REVISION OF DOUBLE ENTRY BOOKKEEPING

chapter coverage

In Chapter 1 we considered how the accounting system of a business might operate. Now we need to look in detail at how the transactions of a business are recorded in the ledger accounts using double entry principles. For Unit 5 you will be required to carry out some detailed entries in the ledger accounts. Therefore it is important that you fully understand the basics of double entry bookkeeping. All of what will be covered in this chapter should be familiar to those of you who studied the Foundation Units 1, 2 and 3 but as this is so vital to your further studies it is worth revising in this chapter.

This is a long chapter but it may well be familiar and is not covering any new ground. The topics that we shall cover are:

- the accounting equation
- what a ledger account looks like
- some rules for double entry
- double entry bookkeeping for cash and credit transactions
- balancing ledger accounts
- preparing a trial balance
- writing up the ledger accounts from the primary records
- entries to the subsidiary ledgers
- accounting for discounts allowed and discounts received
- preparing a bank reconciliation statement

KNOWLEDGE AND UNDERSTANDING AND PERFORMANCE CRITERIA COVERAGE

knowledge and understanding

- the methods of recording information for the organisational accounts of sole traders and partnerships
- the principles of double entry accounting
- the function and form of accounts for income and expenditure
- the function and form of a trial balance and an extended trial balance

PRINCIPLES OF DOUBLE ENTRY BOOKKEEPING

student notes

There are three main principles that underlie the practice of recording transactions in a double entry bookkeeping system:

a) the DUAL EFFECT of transactions – this means that each and every transaction that a business undertakes has two effects on the business

b) the SEPARATE ENTITY CONCEPT – this means that the owner of a business is a completely separate entity to the business itself

c) the ACCOUNTING EQUATION will always balance – the accounting equation is:

ASSETS minus LIABILITIES equals CAPITAL

Assets are items that the business owns.

Liabilities are amounts that are owed to other parties.

The capital of the business is the amount that is owed by the business back to the owner – remember that under the separate entity concept the owner and the business are completely separate entities for accounting purposes.

HOW IT WORKS

Jenny Fisher set up a business selling unusual gifts and decorative items from a small shop. Jenny is not registered for VAT. The transactions for her first month of trading are given below:

1 Feb Paid £12,000 into a business bank account in order to start the business

1 Feb Paid £3,600 by cheque for 6 months' rent on the shop

1 Feb Buys goods for resale by cheque totalling £680

8 Feb Purchases a computer to help with the business accounts for £900 by cheque

8 Feb Purchases more goods for resale from T Trainer on credit for £1,000

12 Feb Cash takings for the first two weeks are banked of £1,380, the cost of the goods that were sold is estimated as £840

17 Feb Sells goods on credit to Jones Stores for £900, the cost of these goods was £550

22 Feb Paid £600 to T Trainer by cheque

student notes

25 Feb Received £700 from Jones Stores

26 Feb Cash takings for the last two weeks are banked of £1,560, the cost of the goods that were sold is estimated to be £950

26 Feb Withdrew £1,200 for her own living expenses by writing a cheque

For each of these transactions we will firstly show the dual effect of the transaction and show that the accounting equation does balance.

1 Feb Paid £12,000 into a business bank account in order to start the business

Effect 1 the bank balance increases
Effect 2 capital increases

Accounting equation:

Assets	–	Liabilities	=	Capital
£12,000	–	£0	=	£12,000

1 Feb Paid £3,600 as 6 months rent on the shop

Effect 1 the bank balance decreases
Effect 2 an expense of rent has been incurred – this decreases the capital of the business

Accounting equation:

Assets	=	£12,000 – 3,600 (bank)	=	£8,400
Capital	=	£12,000 – 3,600 (expense)	=	£8,400

Assets	–	Liabilities	=	Capital
£8,400	–	£0	=	£8,400

1 Feb Buys goods for resale by cheque totalling £680

Effect 1 stocks of goods increase
Effect 2 the bank balance decreases

Accounting equation:

Assets = £8,400 – 680 (bank) + 680 (stock) = £8,400

Assets	–	Liabilities	=	Capital
£8,400	–	£0	=	£8,400

student notes

8 Feb Purchases a computer to help with the business accounts for £900 by cheque

Effect 1	the bank balance decreases
Effect 2	FIXED ASSETS increase

This is a long term asset for use in the business and is therefore classed as a fixed asset.

Accounting equation:

Assets = £8,400 – 900 (bank) + 900 (fixed asset) = £8,400

Assets	–	Liabilities	=	Capital
£8,400	–	£0	=	£8,400

8 Feb Purchases more goods for resale from T Trainer on credit for £1,000

Effect 1	a CREDITOR is now set up – someone the business owes money to
Effect 2	stocks increase

Accounting equation:

Assets = £8,400 + 1,000 (stock) = £9,400
Liabilities = £1,000 (creditor)

Assets	–	Liabilities	=	Capital
£9,400	–	£1,000	=	£8,400

12 Feb Cash takings for the first two weeks are banked of £1,380, the cost of the goods that were sold is estimated as £840

Effect 1	bank balance increases by £1,380
Effect 2	stock decreases by £840
	a PROFIT of (1,380 – 840) £540 has been made

A profit is made when the goods are sold for more than their original cost. The profit is owed back to the owner of the business and as such is added to the capital balance.

student notes

Accounting equation

Assets	=	£9,400 + 1,380 (bank) – 840 (stock)	=	£9,940
Capital	=	£8,400 + 540 (profit)	=	£8,940

Assets	–	Liabilities	=	Capital
£9,940	–	£1,000	=	£8,940

17 Feb Sells goods on credit to Jones Stores for £900, the cost of these goods was £550

Effect 1 a DEBTOR is set up for £900
Effect 2 stocks have decreased by £550
a profit of (900 – 550) £350 has been made

Accounting equation

Assets	=	£9,940 + 900 (debtor) – 550 (stocks)	=	£10,290
Capital	=	£8,940 + £350	=	£9,290

Assets	–	Liabilities	=	Capital
£10,290	–	£1,000	=	£9,290

22 Feb Paid £600 to T Trainer by cheque

Effect 1 bank balance has decreased
Effect 2 creditor is reduced

Accounting equation

Assets	=	£10,290 – 600 (bank)	=	£9,690
Liabilities	=	£1,000 – 600	=	£400

Assets	–	Liabilities	=	Capital
£9,690	–	£400	=	£9,290

25 Feb Received £700 from Jones Stores

Effect 1 bank balance increases
Effect 2 debtor decreases

Accounting equation

Assets	=	£9,690 + 700 (bank) – 700 (debtors)	=	£9,690

Assets	–	Liabilities	=	Capital
£9,690	–	£400	=	£9,290

student notes

26 Feb Cash takings for the last two weeks are banked of £1,560, the cost of the goods that were sold is estimated to be £950

Effect 1	bank balance increases by £1,560
Effect 2	stock decreases by £950
	a profit of (1,560 – 950) £610 has been made

Accounting equation:

Assets	=	£9,690 + 1,560 (bank) – 950 (stock)	=	£10,300
Capital	=	£9,290 + 610 (profit)	=	£9,900

Assets	–	Liabilities	=	Capital
£10,300	–	£400	=	£9,900

26 Feb Withdrew £1,200 for her own living expenses by writing a cheque

Effect 1	bank balance decreases
Effect 2	DRAWINGS of £1,200 have been made

Drawings are the amounts that the owner takes out of the business for his/her own purposes. They are treated as a reduction in the capital ie, a reduction in the amount that the business owes back to the owner.

Accounting equation:

Assets	=	£10,300 – 1,200 (bank)	=	£9,100
Capital	=	£9,900 – 1,200 (drawings)	=	£8,700

Assets	–	Liabilities	=	Capital
£9,100	–	£400	=	£8,700

Activity 1

What are the dual effects of paying money to a creditor by cheque?

student notes

DOUBLE ENTRY BOOKKEEPING

Obviously it would not be possible in practice to draw up the accounting equation each time that a business makes a transaction. For that reason the dual effect of each transaction is recorded in ledger accounts using double entry accounting.

Ledger accounts

A LEDGER ACCOUNT can be in a number of different forms according to the procedures of the particular organisation and whether the accounting system is manual or computerised. However the basic points are that there are ledger accounts for each type of income, expense, asset and liability and each ledger account will have two sides known as the debit and credit sides.

A simple ledger account would look like this:

Title

Date	Details	£	Date	Details	£
DEBIT SIDE			**CREDIT SIDE**		

Due to its appearance such a ledger account is often known as a 'T' account.

When the two effects of a transaction are recorded in the ledger accounts then one entry is on the debit side of an account and the other entry is on the credit side of another account. The trick is to select the right accounts and to get the debit and credit entries the correct way around.

There are some rules that can help you!

Rules for double entry

- if there is a payment made out of the bank account then the entry in the bank account is always a credit and therefore the debit must be to some other account
- if there is a receipt into the bank account then the entry in the bank account is always a debit and therefore the credit must be to some other account
- if a business incurs an expense then this is always a debit entry in the relevant expense account
- if a business earns income then this is always a credit entry in the relevant income account

- the recording of an asset is always a debit entry
- the recording of a liability is always a credit entry
- capital is a special liability of the business, the amount owed back to the owner, and is always therefore a credit entry

This can be summarised in the diagram below:

DEBITS	CREDITS
Money into the business	Money out of the business
Expenses	Income
Assets	Liabilities – including capital

HOW IT WORKS

We will now return to the first month of Jenny Fisher's trading and enter each transaction in the ledger accounts for the period. There are two important differences to note from the drawing up of the accounting equation:

- when a sale was made the profit was calculated in order to add it to the capital balance. In double entry accounting there is no calculation of profit until the end of the accounting period. The only entry that is made when there is a sale is to record the sale in the ledger accounts
- when drawing up the accounting equation the stock figure was adjusted after each purchase and sale. In double entry accounting there is never any entry to the stock account until the end of the accounting period. All purchases are recorded in a purchases account and there is no adjustment to stock levels when a sale is made. This is all dealt with at the end of the accounting period and will be studied in more detail in Chapter 12

Jenny's transactions for the month of February will now be recorded in the ledger accounts.

student notes

1 Feb Paid £12,000 into a business bank account in order to start the business

Debit Bank account – money in
Credit Capital account – creditor

Bank account

Date	Details	£	Date	Details	£
1 Feb	Capital	12,000			

Capital account

Date	Details	£	Date	Details	£
			1 Feb	Bank	12,000

Note that the 'details' recorded are the other side of the double entry as this helps to follow through the double entry accounting.

1 Feb Paid £3,600 as 6 months' rent on the shop

Debit Rent account – expense
Credit Bank account – money out

Bank account

Date	Details	£	Date	Details	£
1 Feb	Capital	12,000	1 Feb	Rent	3,600

Rent account

Date	Details	£	Date	Details	£
1 Feb	Bank	3,600			

student notes

1 Feb Buys goods for resale by cheque totalling £680

Debit Purchases account – expense
Credit Bank account – money out

Purchases account

Date	Details	£	Date	Details	£
1 Feb	Bank	680			

Bank account

Date	Details	£	Date	Details	£
1 Feb	Capital	12,000	1 Feb	Rent	3,600
			1 Feb	Purchases	680

8 Feb Purchases a computer to help with the business accounts for £900 by cheque

Debit Fixed asset account – asset
Credit Bank account – money out

Fixed asset account – computer

Date	Details	£	Date	Details	£
8 Feb	Bank	900			

Bank account

Date	Details	£	Date	Details	£
1 Feb	Capital	12,000	1 Feb	Rent	3,600
			1 Feb	Purchases	680
			8 Feb	Fixed asset	900

student notes

8 Feb Purchases more goods for resale from T Trainer on credit for £1,000

Debit Purchases account – expense
Credit Creditors account – liability

Purchases account

Date	Details	£	Date	Details	£
1 Feb	Bank	680			
8 Feb	Creditor	1,000			

Creditors account

Date	Details	£	Date	Details	£
			8 Feb	Purchases	1,000

12 Feb Cash takings of £1,380 for the first two weeks are banked, the cost of the goods that were sold is estimated as £840

Debit Bank account – money in
Credit Sales account – income

Note that there is no need to know about the cost of the goods sold as in double entry accounting only the purchases and sales are recorded and any profit is dealt with at the end of the accounting period when the financial statements are drawn up.

Bank account

Date	Details	£	Date	Details	£
1 Feb	Capital	12,000	1 Feb	Rent	3,600
12 Feb	Sales	1,380	1 Feb	Purchases	680
			8 Feb	Fixed asset	900

Sales account

Date	Details	£	Date	Details	£
			12 Feb	Bank	1,380

student notes

17 Feb Sells goods on credit to Jones Stores for £900, the cost of these goods was £550

Debit Debtors account – asset
Credit Sales account – income

Debtors account

Date	Details	£	Date	Details	£
17 Feb	Sales	900			

Sales account

Date	Details	£	Date	Details	£
			12 Feb	Bank	1,380
			17 Feb	Debtors	900

22 Feb Paid £600 to T Trainer by cheque

Debit Creditors account – reduction of a liability
Credit Bank account – money out

Creditors account

Date	Details	£	Date	Details	£
22 Feb	Bank	600	8 Feb	Purchases	1,000

Bank account

Date	Details	£	Date	Details	£
1 Feb	Capital	12,000	1 Feb	Rent	3,600
12 Feb	Sales	1,380	1 Feb	Purchases	680
			8 Feb	Fixed asset	900
			22 Feb	Creditors	600

student notes

25 Feb Received £700 from Jones Stores

Debit Bank account – money in
Credit Debtors account – reduction of an asset

Bank account

Date	Details	£	Date	Details	£
1 Feb	Capital	12,000	1 Feb	Rent	3,600
12 Feb	Sales	1,380	1 Feb	Purchases	680
25 Feb	Debtors	700	8 Feb	Fixed asset	900
			22 Feb	Creditors	600

Debtors account

Date	Details	£	Date	Details	£
17 Feb	Sales	900	25 Feb	Bank	700

26 Feb Cash takings of £1,560 for the last two weeks are banked, the cost of the goods that were sold is estimated to be £950

Debit Bank account – money in
Credit Sales account – income

Bank account

Date	Details	£	Date	Details	£
1 Feb	Capital	12,000	1 Feb	Rent	3,600
12 Feb	Sales	1,380	1 Feb	Purchases	680
25 Feb	Debtors	700	8 Feb	Fixed asset	900
26 Feb	Sales	1,560	22 Feb	Creditors	600

Sales account

Date	Details	£	Date	Details	£
			12 Feb	Bank	1,380
			17 Feb	Debtors	900
			26 Feb	Bank	1,560

26 Feb Withdrew £1,200 for her own living expenses

Debit Drawings account – reduction in the liability of capital
Credit Bank account – money out

student notes

Drawings are quite a tricky one to remember – capital is the amount that is owed back to the owner, a credit entry, and drawings are effectively reducing the amount of capital owed to the owner so they must be a debit entry.

Drawings account

Date	Details	£	Date	Details	£
26 Feb	Bank	1,200			

Bank account

Date	Details	£	Date	Details	£
1 Feb	Capital	12,000	1 Feb	Rent	3,600
12 Feb	Sales	1,380	1 Feb	Purchases	680
25 Feb	Debtors	700	8 Feb	Fixed asset	900
26 Feb	Sales	1,560	22 Feb	Creditors	600
			26 Feb	Drawings	1,200

Activity 2

Enter the following transactions for a business in the blank ledger accounts given below. Today's date is 4 March.

a) Sale of goods on credit for £2,400
b) Purchase of goods on credit for £1,800
c) Payment of telephone bill by cheque £140
d) Withdrawal of cash by the owner £500

student notes

Debtors account

Date	Details	£	Date	Details	£

Sales account

Date	Details	£	Date	Details	£

Purchase account

Date	Details	£	Date	Details	£

Creditors account

Date	Details	£	Date	Details	£

Telephone account

Date	Details	£	Date	Details	£

Bank account

Date	Details	£	Date	Details	£

Drawings account

Date	Details	£	Date	Details	£

student notes

BALANCING AND CLOSING OFF THE LEDGER ACCOUNTS

Now that we have entered all of the transactions for the month in the ledger accounts the next stage is to find the closing balance on each account.

HOW IT WORKS

The steps to follow in finding the closing balance on a ledger account will be illustrated using Jenny Fisher's bank account at the end of February.

Step 1 Total both sides of the account making a working note of each total (£6,980 and £15,640). Take the larger total and put this in as the total on both sides of the account leaving a spare line at the bottom of each side.

Bank account

Date	Details	£	Date	Details	£
1 Feb	Capital	12,000	1 Feb	Rent	3,600
12 Feb	Sales	1,380	1 Feb	Purchases	680
25 Feb	Debtors	700	8 Feb	Fixed asset	900
26 Feb	Sales	1,560	22 Feb	Creditors	600
		15,640	26 Feb	Drawings	1,200
					15,640

Step 2 Make the smaller of the two sides of the account add up to this total by putting in the balancing figure and describing it as the balance carried down (which is abbreviated to balance c/d).

Bank account

Date	Details	£	Date	Details	£
1 Feb	Capital	12,000	1 Feb	Rent	3,600
12 Feb	Sales	1,380	1 Feb	Purchases	680
25 Feb	Debtors	700	8 Feb	Fixed asset	900
26 Feb	Sales	1,560	22 Feb	Creditors	600
		15,640	26 Feb	Drawings	1,200
			28 Feb	Balance c/d	8,660
					15,640

student notes

Step 3 Show the same figure below the total on the other side of the account described as the balance brought down (b/d). This is the opening balance at the start of the next month so date it as the first day of the next month.

Bank account

Date	Details	£	Date	Details	£
1 Feb	Capital	12,000	1 Feb	Rent	3,600
12 Feb	Sales	1,380	1 Feb	Purchases	680
25 Feb	Debtors	700	8 Feb	Fixed asset	900
26 Feb	Sales	1,560	22 Feb	Creditors	600
			26 Feb	Drawings	1,200
			28 Feb	Balance c/d	8,660
		15,640			15,640
1 Mar	Balance b/d	8,660			

This shows that Jenny has a balance of £8,660 in the bank account at the start of March.

Activity 3

Given below are all of the remaining ledger accounts for Jenny Fisher which have more than one entry. You are required to balance each one showing the balance carried down and the balance brought down. Note that if there is only one entry in an account, such as the capital account, then this does not need to be balanced as this entry is the closing balance.

Purchases account

Date	Details	£	Date	Details	£
1 Feb	Bank	680			
8 Feb	Creditor	1,000			

Sales account

Date	Details	£	Date	Details	£
			12 Feb	Bank	1,380
			17 Feb	Debtors	900
			26 Feb	Bank	1,560

student notes

Creditors account

Date	Details	£	Date	Details	£
22 Feb	Bank	600	8 Feb	Purchases	1,000

Debtors account

Date	Details	£	Date	Details	£
17 Feb	Sales	900	25 Feb	Bank	700

TRIAL BALANCE

A TRIAL BALANCE is simply a list of all of the balances on the main ledger accounts split between the debit balances brought down and the credit balances brought down. One of the purposes of a trial balance is to serve as a check on the double entry bookkeeping. The total of the debit balances should be equal to the total of the credit balances and if there is an imbalance then this must be investigated and the cause of the imbalance corrected.

At this stage we are simply going to prepare the trial balance – dealing with imbalances and errors will be dealt with in Chapter 11.

HOW IT WORKS

Given below are all of the balanced ledger accounts for Jenny Fisher's first month of trading.

Bank account

Date	Details	£	Date	Details	£
1 Feb	Capital	12,000	1 Feb	Rent	3,600
12 Feb	Sales	1,380	1 Feb	Purchases	680
25 Feb	Debtors	700	8 Feb	Fixed asset	900
26 Feb	Sales	1,560	22 Feb	Creditors	600
		15,640	26 Feb	Drawings	1,200
			28 Feb	Balance c/d	8,660
					15,640
1 Mar	Balance b/d	8,660			

student notes

Capital account

Date	Details	£	Date	Details	£
			1 Feb	Bank	12,000

Rent account

Date	Details	£	Date	Details	£
1 Feb	Bank	3,600			

Fixed asset account – computer

Date	Details	£	Date	Details	£
8 Feb	Bank	900			

Purchases account

Date	Details	£	Date	Details	£
1 Feb	Bank	680	28 Feb	Balance c/d	1,680
8 Feb	Creditor	1,000			
		1,680			1,680
1 Mar	Balance b/d	1,680			

Creditors account

Date	Details	£	Date	Details	£
22 Feb	Bank	600	8 Feb	Purchases	1,000
28 Feb	Balance c/d	400			
		1,000			1,000
			1 Mar	Balance b/d	400

Debtors account

Date	Details	£	Date	Details	£
17 Feb	Sales	900	25 Feb	Bank	700
			28 Feb	Balance c/d	200
		900			900
1 Mar	Balance b/d	200			

student notes

Sales account

Date	Details	£	Date	Details	£
28 Feb	Balance c/d	3,840	12 Feb	Bank	1,380
			17 Feb	Debtors	900
		3,840	26 Feb	Bank	1,560
					3,840
			1 Mar	Balance b/d	3,840

Drawings account

Date	Details	£	Date	Details	£
26 Feb	Bank	1,200			

We will now draw up the trial balance as at 28 February by listing all of the balances b/d as either debit or credit balances.

Trial balance as at 28 February

	Debits	*Credits*
	£	£
Bank	8,660	
Capital		12,000
Rent	3,600	
Fixed asset – computer	900	
Purchases	1,680	
Creditors		400
Debtors	200	
Sales		3,840
Drawings	1,200	
	16,240	16,240

Note how the total of the debit balances is equal to the total of the credit balances – the trial balance balances! This will not always be the case if errors have been made (see later in this Course Companion).

A further point to remember at this stage is that these closing balances at the end of February on these ledger accounts will also be the opening balances at the start of the next month's trading.

student notes

PRIMARY RECORDS AND DOUBLE ENTRY BOOKKEEPING

So far we have taken each transaction as it occurs and entered it into the ledger accounts as a debit and a credit. In practice this would be too time consuming and therefore, as we saw in Chapter 1, all similar transactions are gathered together into the primary records and it is the totals of these primary records that are regularly posted to the ledger accounts.

HOW IT WORKS

In Jenny's second month of trading she decides that as her business is expanding she will organise her accounting records and record the transactions in primary records. Each of these is given below and in turn must be posted to the main ledger accounts. Note that each of the ledger accounts now has an opening balance being the balance at the end of February and therefore the opening balance at the start of March.

Note also that Jenny is now trading on credit with more than one customer and supplier and therefore we will need to open up subsidiary ledger accounts for the sales ledger and purchases ledger. This means that we will now change the name of the debtors and creditors accounts to SALES LEDGER CONTROL ACCOUNT and PURCHASES LEDGER CONTROL ACCOUNT respectively.

Sales on credit

Firstly we have Jenny's Sales Day Book for March – remember that Jenny is not registered for VAT.

Sales day book

Date	*Customer*	*Invoice No.*	*Total*
			£
3 March	Jones Stores	0002	800
11 March	P K Traders	0003	750
23 March	S S Stores	0004	400
			1,950

student notes

This total is then posted as follows:

Debit Sales ledger control account – asset
Credit Sales account – income

Sales ledger control account

Date	Details	£	Date	Details	£
1 Mar	Balance b/d	200			
31 Mar	SDB	1,950			

Sales account

Date	Details	£	Date	Details	£
			1 Mar	Balance b/d	3,840
			31 Mar	SDB	1,950

Note that as the posting is made at the end of the month it is given the date of the last day of the month. Note also that the 'details' are now the primary document from which the entry was posted. This makes it clear where the entry came from but it is also permissible to reference each entry to the other side of the entry ie, the entry in the sales ledger control account would be described as sales and vice versa. The precise treatment will depend upon the policy of the organisation.

Sales returns

Jenny has also had some goods returned from customers and has issued two credit notes. In order to deal with credit notes she has decided to use a sales returns day book.

Sales returns day book

Date	*Customer*	*Credit note No.*	*Total* £
12 Mar	Jones Stores	CN001	50
18 Mar	PK Traders	CN002	30
			80

This must now be posted to the main ledger accounts as:

Debit Sales returns account
Credit Sales ledger control account

student notes

The way in which to remember this posting is that it is precisely the opposite of the double entry for sales as these returns are effectively just reversing the sale.

Sales returns account

Date	Details	£	Date	Details	£
31 Mar	SRDB	80			

Sales ledger control account

Date	Details	£	Date	Details	£
1 Mar	Balance b/d	200	31 Mar	SRDB	80
31 Mar	SDB	1,950			

Subsidiary ledger – the sales ledger

As there are now a number of credit customers Jenny has decided to record the details of the transactions with each customer in the subsidiary ledger, the SALES LEDGER. Each customer has an account – note that only Jones Stores has an opening balance as this was the only credit customer in February. Each individual invoice and credit note must be entered into the individual customers account:

Debit Invoices
Credit Credit notes

Jones Stores

Date	Details	£	Date	Details	£
1 Mar	Balance b/d	200	12 Mar	CN001	50
3 Mar	SDB 0002	800			

PK Traders

Date	Details	£	Date	Details	£
11 Mar	SDB 0003	750	18 Mar	CN002	30

SS Stores

Date	Details	£	Date	Details	£
23 Mar	SDB 0004	400			

student notes

Purchases on credit

Jenny's purchases day book for March is now given. Remember that as she is not registered for VAT she can reclaim no VAT therefore this is not relevant (VAT will be covered in detail in Chapter 4).

Purchases day book

Date	*Supplier*	*Invoice No.*	*Total*
			£
5 Mar	T Trainer	03756	640
12 Mar	J Alison	10468	500
25 Mar	K R Supplies	209735	430
			1,570

This total will now be posted to the main ledger accounts as:

Debit Purchases account – expense
Credit Purchases ledger control account – liability

Purchases account

Date	Details	£	Date	Details	£
1 Mar	Balance b/d	1,680			
31 Mar	PDB	1,570			

Purchases ledger control account

Date	Details	£	Date	Details	£
			1 Mar	Balance b/d	400
			31 Mar	PDB	1,570

Purchases returns

Jenny has also returned some goods to suppliers and has received credit notes. These are recorded in the purchases returns day book.

Purchases returns day book

Date	*Supplier*	*Credit Note No.*	*Total*
			£
10 Mar	T Trainer	743	40
21 Mar	J Alison	C 376	25
			65

student notes

This must now be posted to the main ledger accounts.

Debit Purchases ledger control account
Credit Purchases returns account

As with sales returns the way to remember this posting is that it is the opposite of the double entry for purchases.

Purchases ledger control account

Date	Details	£	Date	Details	£
31 Mar	PRDB	65	1 Mar	Balance b/d	400
			31 Mar	PDB	1,570

Purchases returns account

Date	Details	£	Date	Details	£
			31 Mar	PRDB	65

Subsidiary ledger – the purchases ledger

Just as with the debtors Jenny is now to maintain a subsidiary ledger, the PURCHASES LEDGER, with a ledger account for each credit supplier. The entries in these accounts are:

Invoices Credit
Credit notes Debit

T Trainer

Date	Details	£	Date	Details	£
10 Mar	PRDB	40	1 Mar	Balance b/d	400
			5 Mar	PDB	640

J Alison

Date	Details	£	Date	Details	£
21 Mar	PRDB	25	12 Mar	PDB	500

KR Supplies

Date	Details	£	Date	Details	£
			25 Mar	PDB	430

student notes

Cash receipts

Jenny is now also using a cash receipts book to record any cheque payments received from credit customers and also the takings from the shop that are banked. The cash receipts book is analysed to distinguish between the cash sales and money from debtors as the posting of the two amounts is different.

Jenny has now also offered Jones Stores a settlement discount if they pay within 14 days. Any settlement discounts are recorded in the cash receipts book.

Cash receipts book

Date	*Details*	*Total*	*Cash sales*	*Sales ledger*	*Other*	*Discounts allowed*
		£	£	£	£	£
5 Mar	Jones Stores	200		200		
12 Mar	Jones Stores	720		720		30
14 Mar	Takings	1,730	1,730			
25 Mar	P K Traders	500		500		
30 Mar	Takings	1,550	1,550			
		4,700	3,280	1,420		30

Remember that the cash receipts book is not only a primary record but is also part of the main ledger. The 'total' column is the debit to the bank account and the only posting that is required is the credit entries of the analysis columns.

Credit Sales account with the cash sales total
Credit Sales ledger control account with the sales ledger total

Sales account

Date	Details	£	Date	Details	£
			1 Mar	Balance b/d	3,840
			31 Mar	SDB	1,950
			31 Mar	CRB	3,280

Sales ledger control account

Date	Details	£	Date	Details	£
1 Mar	Balance b/d	200	31 Mar	SRDB	80
31 Mar	SDB	1,950	31 Mar	CRB	1,420

student notes

Discounts allowed

The total of the DISCOUNTS ALLOWED column requires an entire double entry to itself as it is only a memorandum column in the cash receipts book:

Debit Discounts allowed account – expense
Credit Sales ledger control account – reduction of a debtor

The discounts allowed are an expense as they are the price that the business pays for getting its money in faster from its debtors.

Discounts allowed account

Date	Details	£	Date	Details	£
31 Mar	CRB	30			

Sales ledger control account

Date	Details	£	Date	Details	£
1 Mar	Balance b/d	200	31 Mar	SRDB	80
31 Mar	SDB	1,950	31 Mar	CRB	1,420
			31 Mar	CRB – discounts	30

Posting to the subsidiary ledger, the sales ledger

Each of the receipts from credit customers must also be entered into their own accounts in the subsidiary ledger, the sales ledger.

Receipt of cash – credit
Discount allowed – credit

Jones Stores

Date	Details	£	Date	Details	£
1 Mar	Balance b/d	200	12 Mar	CN001	50
3 Mar	SDB 0002	800	5 Mar	CRB	200
			12 Mar	CRB	720
			12 Mar	CRB – discount	30

PK Traders

Date	Details	£	Date	Details	£
11 Mar	SDB 0003	750	18 Mar	CN002	30
			25 Mar	CRB	500

student notes

Cash payments

Jenny also has a cash payments book that is analysed to show the different types of cheque payment that she makes. One of her suppliers, T Trainer, now offers a settlement discount for payment within 21 days and therefore the cash payments book includes a memorandum column for discounts received.

Cash payments book

Date	*Details*	*Cheque No.*	*Total*	*Cash purchases*	*Purchases ledger*	*Other*	*Discounts received*
			£	£	£	£	£
7 Mar	T Trainer	00006	400		400		
12 Mar	Cash purchases	00007	280	280			
18 Mar	T Trainer	00008	560		560		40
21 Mar	Telephone bill	00009	80			80	
25 Mar	Cash purchases	00010	320	320			
31 Mar	J Alison	00011	240		240		
			1,880	600	1,200	80	40

Remember that the cash payments book is not only a primary record but also part of the main ledger. Therefore the 'total' column is the credit entry to the bank account and the only posting required is the debit entries for the analysis column totals.

Debit Purchases account with cash purchases total
Debit Purchases ledger control account with purchases ledger total
Debit Telephone account with 'other' column figure

Purchases ledger control account

Date	Details	£	Date	Details	£
31 Mar	PRDB	65	1 Mar	Balance b/d	400
31 Mar	CPB	1,200	31 Mar	PDB	1,570

Telephone account

Date	Details	£	Date	Details	£
31 Mar	CPB	80			

student notes

Discounts received

The total of the DISCOUNTS RECEIVED column requires a full double entry as this is only a memorandum column in the cash payments book.

Debit Purchases ledger control account – reduction of a creditor
Credit Discounts received account – income

The discounts received account is credited as it is similar to income. It is a benefit given by a supplier in return for paying the outstanding invoices more quickly.

Purchases ledger control account

Date	Details	£	Date	Details	£
31 Mar	PRDB	65	1 Mar	Balance b/d	400
31 Mar	CPB	1,200	31 Mar	PDB	1,570
31 Mar	CPB – discount	40			

Discounts received account

Date	Details	£	Date	Details	£
			31 Mar	CPB	40

Posting to the subsidiary ledger, the purchases ledger

Finally each payment to a credit supplier must be recorded in the supplier's individual account in the subsidiary ledger, the purchases ledger.

Payment – debit
Discount – debit

T Trainer

Date	Details	£	Date	Details	£
10 Mar	PRDB	40	1 Mar	Balance b/d	400
7 Mar	CPB	400	5 Mar	PDB	640
18 Mar	CPB	560			
18 Mar	CPB – discount	40			

J Alison

Date	Details	£	Date	Details	£
21 Mar	PRDB	25	12 Mar	PDB	500
31 Mar	CPB	240			

student notes

Activity 4

What is the double entry for discounts allowed?

All of the postings have now been made from Jenny's primary records into both the main ledger accounts and the subsidiary ledgers. All that now remains is to balance off each of the main ledger accounts and to prepare a trial balance.

BANK RECONCILIATION

The bank balance will be found by balancing the cash payments book and cash receipts book – we will do this first.

The balance on the bank account at the end of February was £8,660 (debit), the total receipts from the cash receipts book were £4,700 in March and the total payments from the cash payments book were £1,880 in March. Therefore the closing balance on the bank account at the end of March can be found:

	£
Opening balance	8,660
Add: receipts	4,700
Less: payments	(1,880)
Closing bank balance	11,480

At this stage Jenny would probably check the accuracy of this figure by performing a bank reconciliation. The bank statement as at 31 March is given below together with the cash receipts book and cash payments book. The bank statement and cash books are compared and ticked when they agree.

student notes

STATEMENT

first national
30 High Street
Benham
DR4 8TT

JENNY FISHER

Account number: 20-26-33 40268134

CHEQUE ACCOUNT

Sheet 011

Date		Paid out	Paid in	Balance
1 Mar	Balance b/f			8,660.00
9 Mar	Credit		200.00✓	8,860.00
13 Mar	Cheque No 00007	280.00✓		8,580.00
15 Mar	Credit		720.00✓	9,300.00
16 Mar	Credit		1,730.00✓	
	Cheque No 00006	400.00✓		10,630.00
19 Mar	Cheque No 00008	560.00✓		10,070.00
24 Mar	Cheque No 00009	80.00✓		9,990.00
28 Mar	Credit		500.00✓	10,490.00
31 Mar	Balance c/f			10,490.00

Cash receipts book

Date	*Details*	*Total*	*Cash sales*	*Sales ledger*	*Other*	*Discounts allowed*
		£	£	£	£	£
5 Mar	Jones Stores	200✓		200		
12 Mar	Jones Stores	720✓		720		30
14 Mar	Takings	1,730✓	1,730			
25 Mar	PK Traders	500✓		500		
30 Mar	Takings	1,550	1,550			
		4,700	3,280	1,420		30

student notes

Cash payments book

Date	Details	Cheque No.	Total	Cash purchases	Purchases ledger	Other	Discounts received
			£	£	£	£	£
7 Mar	T Trainer	00006✓	400		400		
12 Mar	Cash purchases	00007✓	280	280			
18 Mar	T Trainer	00008✓	560		560		40
21 Mar	Telephone bill	00009✓	80			80	
25 Mar	Cash purchases	00010	320	320			
31 Mar	J Alison	00011	240		240		
			1,880	600	1,200	80	40

All of the entries on the bank statement have been ticked and there are three unticked items in the cash book. This means that there is one outstanding lodgement of £1,550 and two unpresented cheques for £320 and £240.

The bank reconciliation statement can now be prepared.

Bank reconciliation at 31 March

	£	£
Bank statement balance		10,490
Less: unpresented cheques		
00010	320	
00011	240	
		(560)
		9,930
Add: outstanding lodgement		1,550
Cash book balance		11,480

The rest of Jenny's main ledger accounts are now given below and balanced where necessary.

Capital account

Date	Details	£	Date	Details	£
			1 Feb	Bank	12,000

Rent account

Date	Details	£	Date	Details	£
1 Feb	Bank	3,600			

student notes

Fixed asset account – computer

Date	Details	£	Date	Details	£
8 Feb	Bank	900			

Sales account

Date	Details	£	Date	Details	£
31 Mar	Balance c/d	9,070	1 Mar	Balance b/d	3,840
			31 Mar	SDB	1,950
			31 Mar	CRB	3,280
		9,070			9,070
			1 Apr	Balance b/d	9,070

Sales returns account

Date	Details	£	Date	Details	£
31 Mar	SRDB	80			

Discounts allowed account

Date	Details	£	Date	Details	£
31 Mar	CRB	30			

Sales ledger control account

Date	Details	£	Date	Details	£
1 Mar	Balance b/d	200	31 Mar	SRDB	80
31 Mar	SDB	1,950	31 Mar	CRB	1,420
			31 Mar	CRB – discounts	30
			31 Mar	Balance c/d	620
		2,150			2,150
1 Apr	Balance b/d	620			

student notes

Purchases account

Date	Details	£	Date	Details	£
1 Mar	Balance b/d	1,680	31 Mar	Balance c/d	3,850
31 Mar	PDB	1,570			
31 Mar	CPB	600			
		3,850			3,850
1 Apr	Balance b/d	3,850			

Purchases returns account

Date	Details	£	Date	Details	£
			31 Mar	PRDB	65

Purchases ledger control account

Date	Details	£	Date	Details	£
31 Mar	PRDB	65	1 Mar	Balance b/d	400
31 Mar	CPB	1,200	31 Mar	PDB	1,570
31 Mar	CPB – discounts	40			
31 Mar	Balance c/d	665			
		1,970			1,970
			1 Apr	Balance b/d	665

Discounts received account

Date	Details	£	Date	Details	£
			31 Mar	CPB	40

Telephone account

Date	Details	£	Date	Details	£
31 Mar	CPB	80			

Drawings account

Date	Details	£	Date	Details	£
26 Feb	Bank	1,200			

student notes

Now each of the balances will be listed in the trial balance.

Trial balance as at 31 March

	Debits	*Credits*
	£	£
Bank	11,480	
Capital		12,000
Rent	3,600	
Fixed assets	900	
Sales		9,070
Sales returns	80	
Discounts allowed	30	
Sales ledger control	620	
Purchases	3,850	
Purchases returns		65
Purchases ledger control		665
Discounts received		40
Telephone	80	
Drawings	1,200	
	21,840	21,840

Activity 5

What are the two main purposes of the trial balance?

CHAPTER OVERVIEW

- the main principles behind double entry accounting are the dual effect of transactions, the separate entity concept and the accounting equation
- the accounting equation is that at any time assets minus liabilities will be equal to capital
- in order to record the transactions of a business double entry accounting is used and the transactions are recorded in ledger accounts
- each ledger account has a debit side and a credit side and each transaction will be recorded in the debit side of one ledger account and the credit side of another ledger account
- payments out of the business are always a credit entry in the bank account and receipts into the business are always a debit entry in the bank account
- expenses and assets are always debit entries
- income and liabilities are always credit entries
- capital is a credit balance as this is a special liability, the amount owed back to the owner
- at the end of each accounting period the ledger accounts must be closed off or balanced
- often a bank reconciliation statement will be prepared as a check on the bank balance
- the trial balance is a list of all of the balances brought down on the main ledger accounts – the total of the debit balances should equal the total of the credit balances
- in practice each transaction will not be entered into the ledger accounts separately, instead they will initially be recorded in the primary records and then the totals of the primary records are posted to the ledger accounts

KEY WORDS

Dual effect each transaction has two effects on a business

Separate entity concept the owner of a business is a completely separate entity from the business itself for accounting purposes

Accounting equation at any point in time the assets of the business minus the liabilities of the business will be equal to the capital of the business

Assets items that the business owns

Liabilities amounts owed to other parties

Capital the amount owed back to the owner by the business

Fixed assets items purchased for long term use in the business

Creditor someone to whom the business owes money

Profit a profit is made where goods are sold for more than they cost

Debtor someone who owes the business money

Drawings amounts taken out of the business by the owner

Ledger account a ledger account is an account with a debit side and a credit side in which double entry accounting takes place

Trial balance a list of all of the debit balances and credit balances in the main ledger at any point in time

Sales ledger control account the main ledger account in which the total of all transactions with credit customers is recorded

Purchases ledger control account the main ledger account in which the total of all transactions with credit suppliers is recorded

CHAPTER OVERVIEW cont.

- for transactions with debtors and creditors each individual invoice, credit note and payment must also be recorded in the debtor's or creditor's account in the subsidiary ledgers – the sales ledger for debtors and the purchases ledger for creditors
- when posting the cash receipts book and the cash payments book you should remember that they are part of the main ledger as well as being primary records – therefore for the cash receipts book only credit entries are required for the analysis columns and for the cash payments book only debit entries are required for the analysis columns
- in the cash receipts and payments book there are memorandum columns for discounts allowed and discounts received respectively – full double entry is required for the total of these discount columns

KEY WORDS

Sales ledger the subsidiary ledger in which there is an account for each credit customer showing the details of every transaction with that customer

Purchases ledger the subsidiary ledger in which there is an account for each credit supplier showing the details of every transaction with that supplier

Discounts allowed cash or settlement discounts taken by credit customers

Discounts received cash or settlement discounts offered by credit suppliers and taken up by the organisation

HOW MUCH HAVE YOU LEARNED?

1 What is the double entry for the following transactions?

a) Sale on credit
b) Purchases for cash
c) Purchase of a fixed asset by cheque
d) Receipt of money from a credit customer
e) Payment of wages by cheque
f) Withdrawal of cash by the owner

2 Given below is a bank account:

Bank account

Date	Details	£	Date	Details	£
1 Mar	Capital	14,000	3 Mar	Purchases	3,500
10 Mar	Sales	4,000	8 Mar	Delivery van	7,400
28 Mar	Sales	6,200	15 Mar	Purchases	15,100
			20 Mar	Wages	1,000
			30 Mar	Telephone	200

What is the balance on this bank account at 31 March?

3 Given below are the transactions of a new business for its first month. The business is not registered for VAT.

1 Mar	Owner pays £20,000 into a business bank account
1 Mar	Fixtures and fittings purchased for the office premises £3,200
4 Mar	Purchases of goods for resale made by cheque for £4,400
6 Mar	Rent paid by cheque £600
10 Mar	Sales for cash £1,800
15 Mar	Sales on credit £4,900
20 Mar	Purchases on credit £2,700
24 Mar	Cash received from credit customers £3,500
28 Mar	Owner withdraws £1,000 in cash
29 Mar	Sales on credit £1,600
30 Mar	Cheque for £1,800 sent to credit supplier
31 Mar	Wages paid by cheque of £900

Write up each of these transactions in the ledger accounts of the business, balance any accounts with more than one entry and then prepare a trial balance as at 31 March.

4 Given below are the primary records of a small business for its first month of trading. The business is not registered for VAT.

Sales day book

Date	*Customer*	*Invoice No.*	*Total*
			£
4 Mar	J Simpson	0001	420
12 Mar	F Barnet	0002	350
18 Mar	H Jerry	0003	180
28 Mar	D Dawson	0004	440
			1,390

Sales returns day book

Date	*Customer*	*Credit note No.*	*Total*
			£
19 Mar	F Barnet	CN 001	40
25 Mar	H Jerry	CN 002	20
			60

Purchases day book

Date	*Customer*	*Invoice No.*	*Total*
			£
1 Mar	L Lilley	89432	590
7 Mar	O Rools	12332	400
24 Mar	R Terry	0532	410
			1,400

Purchases returns day book

Date	*Customer*	*Credit note No.*	*Total*
			£
10 Mar	O Rools	C 357	80

Cash receipts book

Date	Details	Total	Cash sales	Sales ledger	Other	Discounts allowed
		£	£	£	£	£
1 Mar	Capital	15,000			15,000	
7 Mar	Cash sales	930	930			
20 Mar	J Simpson	420		420		
22 Mar	Cash sales	740	740			
31 Mar	F Barnet	300		300		10
		17,390	1,670	720	15,000	10

Cash payments book

Date	Details	Cheque No.	Total	Cash purchases	Purchases ledger	Wages	Other	Discounts received
			£	£	£	£	£	£
2 Mar	Cash purchases	0001	550	550				
6 Mar	Shop fittings	0002	1,100				1,100	
12 Mar	L Lilley	0003	560		560			30
15 Mar	Cash purchases	0004	780	780				
18 Mar	Cash purchases	0005	920	920				
20 Mar	O Rools	0006	310		310			10
31 Mar	Wages		2,200			2,200		
			6,420	2,250	870	2,200	1,100	40

You are required to:

a) post all of the primary record totals to the relevant accounts in the main ledger

b) post the individual entries to the subsidiary ledgers, the sales ledger and the purchases ledger

c) balance all of the main ledger accounts and subsidiary ledger accounts

d) prepare a trial balance as at 31 March

5 The balance on a business's cash book at the end of June is £184.50 but the bank statement shows a balance at the same date of £67.82 overdrawn. There are unpresented cheques at the end of June of £141.35 and outstanding lodgements of £393.67.

Reconcile the bank statement balance to the balance on the cash book at 30 June.

chapter 3: INTRODUCTION TO FINANCIAL STATEMENTS

chapter coverage

In this chapter we shall go a step further than the trial balance and introduce the actual financial statements or final accounts that a business will eventually produce from the trial balance, the profit and loss account and the balance sheet. For Unit 5 you need to be able to prepare a profit and loss account and balance sheet for a sole trader or a partnership. This chapter is just an introduction and this area will be considered in much more detail in Chapters 13, 14 and 15.

This chapter also introduces the regulatory framework within which accountants work and some basic accounting concepts that you need to be aware of. The topics that we shall cover are:

- recognising asset, liability, income and expense balances in the trial balance
- the profit and loss account
- the balance sheet
- the relationship between the ledger accounts and the profit and loss account and the balance sheet
- the regulatory framework for accounting
- accounting policies

KNOWLEDGE AND UNDERSTANDING AND PERFORMANCE CRITERIA COVERAGE

knowledge and understanding

- the relevant legislation and regulations
- the main requirements of relevant SSAPs and FRSs
- the method of closing off revenue accounts
- the need to present accounts in the correct form
- the form of final accounts of sole traders and partnerships
- basic accounting concepts that play a role in the selection of accounting policies – accruals and going concern
- the objectives and constraints in selecting accounting policies – relevance, reliability, comparability, ease of understanding, materiality
- the function and form of a profit and loss account and balance sheet for sole traders and partnerships

student notes

THE MEANING OF THE BALANCES IN A TRIAL BALANCE

In the previous chapter we saw how to prepare a trial balance from the closing balances on the main ledger accounts. We will now consider what the balances in a trial balance represent. Each balance will be one of the following:

- an asset
- a liability
- income
- an expense
- a provision (provisions will be dealt with in later chapters and can be ignored for the purposes of this chapter)

You need to be able to distinguish between each of these types of balances.

HOW IT WORKS

Given below is the trial balance for Hunter Traders, a small business that is not registered for VAT. For each figure it has been stated whether it is an asset, liability, income or expense, with explanation wherever necessary.

	Debits	*Credits*	*Category*
	£	£	
Fixed assets	10,200		asset
Bank	800		asset
Electricity	240		expense
Loan		2,000	liability
Capital		12,760	liability
Carriage outwards	80		expense
Discounts received		280	income
Sales		44,000	income
Opening stock	2,400		(see note below)
Debtors	3,800		asset
Wages	10,400		expense
Discounts allowed	440		expense
Creditors		2,400	liability
Rent	600		expense
Telephone	320		expense
Carriage inwards	160		expense
Drawings	4,000		(see note below)
Purchases	28,000		expense
	61,440	61,440	

student notes

Opening stock – the stock figure in the trial balance is always the opening stock and is technically an expense. This will be explained and expanded upon in Chapter 12.

Drawings – although a debit balance these are neither an expense nor an asset. Drawings are instead a reduction in the liability, capital.

Activity 1

Given below is the trial balance of a small trader N Lawson who is not registered for VAT. In the space next to each balance you are required to state whether the balance is an asset, liability, income or an expense.

	Debits	*Credits*	*Description*
	£	£	
Rent	480		
Motor van	7,400		
Creditors		1,900	
Gas	210		
Discounts received		50	
Carriage outwards	310		
Sales		40,800	
Opening stock	2,100		
Loan		2,000	
Electricity	330		
Capital		7,980	
Telephone	640		
Discount allowed	60		
Purchases	22,600		
Debtors	3,400		
Wages	9,700		
Drawings	4,000		
Carriage inwards	220		
Motor expenses	660		
Bank	620		
	52,730	52,730	

student notes

THE FINANCIAL STATEMENTS

The profit and loss account

The PROFIT AND LOSS ACCOUNT of an organisation is in simple terms:

INCOME minus EXPENSES equals PROFIT OR LOSS

If the income is greater than the expenses then a profit is made. If the expenses exceed the income then a loss has been made.

The profit and loss account is a summary of the activity of the organisation during the year.

However despite the simple concept of the profit and loss account it is normally laid out in a particular manner. For companies this layout is required by law but for other organisations it is normally followed as a matter of best practice.

HOW IT WORKS

The trial balance for Hunter Traders is reproduced below. Below this is the profit and loss account for Hunter Traders, together with an explanation of the important points. Each item denoted as income or expense from the trial balance is used in the profit and loss account. As you work through each figure in the profit and loss account tick it off on the trial balance and you will see that all of the income and expenses are used up.

student notes

Trial balance

	Debits £	Credits £	Category
Fixed assets	10,200		asset
Bank	800		asset
Electricity	240		expense
Loan		2,000	liability
Capital		12,760	liability
Carriage outwards	80		expense
Discounts received		280	income
Sales		44,000	income
Opening stock	2,400		expense
Debtors	3,800		asset
Wages	10,400		expense
Discounts allowed	440		expense
Creditors		2,400	liability
Rent	600		expense
Telephone	320		expense
Carriage inwards	160		expense
Drawings	4,000		reduction of liability
Purchases	28,000		expense
	61,440	61,440	

In order to produce the profit and loss account there is one further figure that is required. This is the value of the closing stock, which for Hunter Traders is £3,200. This will be covered in detail in Chapter 12.

Profit and loss account

	£	£
Sales		44,000
Less: cost of sales		
Opening stock	2,400	
Carriage inwards	160	
Purchases	28,000	
	30,560	
Less: closing stock	(3,200)	
Cost of sales		(27,360)
Gross profit		16,640
Less: expenses		
Electricity	240	
Carriage outwards	80	
Discount allowed	440	
Discount received	(280)	
Wages	10,400	
Rent	600	
Telephone	320	
		(11,800)
Net profit		4,840

Explanation

student notes

Trading account – you can see that the profit and loss account naturally falls into two sections. One ends in gross profit and the other in net profit after deducting the expenses. The top part of the profit and loss account is technically known as the trading account as this is where the sales value is compared to the cost of selling those goods.

Gross profit – the GROSS PROFIT is the profit earned by the trading activities of the business. As you can see it is calculated as the sales value less the cost of those sales. This area will be considered in more detail in Chapter 12.

Carriage inwards and carriage outwards – both of these items are expenses, however they are shown in different places in the profit and loss account. CARRIAGE INWARDS is the cost of getting the purchases into the organisation. As such it is treated as part of the cost of sales. The CARRIAGE OUTWARDS however is the cost of delivering goods to customers and is included lower down the profit and loss account in the expenses section.

Expenses – the second part of the profit and loss account consists of a list of all of the expenses of the business.

Discounts – discounts allowed to customers are an expense of the business and are therefore included in the list of expenses. Discounts received however are similar to income as they are a benefit to the organisation. In this profit and loss account they have been shown as a negative expense in the list of expenses (with brackets around as they are to be deducted from the expenses). However it is also possible to show them as miscellaneous income just beneath the gross profit figure.

Net profit – the NET PROFIT is the final profit of the business after all of the expenses have been deducted.

Activity 2

A business has made sales of £136,700 and its purchases totalled £97,500. The opening stock was £11,300 and the closing stock was £10,600. What is the business's gross profit?

student notes

Balance sheet

Whereas the profit and loss account is a history of the transactions of the business during the accounting period the BALANCE SHEET in contrast is simply a 'snap shot' of the business on the final day of the accounting period.

The balance sheet is a list of all of the assets and liabilities of the business. It is also an expression of the accounting equation. Remember that the accounting equation is:

ASSETS minus LIABILITIES equals CAPITAL

The balance sheet is a vertical form of the accounting equation. It lists and totals the assets of the business and deducts the liabilities. This total is then shown to be equal to the capital of the business.

HOW IT WORKS

We will continue with the example of Hunter Traders. In the trial balance that we ticked off when producing the profit and loss account there are now a number of unticked items. These will all appear in the balance sheet.

Again companies have to produce a balance sheet in a particular format which you do not need to be aware of but most other organisations also produce balance sheets in a similar manner and this is illustrated below for Hunter Traders.

Balance sheet

	£	£	£
Fixed assets			10,200
Current assets:			
Stock	3,200		
Debtors	3,800		
Bank	800		
		7,800	
Current liabilities:			
Creditors		(2,400)	
Net current assets			5,400
			15,600
Long term liabilities:			
Loan			(2,000)
			13,600

student notes

Financed by:

	£
Opening capital	12,760
Add: profit	4,840
	17,600
Less: drawings	(4,000)
	13,600

Explanation

Accounting equation – the balance sheet falls naturally into two parts which are the two sides of the accounting equation – 'assets minus liabilities' and 'capital'.

Fixed assets – fixed assets are always shown as the first assets on the balance sheet being the major long-term assets of the business. The detailed presentation of fixed assets in the balance sheet will be dealt with in Chapter 6.

Current assets – the CURRENT ASSETS of a business are the other shorter term assets. These are listed in particular order starting with the least liquid asset, stock, followed by debtors and then finally the most liquid asset the bank account and then possibly followed by cash in hand or petty cash.

Current liabilities – the CURRENT LIABILITIES of a business are the short term creditors – the other title that is used for these is 'Creditors: amounts payable within one year'.

Net current assets – the NET CURRENT ASSETS figure is a sub-total of the current assets minus the current liabilities. The net current asset total is then added in to the fixed asset total.

Long-term liabilities – the LONG-TERM LIABILITIES are liabilities that are due to be paid after more than one year. In this case we have assumed that the loan is a long term loan, ie, repayable after more than one year. The total for long term liabilities is deducted from the total of fixed assets and net current assets to give the balance sheet total. In terms of the accounting equation this is the total of the assets minus liabilities.

Capital – the capital section of the balance sheet shows the amounts that are owed back to the owner of the business. This consists of the amount of capital owed back to the owner at the start of the accounting period plus the profit that the business has earned (this figure of £4,840 is the net profit taken from the profit and loss account) less the drawings that the owner has taken out of the business during the accounting period. As in this case, the total of the capital section should equal the total of the assets minus the liabilities.

Note that drawings are part of the balance sheet and are not included as expenses – they are a reduction of the amount that is owed to the owner by the business.

student notes

Activity 3

Given below is the trial balance of N Lawson. In the space next to each balance you are to state whether the balance would appear in the profit and loss account or in the balance sheet.

	Debits	*Credits*	*Profit and loss a/c or balance sheet?*
	£	£	
Rent	480		
Motor van	7,400		
Creditors		1,900	
Gas	210		
Discounts received		50	
Carriage outwards	310		
Sales		40,800	
Opening stock	2,100		
Loan		2,000	
Electricity	330		
Capital		7,980	
Telephone	640		
Discount allowed	60		
Purchases	22,600		
Debtors	3,400		
Wages	9,700		
Drawings	4,000		
Carriage inwards	220		
Motor expenses	660		
Bank	620		
	52,730	52,730	

Ledger accounts and the profit and loss account and balance sheet

Before we leave the subject of the financial statements we must consider how the profit and loss account and the balance sheet are prepared from the main ledger accounts.

There is a distinct difference between the profit and loss account ledger accounts and the balance sheet ledger accounts.

Profit and loss account

The profit and loss account is effectively a large ledger account in its own right. This means that each of the balances on income and expense accounts are cleared to this ledger account at the end of the accounting period. The effect of this is that there is no opening balance on the income and expense ledger accounts at the start of the following accounting period.

student notes

Balance sheet

In contrast the balance sheet is a list of all of the balances on the asset and liability accounts. These assets and liabilities will still exist at the start of the next accounting period and therefore the balances on these accounts are simply listed in the balance sheet and then remain in the ledger account as the opening balance at the start of the next accounting period, ie, the next day.

HOW IT WORKS

Given below are the balances on the sales account and sales ledger control account for an organisation at the end of its accounting period.

Sales account

Date	Details	£	Date	Details	£
			31 Dec	Balance b/d	115,000

Sales ledger control account

Date	Details	£	Date	Details	£
31 Dec	Balance b/d	24,000			

Since the sales account is an income account, it is cleared out to the profit and loss account leaving no opening balance on the account at the start of January.

Sales account

Date	Details	£	Date	Details	£
31 Dec	Profit and loss account	115,000	31 Dec	Balance b/d	115,000

In contrast the balance on the sales ledger control account, being an asset, is simply listed in the balance sheet and then remains in the ledger account as the opening balance.

Sales ledger control account

Date	Details	£	Date	Details	£
1 Jan	Balance b/d	24,000			

student notes

Income and expenditure accounts

Sole traders, partnerships and companies all produce a profit and loss account and a balance sheet. Other types of not-for-profit organisations such as clubs and societies do not prepare a profit and loss account as their aim is not necessarily to make a profit. However these organisations do produce something very similar known as an income and expenditure account. An example of an income and expenditure account together with its associated balance sheet are shown below for illustration. You will not be formally assessed on these.

Income and expenditure account for Crowfield Rugby Club for the year ended 31 December 2008

	£	£
Income:		
Subscription income		7,170
Bar profit		3,100
Dinner dance profit		400
		10,670
Less: expenditure		
Loss on sale of grass cutter	100	
Depreciation of grass cutter	250	
Rent and rates	1,300	
Electricity	2,040	
Groundsman's expenses	700	
Club secretary's expenses	900	
Fixtures fees	3,500	
Sundry expenses	200	
		8,990
Surplus of income over expenditure		1,680

Balance sheet as at 31 December 2008

	£	£
Fixed assets at cost		1,000
Less: provision for depreciation		250
Net book value		750
Bar stocks	1,800	
Subscriptions in arrears	30	
Prepayment	300	
Bank	1,550	
		3,680
		4,430
Less: creditors		
Subscriptions in advance	120	
Accruals	240	
		(360)
		4,070

student notes

	£
Accumulated fund at 1 January 2008	2,390
Surplus of income over expenditure	1,680
Accumulated fund at 31 December 2008	4,070

Manufacturing accounts

A further type of accounting statement that some manufacturing organisations will produce is a manufacturing account. This is a structured list of all of the expenses incurred in the production process culminating in the total cost of the goods manufactured in the period. An example of a manufacturing account is given below for illustration. You will not be formally assessed on these.

Manufacturing account for the year ended 31 March 2009

	£	£
Opening stock of raw materials		6,000
Purchases of raw materials		70,000
		76,000
Less: closing stock of raw materials		(8,000)
Direct materials used		68,000
Direct labour		36,000
Direct expenses		1,900
Prime cost		105,900
Production overheads:		
Supervisor's salary	17,000	
Factory rent	8,000	
Machinery depreciation	6,000	
Factory light and heat	4,000	
		35,000
		140,900
Add: opening work in progress		4,000
		144,900
Less: closing work in progress		(4,900)
Manufacturing cost of goods completed		140,000

student notes

THE REGULATORY FRAMEWORK OF ACCOUNTING

The way in which companies prepare their annual financial statements is regulated both by the law and the accounting profession. The purpose of this regulation is to try to ensure that the financial statements of different companies and different types of businesses are as comparable as possible.

Companies Act

The Companies Act 2006 sets out the way in which financial statements should be prepared and gives companies a detailed format of how the profit and loss account and balance sheet should be drawn up, the precise wording that should be used and a great deal of detail about the information that must be shown in the financial statements. For Unit 5 you only have to deal with the accounting transactions and final accounts of sole traders and partnerships, not limited companies. Therefore the details of the Companies Act requirements are not relevant to this syllabus.

Accounting standards

As well as the legal regulation of companies' financial statements the accounting profession also regulates the preparation of financial statements by issuing accounting standards. The first accounting standards were produced around 40 years ago and were known as Statements of Standard Accounting Practice (SSAPs).

The aim of the accounting standards is to reduce the variety of methods of dealing with accounting issues and to set out the best method to use in order to increase the comparability of the financial statements of different organisations.

A number of SSAPs are still in issue although the accounting framework is now under the control of the Accounting Standards Board which issues Financial Reporting Standards (FRSs) with the same aims as the old SSAPs. Companies must follow the requirements of SSAPs and FRSs when preparing financial statements but other non-corporate organisations have more flexibility. However, the SSAPs and FRSs do represent best accounting practice and are followed by most sole traders and partnerships as well.

For the purposes of the Unit 5 syllabus the following SSAPs and FRSs will be covered:

SSAP 5	Accounting for Value Added Tax (Chapter 4)
SSAP 9	Stocks and long-term contracts (Chapter 12)
FRS 15	Tangible fixed assets (Chapter 6)
FRS 18	Accounting policies (see below)

Accounting practice in the UK and elsewhere is increasingly influenced by International Accounting Standards (IASs) and International Financial Reporting Standards (IFRSs), issued by the International Accounting Standards Board (IASB). While these are not yet assessable at Unit 5, they are covered at Intermediate Stage. Chapter 17 of this Course Companion is an introduction to international accounting which you may find useful to glance through at this stage.

student notes

ACCOUNTING POLICIES

When final accounts are being prepared for an organisation they will be prepared according to a number of well known and well understood accounting concepts and also according to the organisation's own accounting policies. In the world of accounting, although there are rules from the Companies Act and from accounting standards as to how to treat items in the final accounts, there are also many choices of accounting treatments. For example some organisations may treat particular costs as part of cost of sales whereas others may treat the same costs as expenses.

The choices that an organisation makes when preparing final accounts are known as their ACCOUNTING POLICIES. The choice of accounting policies that an organisation makes is fundamental to the picture shown by the final accounts and therefore an accounting standard has been issued on this area – FRS 18, Accounting policies.

FRS 18, Accounting policies

FRS 18 sets out the principles that organisations should follow when selecting their accounting policies. The basic principle is that an organisation should select the accounting policies that are judged to be the most appropriate to its particular circumstances.

So how are these most appropriate accounting policies determined?

student notes

Accounting concepts

Over the years a number of accounting concepts have been identified as being fundamental to the preparation of final accounts. Some of these have their origins in the Companies Act whereas others have come about through best accounting practice. FRS 18 identifies two of these concepts as playing a pervasive role in the preparation of final accounts and therefore also in the selection of accounting policies – the GOING CONCERN CONCEPT and the ACCRUALS CONCEPT.

Going concern

FRS 18 requires that final accounts should be prepared on the going concern basis unless the directors believe that the organisation is not a going concern. On the going concern basis, the final accounts are prepared with the underlying assumption that the business will continue for the foreseeable future. This concept or basis affects in particular the values of fixed assets shown in the balance sheet. If the business is a going concern then fixed assets will continue to be shown in the balance sheet at the amount that they cost less accumulated depreciation. However if the business were not a going concern and was due to close down in the near future then fixed assets such as specialised premises or machinery may have a very low value as they would not easily be sold when the business closed.

Accruals

FRS 18 also requires final accounts to be prepared on the accrual basis of accounting. The accrual basis of accounting requires that the effects of transactions are reflected in the final accounts for the period in which they occur and not in the period in which any cash involved is received or paid.

This means that the amount of any income or expense that appear in the final accounts should be the amount that was earned or incurred during the accounting period rather than the amount of cash that was received or paid.

We have already come across examples of this with credit sales and credit purchases. When a sale is made on credit the sales account is credited immediately even though it may be a number of weeks before the cash is actually received from the debtor. In just the same way, when goods are purchased on credit from a supplier, the purchases account is debited immediately although it will be some time before the creditor is paid. We will come across further examples of applying the accrual basis of accounting when we deal with accruals and prepayments in Chapter 8.

Objectives in selecting accounting policies

student notes

As well as the two underlying accounting concepts of going concern and accrual accounting, FRS 18 sets out four objectives against which an organisation should judge the appropriateness of accounting policies to its own particular circumstances. These objectives are:

- relevance
- reliability
- comparability
- understandability

Relevance

Financial information is said to be **relevant** if it has the ability to influence the economic decisions of the users of that information and is provided in time to influence those decisions. Where an organisation faces a choice of accounting policies they should choose the one that is most relevant in the context of the final accounts as a whole.

Reliability

Accounting is not an exact science and as you will see later in this Course Companion many estimates and management decisions have to be made when determining the figures that will appear in the final accounts. Such estimates may never be able to be judged to be correct or not, but the accounting policies chosen by an organisation must ensure that the figures that appear in the final accounts are **reliable**.

There are a number of aspects to providing reliable information in the final accounts:

- the figures should represent the substance of the transactions or events
- the figures should be free from bias, ie they should be neutral
- the figures should be free of material errors
- a degree of caution must be applied in making judgements where there is uncertainty

The latter element, using a degree of caution, is known as PRUDENCE. The prudence concept was initially one of the fundamental accounting concepts stated by the Companies Act and SSAP 2 (now withdrawn and replaced by FRS 18). However, FRS 18 now views prudence as part of the objective of reliability. Prudence is only applicable in conditions of uncertainty and in such conditions it requires more evidence of the existence of an asset or gain than for the existence of a liability or loss. When the value of an asset, liability,

student notes

gain or loss is uncertain then prudence requires a greater reliability of measurement for assets and gains than for liabilities and losses.

Comparability

Information in final accounts is used by many different people and organisations, from the employees and investors in the organisation to its creditors and bank. The information provided in the final accounts is much more useful to these users if it is comparable over time and also with similar information about other organisations. The selection of appropriate accounting policies and their consistent use should provide such comparability.

Understandability

If the final accounts of an organisation are to be useful then they must be understandable. Accounting policies should be chosen to ensure ease of understanding for users of the final accounts who have a reasonable knowledge of business and economic activities and accounting and a willingness to study the information diligently.

Constraints in selecting accounting policies

As well as requiring an organisation's accounting policies to meet these four objectives of relevance, reliability, comparability and ease of understanding, FRS 18 also sets out two constraints on the choice of accounting policies:

- The need to balance the four objectives – particularly where there might be a conflict between relevance and reliability
- The need to balance the cost of providing information with the likely benefit of that information to the users of the final accounts

Activity 4

Can you think of a situation where there might be a conflict between the relevance and reliability of financial information?

OTHER ACCOUNTING CONCEPTS

student notes

As well as the accounting concepts of going concern and accruals there are many other concepts under which final accounts are prepared. The most important of these for the purposes of Unit 5 is MATERIALITY.

Materiality

The MATERIALITY CONCEPT concerns the accounting treatment of "small" or non-material items in the financial statements. What it means in practical terms is that although there are certain rules which underlie the preparation of financial statements these rules do not need to apply to non-material items.

For example we have seen that assets that are for long-term use in the business should be shown as fixed assets in the balance sheet. However small items such as calculators and staplers for use in the office need not be treated as fixed assets if it is decided that they are not material – instead their cost would simply be an expense in the profit and loss account. Similarly the office stationery that is used in the business will be charged as an expense in the profit and loss account. This expense should strictly be adjusted to reflect any stocks of stationery left at the end of the year. However if these amounts are deemed to be immaterial then no adjustment is required.

What is a material amount? The answer to this will depend upon the size of the business itself. In some large businesses the materiality level may be set at something like £5,000. However in a small business it would be much lower maybe with balances of £100 or less being considered immaterial.

If an item in the accounts of an organisation is too small to be material then it cannot be useful to the users of the financial statements and therefore has no relevance. Therefore immaterial items are not considered of importance in the preparation of financial statements.

Statement of Principles for Financial Reporting

The four qualitative characteristics of financial information discussed above – relevance, reliability, comparability, and understandability – were first defined and explained in the STATEMENT OF PRINCIPLES FOR FINANCIAL REPORTING.

student notes

The Statement of Principles was issued by the Accounting Standards Board in December 1999 and it serves as a conceptual framework for accounting and accounting standards. The Statement of Principles is split into eight chapters which each consider various aspects of the concepts behind the preparation of financial statements. These principles embodied in the Statement underlie all of the Financial Reporting Standards (FRSs) that have been issued by the Accounting Standards Board.

CHAPTER OVERVIEW

- debit balances in the trial balance will either be expenses, assets or drawings
- credit balances in the trial balance will either be income or liabilities
- the opening stock figure in the trial balance is an expense
- the profit and loss account shows the income of the business minus the expenses which will then give either a profit or a loss
- the profit and loss account is a historical summary of the activities of the business during the accounting period
- the gross profit is the profit made from the trading activities of the business – this is calculated in the trading account. Once all of the expenses have been deducted then there will be a net profit or net loss
- carriage inwards and outwards are both expenses however carriage inwards is shown in the trading account as part of cost of sales
- discounts allowed are expenses however discounts received can either be shown as income just below gross profit or as a negative expense, ie, as a reduction of the expenses total
- the balance sheet is a 'snap-shot' of the business on the last day of the accounting period listing all of the assets and liabilities of the business
- the balance sheet is a vertical form of the accounting equation showing that the assets minus the liabilities equals the capital balance
- the assets are listed in a particular order starting with the fixed assets and followed by the current assets. The current assets are listed in a particular order starting with the least liquid, stock, and working down to the most liquid, bank and cash balances
- the current liabilities are the creditors of the business that are due to be paid in less than twelve months time – the current liabilities are deducted from the total of the current assets to give a figure known as the net current assets

KEY WORDS

Profit and loss account one of the main financial statements showing the income of the business less the expenses of the business for the last accounting period

Gross profit the profit earned by the business from its trading activities – shown in the trading account

Carriage inwards the cost of getting the stock into the business

Carriage outwards costs of delivering goods to customers

Net profit the final profit of the business after all expenses have been deducted

Balance sheet a list of all of the assets and liabilities of the business on the last day of the accounting period

Current assets the short term assets of the business – stock, debtors and cash and bank balances

Current liabilities liabilities that are due to be paid within one year of the balance sheet date

Net current assets the total of the current assets minus the current liabilities

Long-term liabilities liabilities that are due to be paid more than a year after the balance sheet date

SSAPs Statements of Standard Accounting Practice

FRSs Financial Reporting Standards

CHAPTER OVERVIEW cont.

- the long term liabilities, payable after more than twelve months are deducted from the total of the net current assets and the fixed assets to give the final balance sheet total
- the capital is made up of the opening balance of capital plus the net profit from the profit and loss account minus the owner's drawings
- the profit and loss account is technically a large, summary ledger account and the income and expense ledger accounts are cleared to the profit and loss account at the end of the accounting period leaving no remaining balance on these accounts
- in contrast the balance sheet is a list of the asset and liability account balances on the last day of the accounting period – these balances remain in the ledger accounts to become the opening balances at the start of the next accounting period
- the accounting profession regulates itself by the production of accounting standards and companies must also comply with the legal rules found in the Companies Act 2006
- the accounting standards that have been issued by the profession are Statements of Standard Accounting Practice (SSAPs) and the more recent Financial Reporting Standards (FRSs)
- FRS 18 requires final accounts to be prepared on the going concern basis and under the accrual basis
- a business is a going concern if it will continue for the foreseeable future
- the accrual basis of preparing final accounts is that income and expenses should be included in the final accounts in the period in which they are earned or incurred rather than in the period in which the cash is received or paid
- appropriate accounting policies should be chosen by considering and balancing four objectives – relevance, reliability, comparability and ease of understanding
- the materiality concept allows immaterial items to be treated in a manner which would not be appropriate for material items – the level of materiality will depend upon the size of the business

KEY WORDS

Accounting policies the accounting methods chosen by an organisation to produce its final accounts

Going concern concept final accounts are prepared on the basis that the organisation will continue in business for the foreseeable future

Accruals concept income and expenses are recognised in the period in which they were earned or incurred rather than when the cash was received or paid

Relevance ability to influence the economic decisions of users

Reliability accurate and unbiased recording of the substance of a transaction

Comparability meaningful comparison is possible of financial information over time and between one organisation and another

Understandability ease of understanding for users with reasonable financial knowledge

Materiality the rules of accounting do not need to be applied to immaterial items

Statement of Principles for Financial Reporting a document issued by the Accounting Standards Board to act as a conceptual framework for financial reporting

HOW MUCH HAVE YOU LEARNED?

1 Given below is the trial balance for a small business that is not registered for VAT. You are required to state, in the space next to each balance, whether it is an asset, liability, income or expense and whether the balance would appear in the profit and loss account or the balance sheet.

	Debit	*Credit*	*Type of balance*	*P&L or balance sheet*
	£	£		
Sales		41,200		
Loan		1,500		
Wages	7,000			
Fixed assets	7,100			
Opening stock	1,800			
Debtors	3,400			
Discounts received		40		
Postage	100			
Bank	300			
Capital		9,530		
Rent	500			
Purchases	30,100			
Creditors		2,500		
Discounts allowed	70			
Drawings	3,000			
Electricity	800			
Telephone	600			
	54,770	54,770		

2 Complete the following sentences:

a) The gross profit of a business is the profit from ....

b) Carriage inwards is dealt with in the profit and loss account in the ....

c) The total of the current assets minus the current liabilities is known as ....

d) Current liabilities are ....

e) Long-term liabilities are ....

3 Each of the following statements is an example of which accounting concept?

a) Sales on credit are recognised as sales at the date that the sales invoice is sent out to the customer.

b) Fixed assets are valued in the balance sheet at an amount based on their original cost to the business.

c) Staplers for the office have been charged as an expense to the profit and loss account.

4 Explain each of the four desirable objectives from FRS 18 which should be considered in selecting accounting policies.

chapter 4: VALUE ADDED TAX

chapter coverage

In the chapters so far we have ignored Value Added Tax (VAT). However in this chapter we will consider the effects of VAT on the accounting of businesses and also details of SSAP 5, Accounting for Value Added Tax. The topics that we shall cover are:

- how the VAT system works
- double entry for sales and purchases with VAT
- writing up the ledger accounts from primary records with VAT
- dealing with input VAT in a business that is not registered for VAT
- exempt supplies
- accounting for irrecoverable VAT
- SSAP 5, Accounting for VAT

KNOWLEDGE AND UNDERSTANDING AND PERFORMANCE CRITERIA COVERAGE
knowledge and understanding
■ the main requirements of relevant SSAPs and FRSs

student notes

VALUE ADDED TAX – THE SYSTEM

VAT registration

If the sales of a business exceed a certain amount for a year, currently £64,000, then the business must register for VAT. This means that they have a VAT registration number which must be included on invoices and other business documents.

What it also means is that it must charge VAT on all of its taxable supplies or sales at the standard rate normally of 17.5%. This is known as OUTPUT VAT.

There is however a benefit in that the VAT that the business pays when buying from suppliers or paying expenses can be recovered back from HM Revenue & Customs (HMRC) and is known as INPUT VAT.

Usually every three months the business must complete a VAT return showing the output and input VAT. The excess of output VAT over input VAT must be paid with the VAT return. However if the input VAT exceeds the output VAT then a refund is due from HM Revenue & Customs.

student notes

HOW IT WORKS

Let's follow a simple manufacturing process through the VAT payment process.

Business	Transaction		HMRC VAT due
Supplier of wood	Sells wood to table manufacturer for £160 + VAT of £28		
	Sale value	£160	
	Output VAT	£28	£28
Table manufacturer	Purchases wood from supplier for £160 + VAT of £28 Sells table to retailer for £280 + VAT of £49		
	Sale value	£280	
	Purchases value	£160	
	Output VAT – Input VAT (49 – 28)	£21	£21
Retailer	Purchases table from manufacturer for £280 + VAT of £49 Sells table to customer for £360 + VAT of £63		
	Sale value	£360	
	Purchases value	£280	
	Output VAT – Input VAT (63 – 49)	£14	£14
Customer	Purchases table for £360 + VAT of £63		
	Pays retailer (360 + 63)	£423	£0
Total VAT paid to HM Revenue & Customs			£63

Note that it is the final consumer who bears the cost of the VAT, the table cost him £423 not £360, but the consumer does not have to pay this to HM Revenue & Customs as this has already been done throughout the chain of manufacture and sale.

Activity 1

What are output VAT and input VAT?

student notes

ACCOUNTING FOR VAT

Although a VAT registered business must charge VAT at 17.5% on its sales the business itself makes no profit out of the VAT as it must be paid over to HMRC. This is reflected in the accounting for VAT.

The amount that is recognised as sales is the net of VAT amount. However if the sale is on credit then the amount of the debtor is the full amount including the VAT as this is the amount that the customer must pay. The difference goes to the VAT account, (also sometimes called the VAT control account).

Double entry for sales

Let's summarise the double entry for sales:

Cash sale:
Debit Bank account with the gross amount
Credit Sales account with the net amount
Credit VAT account with the VAT

Credit sale:
Debit Debtors account with the gross amount
Credit Sales account with the net amount
Credit VAT account with the VAT

Double entry for purchases and expenses

Again as with the sales the VAT on purchases and expenses is not a cost to the business as it can be reclaimed from HM Revenue & Customs. Therefore the amount that is recognised as purchases or expenses is again the net amount.

Let's summarise the double entry for purchases:

Cash purchase:
Debit Purchases account with the net amount
Debit VAT account with the VAT
Credit Bank account with the gross amount

Credit purchase:
Debit Purchases account with the net amount
Debit VAT account with the VAT
Credit Creditors account with the gross amount

student notes

HOW IT WORKS

A business makes sales on credit of £20,000 plus VAT and purchases on credit of £12,000 plus VAT. Here are the entries in the ledger accounts for these transactions.

Credit sale

Debtors account

	£		£
Sales (20,000 × 1.175)	23,500		

Sales account

	£		£
		Debtors	20,000

VAT account

	£		£
		Debtors	3,500

Credit purchase

Creditors account

	£		£
		Purchases (12,000 × 1.175)	14,100

Purchases account

	£		£
Creditors	12,000		

VAT account

	£		£
Creditors	2,100	Debtors	3,500

student notes

If the VAT account is balanced at this point then we can see that there is a credit balance brought down of £1,400.

VAT account

	£		£
Creditors	2,100	Debtors	3,500
Balance c/d	1,400		
	3,500		3,500
		Balance b/d	1,400

If a trial balance were drawn up then the balance on the VAT account would appear as a credit balance. This is a creditor, the amount due to HM Revenue & Customs, and would therefore be shown in the balance sheet as a current liability if the financial statements were being drawn up.

Activity 2

A business makes total sales in a month of £84,000 plus VAT and total purchases in the month of £60,000 plus VAT. Write up the VAT account for the month.

VAT account

	£		£

student notes

VAT AND THE PRIMARY RECORDS

As we saw in an earlier chapter, in practice the transactions of a business will initially be recorded in the primary records. If there is a VAT element of these transactions then this must also be recorded in the primary records.

HOW IT WORKS

Given below are some of the primary records of a business that is registered for VAT.

Sales day book

Date	*Customer*	*Invoice No.*	*Gross* £	*VAT* £	*Net* £
2 Mar	L&P Partners	0254	564	84	480
10 Mar	Raine Fnt	0255	376	56	320
21 Mar	Jessops	0256	470	70	400
			1,410	210	1,200

The VAT element of the sales invoices sent out must be shown separately in the sales day book together with the net and gross figures.

Purchases day book

Date	*Supplier*	*Invoice No.*	*Gross* £	*VAT* £	*Net* £
4 Mar	Ogden Ltd	43578	282	42	240
11 Mar	Kipper & Sons	219532	423	63	360
28 Mar	Jill Simms	5621	329	49	280
			1,034	154	880

The VAT element of the invoices from suppliers must also be shown separately in the purchases day book together with the net and gross totals.

student notes

Cash receipts book

Date	Details	Total £	VAT £	Cash sales £	Sales ledger £	Other £
7 Mar	Cash sales	611	91	520		
14 Mar	L&P Partners	564			564	
20 Mar	Cash sales	705	105	600		
30 Mar	Raine Ent	376			376	
		2,256	196	1,120	940	

Note that it is only the cash sales that have the VAT shown in the cash receipts book not the receipts from the sales ledger customers. This is because the VAT on the sales to the credit customers was analysed in the sales day book (and will be posted to the VAT account from there) – to include the VAT element again in the cash receipts book would be double counting.

Cash payments book

Date	Details	Cheque No.	Total £	VAT £	Cash purchases £	Purchases ledger £	Other £
4 Mar	Cash purchases	02456	188	28	160		
15 Mar	Ogden Ltd	02457	282			282	
24 Mar	Cash purchases	02458	141	21	120		
			611	49	280	282	

Just as in the cash receipts book note that the VAT is only analysed for the cash purchases and any other non-purchases ledger expenses as the VAT on the credit purchases was recorded in the purchases day book when the invoice was received.

student notes

Main ledger

We will now post the totals of the primary records to the main ledger accounts.

We will start with the Sales day book totals:

Sales ledger control account

Date	Details	£	Date	Details	£
31 Mar	SDB	1,410			

Sales account

Date	Details	£	Date	Details	£
			31 Mar	SDB	1,200

VAT account

Date	Details	£	Date	Details	£
			31 Mar	SDB	210

Now the Purchases day book:

Purchase ledger control account

Date	Details	£	Date	Details	£
			31 Mar	PDB	1,034

Purchases account

Date	Details	£	Date	Details	£
31 Mar	PDB	880			

VAT account

Date	Details	£	Date	Details	£
31 Mar	PDB	154	31 Mar	SDB	210

student notes

Then the Cash receipts book:

Sales ledger control account

Date	Details	£	Date	Details	£
31 Mar	SDB	1,410	31 Mar	CRB	940

Sales account

Date	Details	£	Date	Details	£
			31 Mar	SDB	1,200
			31 Mar	CRB	1,120

VAT account

Date	Details	£	Date	Details	£
31 Mar	PDB	154	31 Mar	SDB	210
			31 Mar	CRB	196

Finally the Cash payments book:

Purchases ledger control account

Date	Details	£	Date	Details	£
31 Mar	CPB	282	31 Mar	PDB	1,034

Purchases account

Date	Details	£	Date	Details	£
31 Mar	PDB	880	31 Mar	PDB	1,034
31 Mar	CPB	280			

VAT account

Date	Details	£	Date	Details	£
31 Mar	PDB	154	31 Mar	SDB	210
31 Mar	CPB	49	31 Mar	CRB	196

Subsidiary ledgers

Now we must enter each of the individual entries into the individual debtor and creditor accounts in the subsidiary ledgers, the sales ledger and the purchases ledger. The invoice total that is entered into the subsidiary ledger accounts is the gross total as this is the amount that the debtor must pay and that your business must pay its creditors.

student notes

Subsidiary ledger – sales ledger

L&P Partners

Date	Details	£	Date	Details	£
2 Mar	SDB	564	14 Mar	CRB	564

Raine Ent

Date	Details	£	Date	Details	£
10 Mar	SDB	376	30 Mar	CRB	376

Jessops

Date	Details	£	Date	Details	£
21 Mar	SDB	470			

Subsidiary ledger – purchases ledger

Ogden Ltd

Date	Details	£	Date	Details	£
15 Mar	CPB	282	4 Mar	PDB	282

Kipper & Sons

Date	Details	£	Date	Details	£
			11 Mar	PDB	423

Jill Simms

Date	Details	£	Date	Details	£
			28 Mar	PDB	329

Activity 3

Given below are the totals of the purchases day book for a business. What is the double entry for these totals?

student notes

Purchases day book

Gross £	*VAT* £	*Net* £
17,390	2,590	14,800

THE EFFECT OF NON-REGISTRATION FOR VAT

If a business is not registered for VAT because its turnover does not exceed £64,000 then it will not charge VAT on its sales. However if that business buys goods that have VAT charged on them then it will not be able to reclaim this input VAT from HM Revenue & Customs. Therefore the input VAT becomes a cost to the business and must be shown as part of the cost of the goods.

HOW IT WORKS

Jenny Fisher is not registered for VAT. However she buys goods from a credit supplier for £1,000 plus VAT.

When Jenny is accounting for this purchase she must include the VAT as part of the cost of the goods as she cannot reclaim it. The double entry would be:

Creditors account

	£		£
		Purchases	1,175

Purchases account

	£		£
Creditors	1,175		

student notes

EXEMPT SUPPLIES

Some types of supplies of goods are exempt from VAT. These include land, postal services, health and welfare.

If your business buys exempt supplies such as postage costs then these will not include any VAT element.

If your business sells exempt supplies then it will not be charging any VAT on these sales but it can still reclaim all or part of the input VAT that it is charged on its purchases and expenses by agreement with HM Revenue & Customs.

IRRECOVERABLE VAT

Normally a VAT-registered business can reclaim the input VAT on all of its purchases and expenses. However in some cases the VAT cannot be reclaimed and is known as IRRECOVERABLE VAT. The most common example that you might come across is the VAT on the purchase specifically of cars (unless they are for resale) – this is an example of irrecoverable VAT. However, in contrast, the VAT on the purchase of vans is recoverable. So too is VAT on business entertaining.

HOW IT WORKS

A VAT-registered business buys a new car for one of its salesmen at a cost of £10,000 plus VAT. As the VAT on this car is irrecoverable the cost of the car to the business is not £10,000 but £11,750.

SSAP 5 ACCOUNTING FOR VAT

SSAP 5, Accounting for value added tax, adds very little to what has already been covered in this chapter. Its two main requirements are:

- sales, as reported in the profit and loss account, should not include VAT
- irrecoverable VAT should be included in the cost of the item

Activity 4

Your business is not registered for VAT but it buys goods and services that do have VAT charged on them. Explain what effect this has on the accounting for your business.

CHAPTER OVERVIEW

- a business must register for VAT if its sales exceed, currently, £64,000 a year – it will then charge output VAT on its sales usually at the standard rate of 17.5%
- the business will also be able to recover any input VAT paid on its purchases and expenses
- sales and purchases are shown net of VAT and debtors and creditors are shown at the gross amount – the difference, the VAT, is taken to the VAT account

KEY WORDS

Output VAT VAT charged on sales

Input VAT VAT incurred on purchases and expenses

Exempt supplies goods and services that are exempt from VAT

Irrecoverable VAT VAT on a purchase that cannot be recovered

- the balance on the VAT account will normally be a credit balance – this is a creditor balance in the balance sheet, the amount that is owed to HMRC
- in the sales day book the VAT element of the invoices sent out to customers must be shown separately – in just the same way the VAT on suppliers' invoices must be shown separately in the purchases day book
- in the cash receipts book the VAT must only be analysed out for any cash sales as this has already been done for sales on credit in the sales day book
- in the cash payments book the VAT must only be analysed out for any cash purchases and any other non-purchase ledger payments as this has already been done for credit purchases in the purchases day book
- the invoice total to be entered into the subsidiary ledger accounts for debtors and creditors is the gross invoice total
- if a business is not registered for VAT it will not charge VAT on its sales but it will also not be able to recover the VAT on its purchases and expenses – the purchases and expenses must therefore be shown at their VAT-inclusive total in the accounts
- if a business sells supplies that are exempt from VAT then it does not charge any VAT on these sales but it may be able to reclaim all or part of the input VAT that it incurs
- VAT on the purchase of cars that are not for resale is irrecoverable and therefore the VAT must be included as part of the cost of the car in the accounting records. However, VAT on the purchase of vans is recoverable
- SSAP 5, Accounting for VAT, states that sales should be shown net of VAT and that irrecoverable VAT should be included as part of the cost of the item

HOW MUCH HAVE YOU LEARNED?

1 A business that is registered for VAT has made credit sales of £168,000 plus VAT during the month and credit purchases of £126,000 plus VAT. Write up the ledger accounts for these transactions.

2 You are given some of the primary records of a business that is registered for VAT.

Sales day book

Date	*Customer*	*Invoice No.*	*Gross* £	*VAT* £	*Net* £
3 May	F Leonard	03552	185.65	27.65	158.00
12 May	K Olsen	03553	263.20	39.20	224.00
28 May	Claire & Sons	03554	451.20	67.20	384.00
			900.05	134.05	766.00

Sales returns day book

Date	*Customer*	*Credit note No.*	*Gross* £	*VAT* £	*Net* £
16 May	K Olsen	CN 2224	37.60	5.60	32.00

Purchases day book

Date	*Supplier*	*Invoice No.*	*Gross* £	*VAT* £	*Net* £
2 May	Davis & Co	4327	178.60	26.60	152.00
7 May	Norman Bros	21342	336.05	50.05	286.00
22 May	Field & Sons	099807	291.40	43.40	248.00
			806.05	120.05	686.00

Cash receipts book

Date	Details	Total £	VAT £	Cash sales £	Sales ledger £	Other £
7 May	Cash sales	321.95	47.95	274.00		
12 May	F Leonard	185.65			185.65	
18 May	Cash sales	373.65	55.65	318.00		
28 May	K Olsen	225.60			225.60	
		1,106.85	103.60	592.00	411.25	

Cash payments book

Date	Details	Cheque No.	Total £	VAT £	Cash purchases £	Purchases ledger £	Other £
5 May	Cash purchases	38565	227.95	33.95	194.00		
15 May	Davis & Co	38566	178.60			178.60	
21 May	Norman Bros	38567	336.05			336.05	
28 May	Cash purchases	38568	253.80	37.80	216.00		
			996.40	71.75	410.00	514.65	

You are required to:

a) post the totals of the primary records to the main ledger accounts

b) post the individual entries in the primary records to the individual debtor and creditor accounts in the subsidiary ledgers, the sales ledger and the purchases ledger

3 Complete the following sentences:

a) Input VAT is VAT on .... and output VAT is VAT on ....

b) If a business is not registered for VAT then the input VAT that it incurs must be .... in the accounting records.

c) Postage costs are an example of .... supply for VAT purposes.

d) Irrecoverable VAT is .... in the accounting records.

chapter 5: CAPITAL EXPENDITURE

chapter coverage 

In this chapter we start to consider the first element of Unit 5, 'Maintaining records relating to capital acquisition and disposal'. We will be considering the distinction between capital expenditure and revenue expenditure and how to account for and control fixed assets. The topics that we shall cover are:

- the distinction between capital and revenue expenditure
- the costs to be included as capital expenditure
- revenue expenditure
- accounting for capital expenditure
- journal entries for acquisition of fixed assets
- authorisation process for acquisition of fixed assets
- methods of funding the acquisition of fixed assets
- the fixed asset register
- tangible and intangible fixed assets

KNOWLEDGE AND UNDERSTANDING AND PERFORMANCE CRITERIA COVERAGE

knowledge and understanding

- the types and characteristics of different assets and key issues relating to the acquisition and disposal of capital assets
- the relevant legislation and regulations
- the main requirements of relevant SSAPs and FRSs
- how to use plant registers and similar subsidiary records
- how to use the transfer journal
- the distinction between capital and revenue expenditure and what constitutes capital expenditure

Performance criteria – element 5.1

- record relevant details relating to capital expenditure in the appropriate records
- correctly identify and record all acquisition and disposal costs and revenues in the appropriate records
- ensure that the records clearly show the prior authority for capital expenditure and disposal and the approved method of funding and disposal
- ensure that the organisation's policies and procedures relating to the maintenance of capital records are adhered to

CAPITAL EXPENDITURE AND REVENUE EXPENDITURE

student notes

As we have seen in earlier chapters there are a variety of items that a business spends its money on. Some of these will be fairly major long-term assets of the business, some will be assets that are due to be sold shortly and some will be the everyday running expenses of the business.

Fixed assets

Some of the assets that are purchased by a business will be for long-term use in the business – these are known as FIXED ASSETS. Fixed assets are the assets that are necessary for the business to carry on its activities. Typical examples of fixed assets include:

- buildings from which the business operates
- machinery used in the manufacturing process
- delivery vehicles to distribute the goods
- cars for sales representatives
- fixtures and fittings for the office area
- computers for the sales and administration departments

The cost of buying these fixed assets and getting them into operation is known as CAPITAL EXPENDITURE.

All other expenditure of the business, other than on the purchase of fixed assets, is known as REVENUE EXPENDITURE.

The distinction between capital and revenue expenditure

The importance of the distinction between revenue and capital expenditure is due to their differing treatment in the financial statements.

Capital expenditure is classified as a fixed asset and as such is included as an asset in the balance sheet. Revenue expenditure, in contrast, is charged as an expense to the profit and loss account. Suppose therefore that a business spends £20,000 on a new machine for making the organisation's products. If this were mistakenly classified as revenue expenditure then the profit and loss account would have an extra large expense of £20,000 and the balance sheet would not include this major asset of the business.

student notes

What is included in capital expenditure?

Due to the differing treatment of capital and revenue expenditure it is also necessary to ensure that the correct amounts are included in the balance sheet as capital expenditure.

The cost of a fixed asset to be included in the balance sheet, or capitalised, is not just its purchase price. It is the total cost of getting the fixed asset to its correct location and into full working order. Therefore the types of costs that might be included as capital expenditure include:

- the net of VAT cost of the asset (other than cars where the VAT is irrecoverable and therefore must be included in the cost)
- delivery costs
- set up costs
- training costs of training staff to use this particular fixed asset
- any special alterations or equipment required in order to use the fixed asset

FRS 15, Tangible fixed assets, also makes it clear that any major alteration or improvement of the fixed asset would also be treated as capital expenditure.

Revenue expenditure

There will often be other expenses related to the fixed assets of a business and care must be taken to ensure that these are treated as revenue expenditure and charged as expenses in the profit and loss account not capitalised in the balance sheet.

Examples of revenue expenditure which might be confused with capital expenditure might include:

- costs of decorating a new building
- repairs to a building or machinery
- general maintenance costs
- costs of cleaning machinery
- fuel costs
- insurance costs
- servicing and repairs to motor vehicles
- the road fund licence for a vehicle (often included in the invoice for a new vehicle so take care)
- CDs and printer paper for the computer

Assets made by the business's employees

student notes

In some situations fixed assets may not be purchased but are instead made by the business's employees. For example a building firm may build a new set of offices for its own use.

Another situation might be that a business uses its own employees to install a new piece of machinery.

In each case the cost of the fixed asset will include the wages cost of the employees who worked on it together with the cost of any materials that they used. Therefore these wages and materials will be treated as capital expenditure.

HOW IT WORKS

Harris Incorporated have just significantly enlarged the operations of their manufacturing business and as such have purchased a number of major assets.

Purchased a building to use as the factory at a cost of £80,000 plus £1,000 of legal fees

- the legal fees are part of the cost of purchasing the building and therefore are treated as capital expenditure – total capital expenditure £81,000

Carried out £10,000 of building work in order to make the building suitable for the manufacturing process

- again this is part of the cost of the factory and would be treated as capital expenditure

Purchased a TV1 machine for £4,000 which was installed by Harris's own employees using £200 of materials and incurring wages costs of £600

- the installation costs should be treated as capital expenditure as they are a cost of getting the asset into use – total capital expenditure £4,800

student notes

Redecorated a building that was already owned and is used for the sales and administration departments at a total cost of £1,400

- this is all revenue expenditure as these are running expenses of the business – total revenue expenditure £1,400

Purchased a computer to help in the administration department for £1,200 together with computer software costing £400 and a training course for the employees who will be using the computer at a cost of £200. The cost of the computer included £50 of CDs and £20 of printer paper that were delivered with it.

- the cost of the software could be treated as either capital or revenue expenditure – as the cost of this software is quite large it would probably be treated as capital expenditure. The cost of the training course would also be treated as capital expenditure as it is necessary in order to run the computer. The cost of the CDs and the paper is revenue expenditure as this is part of the cost of running the computer – total capital expenditure of £1,730, total revenue expenditure £70

Employed contract cleaners to clean the new TV1 machine after its first week of operations at a cost of £150

- this would be treated as revenue expenditure as it is part of the general running costs of the business – total revenue expenditure £150

Purchased a new delivery van at a cost of £16,400 which included £100 of delivery charges and £200 of road fund licence

- the delivery costs are part of the cost of the fixed asset and are treated as capital expenditure but the road fund licence is a running cost of the vehicle and is treated as revenue expenditure – total capital expenditure £16,200, total revenue expenditure £200

Purchased some office furniture for £1,300 on credit

- total capital expenditure £1,300

student notes

Activity 1

A business has two machines. Machine A has just undergone a major overhaul at a cost of £15,000 which has extended its life to the business by four years. Machine B has just been repaired due to the wearing out of a small working part at a cost of £4,000. Would these costs be treated as capital or revenue expenditure and why?

ACCOUNTING FOR CAPITAL EXPENDITURE

When fixed assets are purchased they are debited to separate fixed asset ledger accounts for each type of fixed asset. The most common classifications of types of fixed assets are:

- land and buildings
- plant and machinery
- motor vehicles
- fixtures and fittings
- computers

The fixed assets may be purchased for cash (ie by cheque) or it may be on credit. The credit entry will therefore either be to the bank account or to the creditors account.

When the business's own employees have been used to make or install fixed assets then the following double entry must be made:

Materials	Debit Fixed asset account Credit Purchases account
Wages	Debit Fixed asset account Credit Wages account

The effect of this is to remove the materials and wages that are capital expenditure from revenue expenditure accounts.

student notes

HOW IT WORKS

We will now return to Harris Incorporated and show how each item of expenditure would be entered into the ledger accounts. All of the purchases were for cash other than the office furniture which was purchased on credit.

Purchased a building to use as the factory at a cost of £80,000 plus £1,000 of legal fees

Land and buildings account

	£		£
Bank	81,000		

Bank account

	£		£
Opening balance (say)	140,000	Land and buildings	81,000

Carried out £10,000 of building work in order to make the building suitable for the manufacturing process

Land and buildings account

	£		£
Bank	81,000		
Bank	10,000		

Bank account

	£		£
Opening balance	140,000	Land and buildings	81,000
		Land and buildings	10,000

Purchased a TV1 machine for £4,000 which was installed by Harris's own employees using £200 of materials and incurring wages costs of £600

Plant and machinery account

	£		£
Bank	4,000		
Purchases	200		
Wages	600		

student notes

Bank account

	£		£
Opening balance	140,000	Land and buildings	81,000
		Land and buildings	10,000
		Plant and machinery	4,000

Purchases account

	£		£
Opening balance (say)	75,000	Plant and machinery	200

Wages account

	£		£
Opening balance (say)	184,000	Plant and machinery	600

Redecorated a building that was already owned and is used for the sales and administration departments at a total cost of £1,400

Buildings maintenance account

	£		£
Bank	1,400	Plant and machinery	200

This is an expense account not a fixed asset account as this is revenue expenditure.

Bank account

	£		£
Opening balance	140,000	Land and buildings	81,000
		Land and buildings	10,000
		Plant and machinery	4,000
		Buildings maintenance	1,400

Purchased a computer to help in the administration department for £1,200 together with computer software costing £400 and a training course for the employees who will be using the computer at a cost of £200. The cost of the computer included £50 of CDs and £20 of printer paper that were delivered with it

student notes

Computers account

	£		£
Bank	1,730		

Stationery account

	£		£
Bank	70		

The CDs and the paper have been charged to an expense account as they are revenue expenditure not capital expenditure.

Bank account

	£		£
Opening balance	140,000	Land and buildings	81,000
		Land and buildings	10,000
		Plant and machinery	4,000
		Buildings maintenance	1,400
		Computers	1,730
		Stationery	70

Employed contract cleaners to clean the new TV1 machine after its first week of operations at a cost of £150

Cleaning costs account

	£		£
Bank	150		

This is an expense account as this is revenue expenditure not capital expenditure.

Bank account

	£		£
Opening balance	140,000	Land and buildings	81,000
		Land and buildings	10,000
		Plant and machinery	4,000
		Buildings maintenance	1,400
		Computers	1,730
		Stationery	70
		Cleaning costs	150

student notes

Purchased a new delivery van at a cost of £16,400 which included £100 of delivery charges and £200 of road fund licence

Motor vehicles account

	£		£
Bank	16,200		

Motor expenses

	£		£
Bank	200		

Again this is an expense account as the road fund licence is not capital expenditure.

Bank account

	£		£
Opening balance	140,000	Land and buildings	81,000
		Land and buildings	10,000
		Plant and machinery	4,000
		Buildings maintenance	1,400
		Computers	1,730
		Stationery	70
		Cleaning costs	150
		Motor vehicles	16,200
		Motor expenses	200

Purchased some office furniture for £1,300 on credit

Fixtures and fittings account

	£		£
Creditors	1,300		

Creditors account

	£		£
		Opening balance (say)	52,000
		Fixtures and fittings	1,300

student notes

Activity 2

A business has recently installed a new machine which cost £17,000 and was purchased on credit. The installation was carried out by its own employees and the wages costs of these employees for the time taken to install the machine are £1,400.

Write up the relevant ledger accounts to reflect the purchase and installation of this machine.

Journal entries

In practice the way in which the acquisition of a fixed asset is recorded in the ledger accounts is by way of a JOURNAL ENTRY.

This is normally the book of original entry for the acquisition of fixed assets.

A journal entry is an instruction to the bookkeeper to make entries in the ledger accounts. Therefore the journal must have equal debit and credit entries together with a brief description of what the entry relates to (the journal will be considered in more detail in Chapter 11).

HOW IT WORKS

student notes

Returning to Harris Incorporated we will now prepare the journal entries for each of the purchases of fixed assets (in practice of course this would be done before the entries are made in the ledger accounts as the journal is the instruction to make the ledger account entries). Today's date is 5 February 2009.

Purchased a building to use as the factory at a cost of £80,000 plus £1,000 of legal fees

Date	*Account*	*Ref*	*Debit*	*Credit*
			£	£
2009				
5 Feb	Land and buildings		81,000	
	Bank			81,000
			81,000	81,000
Being purchase of new factory building				

Note that the reference column would be used to enter the main ledger code for the accounts being debited and credited.

Carried out £10,000 of building work in order to make the building suitable for the manufacturing process

Date	*Account*	*Ref*	*Debit*	*Credit*
			£	£
2009				
5 Feb	Land and buildings		10,000	
	Bank			10,000
			10,000	10,000
Being alterations to new factory				

student notes

Purchased a TV1 machine for £4,000 which was installed by Harris's own employees using £200 of materials and incurring wages costs of £600

Date	*Account*	*Ref*	*Debit*	*Credit*
			£	£
2009				
5 Feb	Plant and machinery		4,800	
	Bank			4,000
	Purchases			200
	Wages			600
			4,800	4,800

Being purchase and installation of TV1 machine

Purchased a computer to help in the administration department for £1,200 together with computer software costing £400 and a training course for the employees who will be using the computer at a cost of £200. The cost of the computer included £50 of CDs and £20 of printer paper that were delivered with it

Date	*Account*	*Ref*	*Debit*	*Credit*
			£	£
2009				
5 Feb	Computers		1,730	
	Stationery		70	
	Bank			1,800
			1,800	1,800

Being purchase of computer

Purchased a new delivery van at a cost of £16,400 which included £100 of delivery charges and £200 of road fund licence

Date	*Account*	*Ref*	*Debit*	*Credit*
			£	£
2009				
5 Feb	Motor vehicles		16,200	
	Motor expenses		200	
	Bank			16,400
			16,400	16,400

Being purchase of new delivery van

student notes

Purchased some office furniture for £1,300 on credit

Date	*Account*	*Ref*	*Debit* £	*Credit* £
2009				
5 Feb	Fixtures and fittings		1,300	
	Creditors			1,300
			1,300	1,300

Being purchase of office furniture

Activity 3

A business has recently purchased four cars for use by its sales force at a total invoiced amount of £79,600 including VAT. This total includes £400 of delivery costs and £800 of road fund licences. The amount due was paid by cheque upon delivery of the cars.

Draft the journal entry for the acquisition of these cars.

AUTHORISATION FOR FIXED ASSET ACQUISITIONS

Clearly the acquisition of fixed assets is a major cost to a business and therefore it must be monitored and controlled. If a fixed asset is required by the business then there will normally be a strict procedure to follow:

- Acquisition application
- Price quotations
- Authorisation of application
- Monitoring of on-going costs

Acquisition application

If an area of a business needs a new fixed asset then this requirement will need to be justified to the owners/managers of the business. The procedure for applying to acquire a new fixed asset will depend upon the nature and the cost of the asset and the organisation and size of the business.

The application to buy a new desk and chair for a new employee in the accounts department may well be a simple memo to the accountant.

student notes✍

The application to purchase a new piece of machinery costing £120,000 is likely to require a much more formal application with many details supporting the need for this acquisition. In larger businesses such applications will probably be dealt with by a capital expenditure committee or at the very least a meeting of the senior management of the business.

Price quotations

As with any purchase that a business makes, when purchasing a fixed asset, it is important that the best possible combination of price, quality and service is found. This may well involve getting detailed quotations from a number of different suppliers. These quotations are likely to differ on price as well as the terms of after sales service and the quality of the product. All of this will be relevant to the managers of the business who will make the decision as to whether to authorise this acquisition.

Authorisation

When considering whether or not to authorise the acquisition of a new fixed asset the management of a business will not only consider the cost of the asset and the terms that are being offered. There are also many other considerations that will go into the authorisation process.

- Can we afford the asset? – the question here is whether the business has enough money to buy the asset (different funding methods will be considered later in the chapter)
- What effect will the new asset have upon staffing levels? A major new production line could mean that new employees are required. A sophisticated computer system may mean that a specialist has to be employed
- New machinery or technology may mean that staff will need to be trained in order to be able to operate the machinery or understand the technology
- What effect will there be on productivity? If a new machine or production line is acquired will this improve the amount of production each hour or day?
- What will be the effect on profitability? Is the fixed asset worthwhile? The costs and benefits of the asset have to be considered over a number of years in order to determine whether this asset will add to the business or detract from it

student notes

Monitoring of costs

Many capital acquisitions a business will make will not be one-off purchases but a development over time. For example if a new factory is being built and stocked with machinery this may well take a number of months. When the initial purchase application was approved the management of the business will have had a price quotation for the job but it is important that all aspects of the job are monitored to ensure that there are no unforeseen cost overruns.

METHODS OF FUNDING

We have already seen that the acquisition of fixed assets is a major expense for any business. Many businesses will not have enough funds in their bank account to purchase large fixed assets by cash. Therefore alternative options have to be considered.

Borrowing

Businesses may borrow the money to acquire new fixed assets either by a LOAN or a MORTGAGE. A loan can be available from banks, building societies and many other providers of finance. A loan for the purchase of a fixed asset will normally be for a fixed amount for any period of time up to about 10 years. Interest will be charged on the amount outstanding and the loan will normally be repaid by monthly or quarterly instalments.

A mortgage might be a more suitable method of borrowing for the purchase of a property. The mortgage loan can be for any amount up to 80% of the value of the property and can be repaid over a period up to around 25 years. The property serves as security for the loan in case the repayments are not made. Interest and capital will normally be paid in monthly instalments.

For any loan the interest will appear in the profit and loss account as an expense each year and the outstanding amount of the loan will appear on the balance sheet as a long term creditor.

Hire purchase

Many fixed assets such as motor vehicles, plant and machinery, office equipment and computers can be purchased under a HIRE PURCHASE AGREEMENT.

Under a hire purchase agreement the business will pay an initial deposit to the finance company and from that point onwards has full use of the asset although the asset remains, in legal terms, as being owned by the finance company. The business will then make regular payments to the finance

student notes

company, usually monthly or quarterly, which are designed to pay off the capital cost of the asset plus the interest charged by the finance company. At the end of the hire purchase period the asset legally becomes owned by the business.

The interest element of the repayments will appear in the profit and loss account as an expense. Although the fixed asset is not legally owned by the business, best accounting practice is that it appears in the balance sheet as a fixed asset at its cost as if it had been purchased outright. There will also be a creditor for the amount still owed to the finance company.

Part exchange

A part exchange deal is very common particularly in the motor trade. If the business wishes to purchase a new car for one of its salesmen it can offer the salesman's current car in PART EXCHANGE. The car dealer will place a value on the old car and deduct this value from the cost of the new car and the business need only pay the difference.

Accounting for part exchange deals will be dealt with in Chapter 7.

FIXED ASSET REGISTER

As we have already seen it is important that a business has strict control over its fixed assets. In order to keep track of all of the fixed assets that the business owns most businesses will keep a fixed asset register (sometimes called a plant register). For each fixed asset that the business acquires a detailed record will be kept in the fixed asset register typically showing the following:

- A description of the asset and possibly a fixed asset number
- Its physical location within the business
- The supplier and the date of purchase
- The cost of the asset
- The estimated life of the asset
- The estimated scrap value of the asset at the end of its life
- The method of depreciation to be applied (see Chapter 6)
- The depreciation percentage
- The amount of depreciation charged each year
- The provision for depreciation at the end of each year
- The net book value of the asset at the end of each year (see Chapter 6)
- Eventually the details of the disposal of the asset including sale proceeds and any profit or loss on disposal (see Chapter 7)

HOW IT WORKS

student notes

Kendall Engineering have just purchased a new machine, the FD254, from Leyland Machinery for £120,000. Today's date is 1 March 2009 and the machine is allocated fixed asset number 02635. The machine is located in the factory and is expected to be used for 5 years after which it will have an estimated scrap value of £20,000.

We will now enter these initial details in the fixed asset register.

FIXED ASSET REGISTER

Fixed asset number 02635
Description Machine FD254
Location Factory
Supplier Leyland Machinery

Date	Cost £	Expected life (years)	Estimated scrap value £	Depreciation method	Depreciation rate	Depreciation charge for the year £	Provision at end of the year £	Net book value at end of year £	Disposal proceeds £	Profit or loss on disposal £
2009 1 Mar	120,000	5	20,000							

student notes

In Chapters 6 and 7 the remaining entries in the fixed asset register will be considered.

TANGIBLE AND INTANGIBLE FIXED ASSETS

The types of fixed assets that we have considered so far, land, buildings, machinery, motor vehicles, computers etc are all TANGIBLE FIXED ASSETS. Tangible fixed assets are assets that have a physical form.

However there are also other types of fixed assets, INTANGIBLE FIXED ASSETS. These are still fixed assets, ie, they are for long term use within the business, but they have no physical form. One of the most common forms of intangible fixed assets is goodwill. We will consider this further when dealing with partnerships.

Goodwill

Many businesses will have an intangible fixed asset known as GOODWILL. Technically this means that the business as a whole is worth more than the sum of its net assets. The goodwill, the extra value, will have been created by such things as good quality products, excellent after sales service, good location, loyal workforce etc. The goodwill is a true asset of the business as it will mean that the business makes more sales and earns more profit. However in most cases the goodwill will not appear on the balance sheet due to difficulties in measuring it reliably in monetary terms.

CHAPTER OVERVIEW

- capital expenditure is the cost of acquiring fixed assets, assets for long term use in the business rather than for sale
- revenue expenditure is all other business expenditure
- the costs to be included as the cost of a fixed asset are the costs involved in purchasing the asset and getting it into working order – these are then included in the balance sheet as fixed assets
- revenue expenditure is charged to the profit and loss account as expenses
- the double entry for acquiring a fixed asset is to debit the relevant fixed asset account and to credit either bank or creditors depending upon whether the asset was purchased for cash or on credit
- if a fixed asset has been made or installed by the business's own workforce then the materials and wages costs are debited to the fixed asset account and credited to purchases and wages respectively
- the entries to the ledger accounts are initiated by a journal entry instructing the bookkeeper to account for the acquisition of the fixed assets
- control and monitoring of fixed assets is extremely important and a fixed asset should only be acquired if its acquisition application is authorised
- many fixed assets will not be acquired for cash but will be financed by a loan or purchased on a hire purchase agreement
- old assets can often be given in part-exchange for a new asset in order to reduce the cost of the new asset
- the details of all fixed assets will be kept in a fixed asset register
- tangible fixed assets are assets that have a physical form – some businesses will also have intangible fixed assets such as goodwill

KEY WORDS

Fixed assets assets acquired for long term use within the business

Capital expenditure expenditure on acquiring fixed assets

Revenue expenditure all other expenditure – therefore any expenditure that is not the acquisition or major improvement of fixed assets

Journal entry an instruction to the bookkeeper to put through a double entry in the ledger accounts

Acquisition application an application by an area of the business to purchase a fixed asset

Loan a fixed amount borrowed from a bank or building society etc which is to be repaid over a fixed period of time on which interest is paid on the outstanding amount

Mortgage a specific type of loan for the purchase of buildings where the building itself acts as security for the loan

Hire purchase agreement a method of financing the purchase of a fixed asset where an initial deposit is paid to the finance company followed by a fixed number of instalments after which the asset is owned by the business

Part exchange a method of reducing the cost of a new asset by offering an old asset in part exchange

Fixed asset register a record of the details of all of the fixed assets of the business individually

Tangible fixed assets assets for long term use within the business that have a physical form

Intangible fixed assets assets for long term use within the business that have no physical form

Goodwill the difference between the value of the business as a whole and the total of the value of all of its net assets

HOW MUCH HAVE YOU LEARNED?

1 For each of the following transactions state the amounts that should be treated as capital expenditure and the amounts that should be treated as revenue expenditure.

a) A machine is purchased on credit at a total cost of £15,800. This includes delivery costs of £350, installation costs of £550 and a supply of lubricating oil for the machine costing £100

b) A building plot is purchased for £60,000 plus surveyor's fees of £600 and legal fees of £500

c) A new computer system is installed at a cost of £65,000. The computer room has had to be re-wired for this system at a cost of £3,600 and while the electricians were in the building the sales department lighting system was repaired at a cost of £800

2 Draft the necessary journal entries for each of the following fixed asset acquisitions.

a) Desks and chairs for the head office at a cost of £4,200, paid for by cheque

b) A new computer purchased on credit at a total cost of £2,400 including £100 of rewritable CDs

c) A new machine purchased at a cost of £9,600 by cheque and installed by the business's own employees using materials costing £200 and incurring wages costs of £800

3 If a machine is purchased under a hire purchase agreement when would it appear as a fixed asset in the business's balance sheet?

a) On the date of payment of the deposit
b) On the date of the final instalment
c) Never

Is the answer a), b) or c)?

4 What details would you expect to find in a fixed asset register?

chapter 6: DEPRECIATION OF FIXED ASSETS

chapter coverage

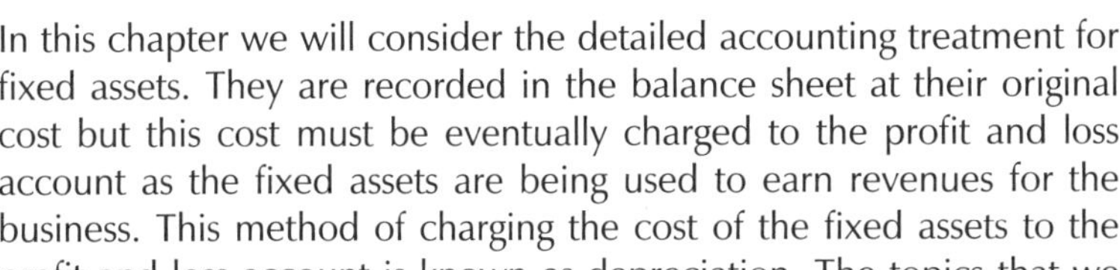

In this chapter we will consider the detailed accounting treatment for fixed assets. They are recorded in the balance sheet at their original cost but this cost must be eventually charged to the profit and loss account as the fixed assets are being used to earn revenues for the business. This method of charging the cost of the fixed assets to the profit and loss account is known as depreciation. The topics that we shall cover are:

- the purpose of depreciation
- the accounting concepts that underlie depreciation
- the straight line method of depreciation
- estimated residual values
- the reducing balance method of depreciation
- comparison of the two methods of depreciation
- depreciation policies
- accounting for depreciation
- recording depreciation in the fixed asset register

KNOWLEDGE AND UNDERSTANDING AND PERFORMANCE CRITERIA COVERAGE

knowledge and understanding

- the main requirements of relevant SSAPs and FRSs
- methods of depreciation and when to use each of them: straight line; reducing balance
- how to use plant registers and similar subsidiary records
- how to use the transfer journal
- the principles of double entry accounting
- the objectives of making provisions for depreciation and other purposes

Performance criteria – element 5.1

- correctly calculate and record depreciation charges and other necessary entries and adjustments in the appropriate records
- ensure that the organisation's policies and procedures relating to the maintenance of capital records are adhered to

WHAT IS DEPRECIATION?

student notes

We will start with the technical definition of DEPRECIATION from FRS 15, Tangible fixed assets.

'Depreciation is the measure of the cost .... of the economic benefits of the tangible fixed asset that have been consumed during the period. Consumption includes the wearing out, using up or other reduction in the useful economic life of a tangible fixed asset whether arising from use, effluxion of time or obsolescence through either changes in technology or demand for goods and services produced by the asset.'

Now we will consider what this actually means.

The first element of the definition regards the accounting concept of accruals. As we have seen when a fixed asset is purchased its entire cost is included in the relevant fixed asset account and is then recorded as a fixed asset in the balance sheet. According to the accruals concept all of the costs involved in producing the income of the business during a period should be charged to the profit and loss account as an expense in the same period.

If fixed assets are used in the business then they are earning income for the business. Therefore a part of their cost should be charged to the profit and loss account each period in order to accord with the accruals concept – this is the depreciation charge.

The FRS 15 definition talks about the amount of the cost of the fixed asset that is 'consumed' or used up during the period as being the depreciation charge. This amount has to be estimated for each type of fixed asset. Different types of asset will be consumed or depreciated in different ways:

- Machinery, motor vehicles, office furniture will tend to wear out through use
- Leases on buildings will be consumed by the passage of time as the lease term diminishes
- Computer equipment will tend to become obsolete as technology advances

The aim of depreciation therefore is to charge the amount of the cost of the fixed asset that has been consumed during the period to the profit and loss account as an expense in order to match with the income that the fixed asset has earned in the period.

The only type of fixed asset that is not required to be depreciated is freehold land, since it has an infinite life so is not consumed in the business.

student notes

The other aspect of depreciation is that if some of the cost of the asset has been consumed then the asset itself will be worth less than its original cost. This is reflected in the balance sheet where the fixed assets are shown at their cost less all of the depreciation charged to date, or consumed so far. This is known as the NET BOOK VALUE of the fixed asset.

COST	–	DEPRECIATION TO DATE	=	NET BOOK VALUE

METHODS OF CALCULATING DEPRECIATION

The amount of depreciation that is charged on a fixed asset each year is an estimate of how much of the cost of that asset has been consumed during the year. In order to make such estimates organisations will have DEPRECIATION POLICIES. These policies will state the method that is used for the depreciation of each type of fixed asset and this method should generally be used every year in order to be comparable (see Chapter 3).

The two most commonly used methods of depreciation used are:

- the straight line method
- the reducing balance method

Straight line method of depreciation

The aim of the STRAIGHT LINE METHOD of depreciation is to charge the same amount of depreciation on the fixed asset each year of the asset's life.

In order to be able to calculate the depreciation charge for a fixed asset under this method we will need to know the original cost of the asset and its ESTIMATED USEFUL ECONOMIC LIFE. This is the time period over which it is estimated that the fixed asset will be used within the business.

HOW IT WORKS

Nick Waldron has recently set up a retail venture known as N W Traders. One of the fixed assets that has been purchased is an item of machinery that has cost £8,000 and which it is estimated will be used in the business for 8 years after which it will have to be replaced due to technological changes and will have no resale value at that date. The machine is to be depreciated using the straight line method.

The annual depreciation charge is calculated as:

$$\frac{\text{Original cost of the asset}}{\text{Estimated useful economic life of the asset}}$$

Therefore each year the depreciation charge for this asset will be:

$$\frac{£8{,}000}{8 \text{ years}} = £1{,}000 \text{ per annum}$$

Each year £1,000 will be charged to the profit and loss account as an expense and each year a further £1,000 will be deducted from the cost of the fixed asset in the balance sheet when showing it at its net book value. Therefore by the end of the asset's estimated useful economic life its net book value will be:

Cost – depreciation to date

£8,000 – (8 × £1,000) = zero

Activity 1

Using the fixed asset details given above what will be the net book value of the asset after it has been owned by NW Traders for three years?

Estimated residual value

In the previous example we were told that the asset would be worthless by the end of its useful economic life. However many fixed assets that a business purchases are likely to be sold on in the second hand market at the end of their useful life to the business. This is probably especially the case with motor vehicles which may be kept for three or four years and then replaced. Such assets will have a resale value at the date of their sale.

When you are using straight line depreciation, at the time that the fixed asset is purchased not only must the useful economic life of the asset be estimated but an estimate must also be made of the scrap value or resale value at the end of this period. This is known as the asset's ESTIMATED RESIDUAL VALUE. The amount that is to be depreciated over the asset's life is:

COST – ESTIMATED RESIDUAL VALUE

Note that when reducing balance depreciation is the method used, the percentage applied has been calculated by taking into account the asset's estimated useful life and its estimated residual value. All you need to do therefore is to apply the given percentage to the asset's net book value.

student notes

HOW IT WORKS

N W Traders has also purchased a motor van for deliveries for £16,000 and it is estimated that it will be used for three years and then sold for an estimated amount of £5,500 at the end of the three years.

The relevant figures for this fixed asset are therefore:

Cost	£16,000
Estimated useful economic life	3 years
Estimated residual value	£5,500

Using the straight line method of depreciation the annual charge for depreciation will be:

$$\frac{\text{Original cost} - \text{estimated residual value}}{\text{Estimated useful economic life}} = \frac{£16{,}000 - 5{,}500}{3 \text{ years}}$$

$$= £3{,}500 \text{ per annum}$$

At the end of each year of the van's life this is how it will appear at its net book value in the balance sheet:

End of year 1	£16,000 – £3,500	=	£12,500
End of year 2	£16,000 – £7,000	=	£9,000
End of year 3	£16,000 – £10,500	=	£5,500

Activity 2

A business has purchased a fixed asset for a cost of £22,000 which has an estimated useful economic life of 4 years and an estimated resale value at the end of this period of £9,000.

What is the annual depreciation charge using the straight-line method? What is the net book value of the asset after two years?

student notes

Reducing balance method of depreciation

The aim of the REDUCING BALANCE METHOD of depreciation is to have a higher charge for depreciation in the early years of the fixed asset's life and a lower charge in later years. This often reflects the pattern of the consumption or loss of value of assets such as motor vehicles that tend to lose more of their value in the early years of their life than the later years.

In order to calculate the annual depreciation charge using the reducing balance method the depreciation is calculated as a fixed percentage of initially the original cost of the asset and thereafter the net book value (NBV) of the asset. The determination of the percentage rate is a complicated calculation which you do not need to carry out – you will be given the percentage rate to use.

HOW IT WORKS

N W Traders has purchased a motor van for deliveries for £16,000 and it is estimated that it will be used for three years and then sold for an estimated amount of £5,500 at the end of the three years.

This van is to be depreciated under the reducing balance method at a rate of 30% per annum.

		Annual depreciation charge
	£	£
Original cost	16,000	
Year 1 depreciation 16,000 x 30%	4,800	4,800
NBV at end of year 1	11,200	
Year 2 depreciation 11,200 x 30%	3,360	3,360
NBV at end of year 2	7,840	
Year 3 depreciation 7,840 x 30%	2,352	2,352
NBV at end of year 3	5,488	

You can see from the calculations that the depreciation charge is higher in year 1 and subsequently decreases. You can also see that the calculations have brought the net book value of the asset down to approximately its estimated residual value, £5,500, at the end of its three year useful economic life.

student notes

Activity 3

A business has purchased a fixed asset for a cost of £22,000 which has an estimated useful economic life of four years and an estimated resale value at the end of this period of £9,000.

You are to show the depreciation charge for each year of the asset's life and the net book value at the end of each year of the asset's life if it is to be depreciated using the reducing balance method at a rate of 20%.

Comparison of straight line and reducing balance methods

If we return to the N W Traders motor van we can compare the annual depreciation charge and net book value under each of the two methods of depreciation.

	Depreciation charge		*Net book value*	
	Straight line	*Reducing balance*	*Straight line*	*Reducing balance*
	£	£	£	£
Year 1	3,500	4,800	12,500	11,200
Year 2	3,500	3,360	9,000	7,840
Year 3	3,500	2,352	5,500	5,488
	10,500	10,512		

We can see that under both methods the total depreciation charged over the three years is approximately £10,500 and the net book value of the asset at the end of the three years is approximately £5,500 (the small difference is due to rounding when calculating the reducing balance percentage rate). However the depreciation charge is spread differently over the years.

In year 1 the depreciation charge under the reducing balance method is higher than the straight line method but by year 3 the reducing balance charge is significantly lower than the straight line charge.

Choice of method

FRS 15 allows businesses to choose which method of depreciation is most appropriate to their fixed assets. Most businesses will choose different depreciation methods and rates for its different types of fixed assets depending upon what is deemed to be most appropriate. The straight line method will often be used for fixed assets that are likely to be kept for their entire useful lives and have low expected resale values, such as machinery and office fixtures and fittings. The reducing balance method however is more appropriate for assets such as motor vehicles that lose more of their value in early years and are likely to be sold before the end of their lives.

However once the depreciation method and rates have been set they should only be changed if the managers or owner of the business have good reason to change them. This is in order to comply with the accounting concept of consistency which states that items in the accounting records should be dealt with in the same manner each year.

student notes

Description of depreciation policies

In the examples so far we have seen how to calculate the depreciation for an individual fixed asset by looking at the original cost of the asset, the estimated useful life and the estimated residual value. In some assessments you will need to be able to calculate the depreciation for a single asset. However in many assessments or exams you will need to calculate the depreciation charge for the year for an entire class of assets and in order to do this you will be told the depreciation policy for that class of fixed asset.

HOW IT WORKS

Harris Incorporated has a number of different classes of fixed assets. These include buildings and motor vehicles. The depreciation policies for these two classes of fixed assets are:

- buildings – depreciated on the straight line basis at a rate of 2% per annum
- motor vehicles – depreciated at a rate of 25% on the reducing balance basis

In order to determine the depreciation charge for each class of fixed asset for the year certain information is required.

As the buildings are being depreciated on the straight line basis what is required is the cost of the buildings at the end of the year which we will suppose is £100,000.

For the motor vehicles the policy is to use the reducing balance basis and therefore the figure that is required is the net book value of the motor vehicles at the end of the year, in this case this is £40,000.

student notes

The depreciation charge for the year for each class of fixed assets is therefore:

Buildings	£100,000 x 2%	=	£2,000
Motor vehicles	£ 40,000 x 25%	=	£10,000

Assets purchased part way through the year

Sometimes you must take care when reading a business's depreciation policy in an assessment or exam. If fixed assets are purchased part of the way through the year then the business has a choice whether to depreciate the new asset for the entire year or only for the period since it was purchased.

This choice must be made and then will be expressed in the depreciation policy. The two alternatives are normally expressed as follows:

> 'A full year's depreciation charge is to be made in the year of acquisition and none in the year of disposal' – this means that no matter when the new asset was purchased in the year a full year's depreciation is charged in that year.
>
> 'Depreciation is charged at 10% per annum on cost' – the words per annum show that the depreciation charge must be based upon the number of months in the year that the asset has been owned.

HOW IT WORKS

Two businesses purchase a piece of machinery on 1 April 2008 for £20,000 and both businesses have an accounting period which runs from 1 January to 31 December.

Business A depreciates its machinery at 10% on the straight-line basis with a full year's charge in the year of acquisition.

Business B depreciates its machinery at 10% per annum on the straight-line basis.

The depreciation charges for each business in the year of acquisition for this machinery is:

A	£20,000 x 10%	=	£2,000
B	£20,000 x 10% x 9/12	=	£1,500 (as the asset has only been owned for 9 months of the year)

student notes

ACCOUNTING FOR DEPRECIATION

The accounting entries for the annual depreciation charge reflect the treatment of depreciation that we have already discussed.

Each year the profit and loss account is charged with the DEPRECIATION EXPENSE for the year. This is taken as a debit entry (an expense) in the depreciation expense account.

The accumulated depreciation that has been charged to date on the fixed assets is deducted from their cost to give the net book value – this accumulated depreciation is known as the PROVISION FOR DEPRECIATION. All provisions are credit entries as they are the reduction in the value of an asset (a debit entry). Therefore the depreciation for the year is entered as a credit in the provision for depreciation account.

To summarise, the double entry for the depreciation charge for the year is:

Debit Depreciation expense account
Credit Provision for depreciation account

Note that there are no entries to the fixed asset at cost account. This remains with the original cost and is not changed.

HOW IT WORKS

We shall now return to N W Traders who purchased a motor van for deliveries for £16,000 with an estimated useful economic life of three years and an estimated residual value of £5,500. The annual depreciation charge calculated on the straight line basis is:

$$\frac{£16{,}000 - 5{,}500}{3\text{ years}} = £3{,}500$$

We will now record this in the ledger accounts for each of the three years.

student notes

Year 1

The depreciation charge of £3,500 is debited to the depreciation expense account and credited to the provision for depreciation account.

Depreciation expense

	£		£
Provision for depreciation	3,500		

Provision for depreciation

	£		£
		Depreciation expense	3,500

At the end of the year as the depreciation expense account is a profit and loss account item it will be cleared to the profit and loss account and will therefore have no remaining balance on it.

Depreciation expense

	£		£
Provision for depreciation	3,500	Profit and loss account	3,500

The provision for depreciation account however will appear in the balance sheet and the balance will remain as the opening balance for year 2.

Provision for depreciation

	£		£
Balance c/d	3,500	Depreciation expense	3,500
		Year 2 Balance b/d	3,500

In the financial statements at the end of year 1 the depreciation would be treated as follows:

Profit and loss account

	£
Expenses:	
Depreciation expense	3,500

Balance sheet

Fixed assets	*Cost*	*Accumulated depreciation*	*Net book value*
	£	£	£
Motor van	16,000	3,500	12,500

Year 2

The depreciation charge of £3,500 is debited to the depreciation expense account and credited to the provision for depreciation account.

Depreciation expense

	£		£
Provision for depreciation	3,500		

Provision for depreciation

	£		£
		Year 2 Balance b/d	3,500
		Depreciation expense	3,500

At the end of the year as the depreciation expense account is a profit and loss account item it will be cleared to the profit and loss account and will therefore have no remaining balance on it.

Depreciation expense

	£		£
Provision for depreciation	3,500	Profit and loss account	3,500

student notes

student notes

The provision for depreciation account however will appear in the balance sheet and the balance will remain as the opening balance for year 3.

Provision for depreciation

	£		£
Balance c/d	7,000	Year 2 Balance b/d	3,500
		Depreciation expense	3,500
	7,000		7,000
		Year 3 Balance b/d	7,000

In the financial statements at the end of year 2 the depreciation would be treated as follows:

Profit and loss account

	£
Expenses:	
Depreciation expense	3,500

Balance sheet

Fixed assets	*Cost*	*Accumulated depreciation*	*Net book value*
	£	£	£
Motor van	16,000	7,000	9,000

Year 3

The depreciation charge of £3,500 is debited to the depreciation expense account and credited to the provision for depreciation account.

Depreciation expense

	£		£
Provision for depreciation	3,500		

Provision for depreciation

	£		£
Provision for depreciation	3,500	Year 3 Balance b/d	7,000
		Depreciation expense	3,500

At the end of the year as the depreciation expense account is a profit and loss account item it will be cleared to the profit and loss account and will therefore have no remaining balance on it.

student notes

Depreciation expense

	£		£
Provision for depreciation	3,500	Profit and loss account	3,500

The provision for depreciation account however will appear in the balance sheet and the balance will remain.

Provision for depreciation

	£		£
Balance c/d	10,500	Year 3 Balance b/d	7,000
		Depreciation expense	3,500
	10,500		10,500
		Balance b/d	10,500

In the financial statements at the end of year 3 the depreciation would be treated as follows:

Profit and loss account

	£
Expenses:	
Depreciation expense	3,500

Balance sheet

Fixed assets	*Cost*	*Accumulated depreciation*	*Net book value*
	£	£	£
Motor van	16,000	10,500	5,500

Activity 4

A business which has just completed its first year of business has machinery costing £120,000. The depreciation policy is to depreciate machinery at the rate of 20% on the straight line basis.

Show the ledger entries for the depreciation for the first year and the entries in the profit and loss account and balance sheet at the end of the year.

student notes

DEPRECIATION AND THE FIXED ASSET REGISTER

You will remember from the previous chapter that all details for all fixed assets are kept in the fixed asset register, this includes entries for the annual depreciation charge.

HOW IT WORKS

From an earlier example Kendall Engineering have just purchased a new machine, the FD254, from Leyland Machinery for £120,000. The machine is to be depreciated on the reducing balance basis at a rate of 30% per annum with a full years charge in the year of purchase. It is now 31 December 2008 and the entries relating to depreciation for the first year are now to be made.

student notes

FIXED ASSET REGISTER

Fixed asset number 02635
Description Machine FD254
Location Factory
Supplier Leyland Machinery

Date	Cost £	Expected life (years)	Estimated scrap value £	Depreciation method	Depreciation rate	Depreciation charge for the year £	Provision at end of the year £	Net book value at end of year £	Disposal proceeds £	Profit or loss on disposal £
2008 1 Mar	120,000	5	20,000	Reducing balance	30%					
31 Dec						36,000	36,000	84,000		

CHAPTER OVERVIEW

- depreciation is a method of applying the accruals concept by charging some of the cost of fixed assets to the profit and loss account each year that they are used by the business
- the amount to be charged is an estimate of the amount of the cost that has been 'consumed' in the accounting period – this is estimated by calculating the depreciation charge either under the straight line method or the reducing balance method
- the cost of the fixed asset minus the depreciation charged to date is known as the net book value
- the straight line method of depreciation ensures that the same amount of depreciation is charged for each year of the asset's life
- straight line depreciation is calculated as the cost of the asset minus the estimated residual value spread over the useful economic life of the asset
- the reducing balance method of depreciation charges a larger amount of depreciation in the early years of the asset's life and a lower amount in the later years of its life
- reducing balance depreciation is calculated by applying a fixed percentage to the net book value of the fixed asset
- care has to be taken over the precise depreciation policy of a business – some businesses charge a full years depreciation on an asset no matter when it was purchased during the year – other businesses will charge depreciation only for the months that the asset has been owned in the first year
- when accounting for the depreciation charge it is debited to the depreciation expense account and credited to the provision for depreciation account
- the depreciation expense account is cleared to the profit and loss account at the end of each year but the provision for depreciation account is listed in the balance sheet and the balance is then carried down as the opening balance for the following period
- the depreciation charge is shown as an expense in the profit and loss account

KEY WORDS

Depreciation the annual charge to the profit and loss account to reflect the use of the fixed asset during the period

Net book value the cost of the fixed asset minus the depreciation charged to date

Depreciation policies the stated methods and rates of depreciation for a business

Straight line method a method of calculating the depreciation charge to give the same amount of depreciation charge each year

Estimated useful economic life the period over which the business estimates that the fixed asset will be used

Estimated residual value the anticipated resale value of the fixed asset at the end of its useful economic life to the business

Reducing balance method method of calculating depreciation so that a larger amount is charged in the earlier years and smaller amounts in subsequent years

Depreciation expense the amount of depreciation charged to the profit and loss account each year

Provision for depreciation the balance sheet account that records the accumulated depreciation to date on a fixed asset

CHAPTER OVERVIEW cont.

- the balance on the provision for depreciation account is shown in the balance sheet deducted from the cost of the fixed asset and as a balance sheet account the balance is carried down as the opening balance for the following accounting period
- the depreciation method, rate, charge for the year, provision for depreciation and net book value are all recorded in the fixed asset register

HOW MUCH HAVE YOU LEARNED?

1 What is the main purpose of depreciation? Refer to the main accounting concept that underlies the requirement to depreciate fixed assets.

2 A business has a machine that was purchased on 1 January 2007 costing £11,500 with an estimated useful economic life of five years and an estimated residual value of £2,500. The policy is to depreciate machinery on the straight line basis.

What is the depreciation charge for the year ended 31 December 2008 and what is the net book value of the machine at this date?

3 A business owns a car that was purchased on 1 January 2007 costing £16,400. It has an estimated useful economic life of three years and an estimated residual value of £4,500 at that date. The car is to be depreciated at 35% each year on the reducing balance basis.

What is the depreciation charge for the year ended 31 December 2008 and what is the net book value of the car at this date?

4 Why might the reducing balance method of depreciation be used in preference to the much simpler straight-line method?

5 A business has machinery with a cost of £240,000 and depreciation to date at the start of the year of £135,000. The policy is to depreciate the machinery at the rate of 30% on the reducing balance basis.

What is this year's depreciation charge?

6 A business purchased a delivery lorry for £24,000 on 1 June 2008 which is to be depreciated on the straight-line basis at a rate of 20% per annum.

What is the depreciation charge for the accounting year ending 31 December 2008?

7 A business buys a machine for £120,000 on 31 October 2006 which is to be depreciated at the rate of 15% straight-line with a full year's depreciation in the year of acquisition.

You are required to:

a) write up the depreciation expense account and provision for depreciation account for the years ending 31 December 2006, 2007 and 2008

b) show the extract from the balance sheet for this machine at 31 December 2006, 2007 and 2008

chapter 7: DISPOSAL OF FIXED ASSETS

chapter coverage

Having considered the acquisition of fixed assets and their accounting treatment during their lives we must now consider the process of selling a fixed asset when it is of no more use to the business. In this chapter we will also consider the relationship between the fixed asset register and the actual fixed assets held. At regular intervals the details of fixed assets in the fixed asset register should be checked to the actual assets held on the premises. The topics that we shall cover are:

- authorisation of disposal of fixed assets
- accounting for disposals of fixed assets
- profit and loss on disposal
- part exchange deals
- disposals and the fixed asset register
- physical checks of fixed assets to the fixed asset register

KNOWLEDGE AND UNDERSTANDING AND PERFORMANCE CRITERIA COVERAGE

knowledge and understanding

- the types and characteristics of different assets and key issues relating to the acquisition and disposal of capital assets
- the accounting treatment of capital items sold, scrapped or otherwise retired from service
- how to use plant registers and similar subsidiary records
- the methods of funding: part exchange deals

KNOWLEDGE AND UNDERSTANDING AND PERFORMANCE CRITERIA COVERAGE

Performance criteria – element 5.1

- ensure the organisation's records agree with the physical presence of capital items
- correctly identify and record all acquisition and disposal costs and revenues in the appropriate records
- ensure the records clearly show the prior authority for capital expenditure and disposal and the approved method of funding and disposal
- correctly calculate and record the profit and loss on disposal in the appropriate records
- identify and resolve or refer to the appropriate person any lack of agreement between physical items and records
- make suggestions for improvements in the way the organisation maintains its capital records where possible to the appropriate person

AUTHORISATION OF DISPOSAL OF FIXED ASSETS

student notes

When a fixed asset is purchased it is important that the procedures are correctly carried out to ensure that this is a fixed asset that the business requires and that this is the best supplier for this asset. Similarly when a fixed asset is to be disposed of control is also important.

The first question that has to be asked is if this asset is truly no longer needed by the business.

In some cases it may be the business policy to dispose of particular assets after a certain period – for example many businesses replace their motor vehicles after three or four years as a matter of policy.

Alternatively the asset may have reached the end of its useful life – for example a machine may no longer be worthwhile running as its running costs are greater than the benefits that it gives.

Changes in technology may also require assets to be replaced – for example a computer that served the purposes of the business four years ago might need to be replaced by a more up to date model.

Fixed assets may also simply wear out such as office fixtures and fittings that are now so shabby that they must be replaced.

Method of disposal

Some assets that are worthless will simply be scrapped. However many fixed assets although of no use to the business itself can be sold to a third party.

This may be a straight sale to an unrelated party, a part exchange deal (see later in the chapter) or a sale to an employee. In many cases assets such as business cars may be sold to the person in the business who uses the car once the business decides to replace it.

Whatever the method of disposal of the asset the resale value is obviously important to the business as this is the amount that it will receive for the asset. This resale value is an uncertain amount which will normally be the subject of negotiations and it is therefore important that there is good management control of this area.

It would be easy for an asset to be sold to an employee, a third party or part exchanged for an amount that was much less than its market worth. Therefore it is important that a fixed asset disposal form is filled out and authorised by the appropriate person within the business before any asset is sold or scrapped.

student notes

ACCOUNTING FOR DISPOSALS

When a fixed asset is sold there are two effects on the accounts of the business:

- All accounting entries for the asset must be removed from the accounting records
- Any profit or loss on the disposal of the asset must be calculated and accounted for

All of this can be done in one ledger account – the DISPOSALS ACCOUNT.

The first step is to remove the cost of the fixed asset and the provision for depreciation for that asset from the ledger accounts – these amounts are taken out of the relevant accounts and put into the disposal account:

Debit Disposal account
Credit Fixed asset at cost account

- with the original cost of the asset

Debit Provision for depreciation account
Credit Disposal account

- with the accumulated depreciation on the asset up to the date of sale

This has removed all traces of the asset sold from the ledger accounts – now we must deal with the sale proceeds:

Debit Bank or Debtors
Credit Disposal account

- with the sale proceeds – if a cheque or cash is received then the bank account will be debited, if the sale is made on credit then the debtors account will be debited

The final step is to calculate the balance on the disposal account – this will be either a PROFIT OR LOSS ON DISPOSAL and will be transferred to the profit and loss account as an expense if it is a loss or as sundry income if it is a profit.

HOW IT WORKS

student notes

Harris Incorporated had purchased a machine on 1 January 2006 for £15,000. This was to be depreciated on the straight line basis at a rate of 20% per annum. The machine was sold for £5,000 on 31 December 2008.

Before we look at the accounting entries for this sale we will think about what has happened here first. The machine was owned for the whole of 2006, 2007 and 2008 and therefore had three years of depreciation charges at £3,000 (£15,000 x 20%) per annum.

	£
Cost of machine	15,000
Provision for depreciation	9,000
Net book value at 31 December 2008	6,000
Sale proceeds	5,000
Loss on sale	1,000

At the date of the disposal the machine had a net book value of £6,000 but was sold for only £5,000. Therefore a loss was made on the disposal of £1,000.

Now we will consider the accounting entries:

Debit Disposal account
Credit Fixed asset at cost account

- **with the original cost of the asset**

Machine at cost account

		£			£
2006			2008		
1 Jan	Bank	15,000	31 Dec	Disposal	15,000

Disposal account

		£			£
2008					
31 Dec	Machine	15,000			

student notes

Debit Provision for depreciation account
Credit Disposal account

- **with the accumulated depreciation on the asset up to the date of sale**

Provision for depreciation account

		£			£
2006			2006		
31 Dec	Balance c/d	3,000	31 Dec	Depreciation	3,000
		3,000			3,000
2007			2007		
31 Dec	Balance c/d	6,000	1 Jan	Balance b/d	3,000
			31 Dec	Depreciation	3,000
		6,000			6,000
2008			2008		
31 Dec	Disposal	9,000	1 Jan	Balance b/d	6,000
			31 Dec	Depreciation	3,000
		9,000			9,000

Disposal account

		£			£
2008			2008		
31 Dec	Machine	15,000	31 Dec	Provision	9,000

Debit Bank or Debtors account
Credit Disposal account

- **with the sale proceeds**

Disposal account

		£			£
2008			2008		
31 Dec	Machine	15,000	31 Dec	Provision	9,000
			31 Dec	Bank – proceeds	5,000

Finally balance the disposal account to find the profit or the loss on disposal:

Disposal account

		£			£
2008			2008		
31 Dec	Machine	15,00	31 Dec	Provision	9,000
		15,000	31 Dec	Bank – proceeds	5,000
			31 Dec	P&L – loss	1,000
					15,000

The full double entry for this loss on disposal is a credit in the disposal account and a debit (an expense) to the profit and loss account.

In practice it is unlikely that each fixed asset will have its own account for cost and accumulated depreciation. Instead there will be a cost and provision for depreciation account for each type or class of fixed assets, ie. machinery, fixtures and fittings, motor vehicles etc. This will mean that when the entries are made to remove the cost and accumulated depreciation for the asset disposed of a balance will remain on the cost and provision accounts.

student notes

Activity 1

A business purchased a motor car for £11,200 on 1 January 2007 and this car was sold for £5,000 on 31 December 2008. The depreciation policy for the motor car was 30% per annum on the reducing balance basis, with a full year's charge in the year of disposal.

a) Calculate the net book value of the car on 31 December 2008

b) Determine any profit or loss that has been made on the disposal

c) Write up the motor car at cost account, the provision for depreciation on the motor car account and the disposal account

Under or over depreciation

In many cases the profit or loss on the disposal of an asset is not described as such – an alternative description is:

- profit on disposal – OVER DEPRECIATION
- loss on disposal – UNDER DEPRECIATION

The profit or loss is simply a comparison of the net book value of the asset and the sale proceeds. The net book value of the asset is dependent upon the depreciation that has been charged during the years of use of the asset. The aim of the depreciation charge is to charge to the profit and loss account each year an estimate of the amount of the cost of the asset that has been consumed each year. If this estimate was totally accurate then the sale proceeds of the asset would be equal to the net book value – however as the depreciation charge is just an estimate this is often not the case leading to the proceeds being either more or less than the net book value.

This is not really a profit or a loss; it is simply the fact that if the proceeds are more than the net book value then too much depreciation has been charged, over depreciation or a profit on disposal, whilst if the proceeds are less than the net book value too little depreciation has been charged, under depreciation or a loss on disposal.

student notes

Date of disposal

Some care must be taken with the depreciation policy details when an asset is disposed of part of the way through the year. Depreciation should be charged on the asset up to the date of disposal according to the depreciation policy of the organisation.

HOW IT WORKS

Two businesses purchase a piece of machinery on 1 August 2006 for £3,600. Both businesses have an accounting period which runs from 1 January to 31 December. Both businesses sell the asset on 31 October 2008 for £2,800.

Business A depreciates its machinery at 10% on the straight-line basis with a full year's charge in the year of acquisition and none in the year of sale.

Business B depreciates its machinery at 10% per annum on the straight-line basis.

The profit or loss on disposal for each business is:

	Business A		*Business B*
	£		£
Cost	3,600		3,600
Depreciation –			
to 31 December 2006	(360)	x 5/12	(150)
to 31 December 2007	(360)		(360)
to 31 October 2008	–	x 10/12	(300)
Net book value	2,880		2,790
Sale proceeds	2,800		2,800
Loss on disposal	80	Profit	10

PART EXCHANGE OF AN ASSET

In many cases when a business is selling a fixed asset it will be in order to replace it with a new or newer model. This is often done by means of a PART EXCHANGE, most frequently in the case of motor vehicles.

This means that when the new asset is purchased the old asset is taken as part of the purchase price – a PART EXCHANGE ALLOWANCE is given on the old asset in order to reduce the cash price of the new asset. This part exchange allowance is therefore part of the price of the new asset as well as the cash that is also paid. The part exchange allowance is also effectively the sale proceeds of the old asset.

This is reflected in the accounting for the sale of the old asset and the purchase of the new asset. The entries to the disposal account for the sale of the old asset are largely the same as in a straight sale – the cost of the asset and the provision for depreciation on the asset are removed from the cost and provision accounts and entered into the disposal account.

There are no cash proceeds for the sale of the old asset but the part exchange allowance is treated as the sale proceeds as follows:

Debit Fixed asset at cost account
Credit Disposal account

- **with the part exchange allowance**.

The credit to the disposal account allows a profit or loss on disposal to be determined by comparing the part exchange allowance with the net book value. The debit to the fixed asset at cost account recognises that the part exchange allowance is part of the cost of the new asset together with the remainder of the cash cost which will be debited to the fixed asset at cost account and credited to the bank account.

student notes

HOW IT WORKS

Harris Incorporated are buying a new motor car for a salesman with a list price of £12,000. They have come to an agreement with the car dealer that he will take the salesman's old car in part exchange with a part exchange value of £3,800.

The old car had cost £13,500 on 1 January 2006 and at the date of disposal, 30 June 2008, had accumulated depreciation charged to it of £9,250.

The profit or loss on disposal of the old car can first be calculated:

	£
Cost	13,500
Accumulated depreciation	9,250
Net book value	4,250
Part exchange allowance	3,800
Loss on disposal	450

The cash cost of the new car can also be calculated:

	£
List price	12,000
Less: part exchange allowance	(3,800)
Cash cost	8,200

student notes

Now we will deal with the entries in the ledger accounts:

Motor car at cost account

		£			£
2006			2008		
1 Jan	Bank	13,500	30 Jun	Disposal	13,500
2008			2008		
30 Jun	Bank	8,200	30 Jun	Balance c/d	12,000
30 Jun	Disposal	3,800			
		12,000			12,000
1 Jul	Balance b/d	12,000			

Note that the cost of the old car has been removed and taken to the disposal account and the cost of the new car in full, £12,000, has been entered into the account by making two entries, one to the bank account for the cash cost and one to the disposal account for the part exchange allowance, effectively the proceeds of sale of the old car.

Disposal account

		£			£
2008			2008		
30 Jun	Disposal	9,250	30 Jun	Balance b/d	9,250

Disposal account

		£			£
2008			2008		
30 Jun	Motor car at cost	13,500	30 Jun	Motor car depreciation	9,250
			30 Jun	Motor car at cost – allowance	3,800
			30 Jun	Loss on disposal	450
		13,500			13,500

student notes

Activity 2

A business purchased a car on 1 March 2006 costing £10,000. This car was part exchanged for a new car with a total list price of £11,000 on 31 May 2008. At the date of the part exchange the old car had £5,500 of accumulated depreciation charged to it. The part exchange allowance given on the old car was £4,800.

Show the accounting entries necessary to record the sale of the old car and purchase of the new car.

DISPOSAL OF A FIXED ASSET AND THE FIXED ASSET REGISTER

We have already seen how entries should be made in the fixed asset register when a fixed asset is purchased and each year of its life to record the depreciation. When a fixed asset is sold the entries in the fixed asset register are then completed with entries being made for the disposal proceeds and any profit or loss on disposal.

HOW IT WORKS

We have seen in an earlier example a machine purchased by Kendall Engineering for £120,000 on 1 March 2008. It is being depreciated at 30% reducing balance with a full years charge in the year of acquisition but none in the year of disposal. Let us now complete the picture supposing that this machine was sold on 1 February 2010 for £50,000.

student notes

FIXED ASSET REGISTER

Fixed asset number 02635
Description Machine FD254
Location Factory
Supplier Leyland Machinery

Date	*Cost* £	*Expected life (years)*	*Estimated scrap value* £	*Depreciation method*	*Depreciation rate*	*Depreciation charge for the year* £	*Provision at end of year* £	*Net book value at end of year* £	*Disposal proceeds* £	*Profit or loss on disposal* £
2008										
1 Mar	120,000	5	20,000	Reducing balance	30%					
31 Dec						36,000	36,000	84,000		
2009										
31 Dec						25,200	61,200	58,800		
2010										
1 Feb									50,000	(8,800)

student notes

Activity 3

On 1 May 2005 Kendall Engineering had purchased a fork lift truck type XC355 which is used in the warehouse from Leyland Machinery for £34,000. The truck was given the fixed asset number 24116 and had an expected life of four years and an estimated residual value of £6,250.

The truck is depreciated at 30% on the reducing balance with a full year's charge in the year of acquisition and none in the year of disposal. The business's year end is 31 December. The truck was sold on 20 March 2008 for £10,500.

Make all the entries required for this truck in the fixed asset register given below.

student notes

FIXED ASSET REGISTER

Fixed asset number
Description
Location
Supplier

Date	*Cost* £	*Expected life (years)*	*Estimated scrap value* £	*Depreciation method*	*Depreciation rate*	*Depreciation charge for the year* £	*Provision at end of year* £	*Net book value at end of year* £	*Disposal proceeds* £	*Profit or loss on disposal* £

CHECKING PHYSICAL ASSETS TO THE FIXED ASSET REGISTER

student notes

The main reason for keeping the fixed asset register is to help in the control of the fixed assets of a business. Fixed assets are often very expensive items and in some cases are also easily portable, such as laptop computers. Once a fixed asset has been purchased by the business it is important to check that the asset is still within the business on a fairly regular basis.

This will be done by checks being made in two ways:

- That every fixed asset in the fixed asset register exists within the organisation
- That every fixed asset in the business is recorded in the fixed asset register.

It is unlikely that all the fixed assets of the business will be checked at the same time in this manner but most businesses will have a rolling policy of checking categories of fixed assets regularly such that all assets are checked once a year.

This physical check of the assets may show that there are some discrepancies:

- Some assets that exist in the business are not in the fixed asset register – this means that when the asset was purchased no entries were made for the asset in the fixed asset register
- Some entries in the fixed asset register are not up to date – the depreciation charge each year may not have been entered
- There is no physical asset when one is recorded in the fixed asset register – this may mean that an asset has been sold or scrapped but this has not been recorded in the fixed asset register or at worst the asset has been stolen.

Any discrepancies found when carrying out this physical check must be reported to management to be dealt with appropriately.

Maintenance of capital records

In the last few chapters we have looked at the details of the maintenance of records of capital expenditure. This is a hugely important area with far-reaching consequences for any organisation, of whatever size. Consider the importance of authorisation for acquisitions, methods of funding, depreciation methods, recording of fixed assets in an independent fixed asset register, checking of physical assets to the fixed asset register on a regular basis and authorisation for disposals. Be prepared to think about whether there are any ways in which there might be improvements made in an organisation's methods of maintaining its capital records. If any such suggestions were to be made then this must of course be to the appropriate person within the organisation. In a large organisation there may be an individual specifically in charge of fixed assets otherwise it may be the managing director, finance director or the owner of the business.

CHAPTER OVERVIEW

- it is as important that the disposal of fixed assets is properly controlled and authorised as the acquisition of fixed assets
- the accounting for the disposal takes place in the disposal account by entering the original cost and accumulated depreciation on the asset being disposed of together with the disposal proceeds
- the final balance on the disposal account will be either a profit on disposal which will be shown in the profit and loss account as sundry income or a loss on disposal which will be an expense in the profit and loss account
- a profit on disposal is often called over depreciation and a loss on disposal, under depreciation
- in some cases a fixed asset will be disposed of by it being part exchanged in the purchase of a replacement asset – the part exchange allowance is treated as the sale proceeds of the old asset and part of the cost of the new asset
- when a fixed asset is disposed of the date of disposal, proceeds and the profit or loss should be recorded in the fixed asset register
- on a regular basis the physical fixed assets that a business has should be checked to the entries in the fixed asset register – any discrepancies should be reported to the appropriate person in the organisation for any required action to be taken

KEY WORDS

Disposals account the ledger account used to record all aspects of the disposal of the fixed asset

Profit or loss on disposal the difference between the net book value of the asset at the date of disposal and the sale proceeds

Over depreciation a profit on disposal

Under depreciation a loss on disposal

Part exchange a method of disposal whereby the old asset is given in part exchange for a new asset

Part exchange value the value assigned to the old asset being part exchanged by the supplier of the new asset

HOW MUCH HAVE YOU LEARNED?

1 A business purchases a computer on 1 April 2005 for £2,200. This is then sold on 14 May 2008 for £200. The depreciation policy is to depreciate computers on a reducing balance basis at a rate of 40% with a full year charge in the year of acquisition and none in the year of disposal. The business's accounting year ends on 31 December.

a) Calculate the profit or loss on the sale of this computer.

b) Show all of the accounting entries for this computer from the date of purchase through to the date of sale.

2 A business purchases a machine on 1 October 2006 for £7,200 and this machine is then sold on 31 July 2008 for £3,800. The machine is depreciated at a rate of 25% per annum on the straight line basis. The business's year end is 30 November.

a) Calculate the profit or loss on the sale of this machine.

b) Show all of the accounting entries for this machine from the date of purchase through to the date of sale.

3 a) A loss on disposal can also be described as ....

b) A profit on disposal can also be described as ....

4 A business is purchasing a new motor van with a list price of £16,700 on 30 April 2008. The car dealer has agreed to take an old motor van in part exchange requiring the business to pay only £12,200 for the new van. The old van had originally cost £13,600 on 1 July 2005 and the provision for depreciation on this van at 30 April 2008 totalled £9,000.

Show the accounting entries required in the ledger accounts on 30 April 2008 to deal with the purchase of this new van and the part exchange of the old van.

5 A business purchases a computer with a serial number 1036525 for £4,800 from Timing Computers Ltd on 1 March 2006. The computer is allocated an internal fixed asset number 10435 and is to be used in the sales department.

The computer is thought to have a four year useful life and a scrap value at the end of that period of just £600. It is to be depreciated on the reducing balance basis at a rate of 40% with a full year's charge in the year of acquisition and none in the year of disposal. The business's year end is 31 July.

On 27 June 2008 the computer was in fact sold for £700.

Record all of these details on the fixed asset register given.

FIXED ASSET REGISTER

Fixed asset number
Description
Location
Supplier

Date	*Cost £*	*Expected life (years)*	*Estimated scrap value £*	*Depreciation method*	*Depreciation rate*	*Depreciation charge for the year £*	*Provision at end of year £*	*Net book value at end of year £*	*Disposal proceeds £*	*Profit or loss on disposal £*

chapter 8: ACCRUALS AND PREPAYMENTS

chapter coverage

In this chapter we will consider the accounting treatment of income and expenses, in particular in the context of the fundamental accounting concept of accruals. The topics that we shall cover are:

- accounting for sales and purchases
- accounting for expenses
- accounting for accruals of expenses
- accounting for prepayments of expenses
- accounting for accruals of income
- accounting for prepayments of income

KNOWLEDGE AND UNDERSTANDING AND PERFORMANCE CRITERIA COVERAGE

knowledge and understanding

- the methods of recording information for the organisational accounts of sole traders and partnerships
- accounting treatment of accruals and prepayments
- the principles of double entry accounting
- the methods of analysing income and expenditure
- the function and form of accounts for income and expenditure

Performance criteria – element 5.2

- correctly identify, calculate and record appropriate adjustments

student notes

THE ACCRUALS CONCEPT

In Chapter 3 the accounting concept of accruals or matching was considered. The basic principle of the ACCRUALS CONCEPT is that the amount of income and expense that is included in the financial statements for an accounting period should be the income earned and the expenses incurred during the period rather than the cash received or paid. In this chapter we shall start to look at the practical application of this concept to the maintaining of financial records and the preparation of final accounts.

Sales and purchases

When sales are made then either the cash is received now or the sale is made on credit. Either way the sale is recorded as soon as it is made. If the sale is on credit then a debtor is set up and the sale is recorded in the sales account. Therefore even though the money has not yet been received the sale has been included in the ledger accounts.

In just the same way when an invoice is received from a credit supplier this is recorded as a purchase and a creditor. Even though the money has not yet been paid to the supplier the purchase has been recorded.

Therefore our system for recording sales and purchases automatically applies the accruals concept.

Expenses

The system for recording expenses is however different. Expenses will be recorded in the ledger accounts when the payment for the expense is made.

When the rent is due it will be paid and the double entry will be:

Debit Rent account
Credit Bank account

When the telephone bill arrives it will be paid and the double entry will be:

Debit Telephone account
Credit Bank account

This system means that initially the only expenses that are recorded in the ledger accounts are those that have been paid rather than those that were incurred in the period.

Therefore at the end of each accounting period each expense must be considered to ensure that the full amount of that expense that has been incurred in the period is shown as the expense rather than just the amount that has been paid.

student notes

ACCRUALS OF EXPENSES

An ACCRUAL is an amount of an expense that has been incurred during the accounting period but has not yet been paid for. As it has not yet been paid for then it does not appear in the expense ledger account.

The accounting treatment for an accrual is twofold:

- It must be added to the balance in the expense account to ensure that all of the expense incurred in the period is included in the profit and loss account
- It will be shown as a type of creditor, called an accrual, in the balance sheet

Activity 1

A business has paid £1,110 of telephone bills during the accounting year. After the year end it receives a further bill for £260 which also relates to that accounting year.

What effect will this have on the figures to be included in the accounting year's financial statements?

HOW IT WORKS

Dawn Fisher runs a business designing and selling T shirts. On 31 March 2009 she completed her first year of trading. Her electricity account shows a debit balance of £780 but on 5 April she receives an electricity bill for the three months to 31 March for £410.

This must be included in her accounts for the year by increasing the electricity expense by £410 and showing a creditor, an accrual for £410 in the balance sheet.

There are two methods of accounting for this accrual:

- Using an accruals account
- Showing a balance carried down on the electricity account

student notes

Accruals account method

Under this method a separate accruals account is maintained. In order to increase the expense the double entry is:

Debit	Electricity account	£410
Credit	Accruals account	£410

Electricity account

Date	Details	£	Date	Details	£
31 Mar	Balance b/d	780	31 Mar	Profit & loss a/c	1,190
31 Mar	Accruals	410			
		1,190			1,190

Accruals account

Date	Details	£	Date	Details	£
			31 Mar	Electricity	410

The electricity account now shows the total amount of electricity expense incurred in the year and the accruals account shows a credit balance that will be listed in the balance sheet as an accrual at the year end.

When the electricity bill is eventually paid the electricity account should not be debited as we are now into a new accounting year and this bill is for the previous year. Therefore the double entry will be:

Debit	Accruals account
Credit	Bank account

Suppose that Dawn paid the electricity bill on 20 April:

Accruals account

Date	Details	£	Date	Details	£
20 Apr	Bank	410	31 Mar	Electricity	410

The accrual, or creditor, has now been cancelled out as it has been paid and the electricity account has not been charged with an expense that was in fact for the previous accounting year.

student notes

Balance carried down method

Using this alternative method no separate accruals account is necessary – all of the double entry takes place in the expense account.

The method is to debit the electricity account with the accrual and to complete the double entry by bringing down a credit balance on the electricity account which will be listed in the balance sheet as an accrual.

Electricity account

Date	Details	£	Date	Details	£
31 Mar	Balance b/d	780	31 Mar	Profit & loss a/c	1,190
31 Mar	Accruals c/d	410			
		1,190			1,190
			1 Apr	Balance b/d	410

Again the profit and loss account is charged with the full amount of the electricity used in the period and the credit balance on the electricity account is listed in the balance sheet as an accrual.

When the electricity bill is paid it should be debited to the electricity account as this cancels out the accrual balance leaving the account with a zero balance with which to start the next accounting period.

Accruals account

Date	Details	£	Date	Details	£
20 Apr	Bank	410	1 Apr	Balance b/d	410

Activity 2

A business has a balance of £2,600 on its telephone expense account for the year ended 31 December 2008. On 12 January 2009 it received a telephone bill which included £480 of call charges for the three months ended 31 December 2008.

Using a separate accruals account show the accounting entries necessary to deal with this additional bill.

student notes

PREPAYMENTS OF EXPENSES

A PREPAYMENT is the opposite of an accrual. It is an amount of an expense that has been paid already but relates to the following accounting period. As it has already been paid then it will appear as part of the balance in the expense account but it does not relate to that accounting period and therefore should be removed.

The accounting effect for a prepayment is:

- to remove the prepayment from the expense account therefore reducing the expense to the amount actually incurred in the period
- to show the prepayment as a type of debtor in the balance sheet, known as a prepayment

HOW IT WORKS

Dawn's insurance premiums are paid on 30 June each year in advance for the following year. On 30 June 2008 Dawn paid her first premium of £1,200 and the insurance account reflects this with a debit balance of £1,200. However only the period from 30 June 2008 to 31 March 2009 (9 months) actually relates to the current accounting period. The remaining 3 months of premium are an expense of the next accounting period and therefore must be removed from the insurance account balance. As with the accruals accounting there are the same two methods of accounting for this.

Prepayments account method

Using this method a separate prepayments account is set up. The double entry for the amount of the prepayment £300 (£1,200 x 3/12) is:

Debit Prepayments account
Credit Insurance account

Insurance account

Date	Details	£	Date	Details	£
31 Mar	Balance b/d	1,200	31 Mar	Prepayment	300
			31 Mar	Profit & loss a/c	900
		1,200			1,200

Prepayments account

Date	Details	£	Date	Details	£
31 Mar	Insurance	300			

student notes

The expense shown in the profit and loss account is now the correct figure, £900, for the nine months of insurance in the accounting period and the prepayments account has a debit balance which will be recorded in the balance sheet as a debtor, a prepayment.

This £300 however is an expense of the next accounting period and therefore after the year end accounting has been completed an adjustment must be made to put the £300 back into the insurance account. This is done by:

Debit Insurance account
Credit Prepayments account

Insurance account

Date	Details	£	Date	Details	£
31 Mar	Balance b/d	1,200	31 Mar	Prepayment	300
			31 Mar	Profit & loss a/c	900
		1,200			1,200
1 Apr	Prepayments	300			

Prepayments account

Date	Details	£	Date	Details	£
31 Mar	Insurance	300	1 Apr	Insurance	300

Now the insurance account shows the £300 that relates to the next accounting period and the prepayments account no longer has a balance.

Balance carried down method

The accounting using this method is just the opposite of the entries made for accruals. The expense account is credited to reduce the expense for the period and to complete the double entry a debit balance is brought down to be shown in the balance sheet as a prepayment.

Insurance account

Date	Details	£	Date	Details	£
31 Mar	Balance b/d	1,200	31 Mar	Profit & loss a/c	900
			31 Mar	Balance c/d	300
		1,200			1,200
1 Apr	Prepayments	300			

student notes

The insurance account now shows a debit balance that will be listed as a prepayment among the current assets in the balance sheet. This balance is also the start of the following period's insurance expense and therefore no further adjustments are necessary.

Activity 3

A business pays rent for its premises quarterly in advance. The last payment was on 1 November 2008 for the following three months for £900. The business's year end is 31 December. The balance on the rent account at 31 December was £3,200.

Using only the rent account show how this prepayment would be accounted for.

ACCRUALS OF INCOME

We have already seen earlier in the chapter that the main income of a business, its sales, are automatically accounted for on the accruals basis by recognising debtors for credit sales. However some businesses do also have other sources of miscellaneous income which must also be accounted for according to the accruals concept.

An ACCRUAL OF INCOME is an amount of income that is due for the accounting period but has not yet been received. For accounting purposes the effect of this is:

- add the accrual to the balance on the income account to show the full amount of income due for the period
- show the amount due as a form of debtor in the balance sheet, income receivable

HOW IT WORKS

Dawn Fisher sells some clothes made by another business and is paid a commission for the amounts that she sells. The commission received for the year to 31 March 2009 has been £2,300 but there is a further £400 due for March commissions.

The accounting methods and entries are the same as for accruals and prepayments of expenses but you do need to think quite carefully about the entries as we are now dealing with income and not expenses.

student notes

Commission receivable account

Commission account

Date	Details	£	Date	Details	£
31 Mar	Profit & loss a/c	2,700	31 Mar	Balance b/d	2,300
			31 Mar	Commission receivable	400
		2,700			2,700

Commission receivable

Date	Details	£	Date	Details	£
31 Mar	Commission	400			

The full amount of commission for the period, £2,700, is credited to the profit and loss account and a debtor is shown in the balance sheet for the commission receivable.

Balance carried down method

Commission account

Date	Details	£	Date	Details	£
31 Mar	Profit & loss a/c	2,700	31 Mar	Balance b/d	2,300
			31 Mar	Commission receivable c/d	400
		2,700			2,700
1 Apr	Balance b/d	400			

Again the correct amount is credited to the profit and loss account and the debit balance on the account is listed in the balance sheet as commission receivable.

PREPAYMENTS OF INCOME

It is also possible for income from another party to be prepaid. A PREPAYMENT OF INCOME is miscellaneous income that has already been received for the following accounting period.

The accounting effect of this is:

- the prepayment must be deducted from the amount of income recorded in order that the income in the profit and loss account is the income for the period
- the prepaid income is listed in the balance sheet as a creditor, income received in advance

student notes

HOW IT WORKS

Dawn Fisher sublets some of her premises to a local artist for a quarterly rental payable in advance of £250. The rental income account at 31 March 2009 shows a credit balance of £1,000 but this includes £250 paid on 28 March for the following quarter.

Income prepayment account

Rental income

Date	Details	£	Date	Details	£
31 Mar	Income prepayment	250	31 Mar	Balance b/d	1,000
31 Mar	Profit & loss a/c	750			
		1,000			1,000

Income prepayment

Date	Details	£	Date	Details	£
			31 Mar	Rental income	250

The profit and loss account shows the income due for the period and the income prepayment account balance will be listed in the balance sheet as a form of creditor, income received in advance.

Balance carried down method

Rental income

Date	Details	£	Date	Details	£
31 Mar	Profit & loss a/c	750	31 Mar	Balance b/d	1,000
31 Mar	Balance c/d	250			
		1,000			1,000
			1 Apr	Balance b/d	250

Again the income appearing in the profit and loss account is the correct amount of £750 and a credit balance of £250, income received in advance, is listed in the balance sheet.

Activity 4

A business shows a balance on its rental income account of £3,400. This includes rental income for the next accounting period paid in advance of £800.

Describe what effect this would have on the accounting entries in the profit and loss account and the balance sheet.

CHAPTER OVERVIEW

- financial statements should be prepared according to the accruals concept which means that the income and expenses that are recognised should be those that have been earned or incurred in the period not just the amounts of cash that have been received or paid
- by setting up debtor and creditor accounts for sales and purchases on credit then sales and purchases are automatically recorded according to the accruals concept – the sale and purchase is recognised when it is made not when the cash is received or paid
- expenses are however treated differently – they will only be recorded in the expense ledger account when they are actually paid, therefore at the end of each accounting year each expense account must be considered carefully to ensure that the balance represents the full amount of that expense that has been incurred in the period
- an accrual is an amount of expense that has been incurred but has not yet been paid and is therefore not yet recorded in the expense ledger account – this accrual must be added to the expense balance and shown in the balance sheet as a creditor, an accrual
- a prepayment is the opposite of an accrual – it is an amount of expense that has been paid and therefore appears in the ledger account but it relates to the following accounting period – this must be removed from the ledger account balance and is shown in the balance sheet as a form of debtor, a prepayment
- many businesses will have sources of miscellaneous income – these can also be either accrued or prepaid
- an accrual of income is an amount that is due for the period but has not been received – this must be added to the income account balance and included in the balance sheet as a form of debtor, income receivable
- a prepayment of income is where income has been received but it actually relates to the following accounting period – this must be deducted from the income account balance and shown in the balance sheet as a creditor, income received in advance

KEY WORDS

Accruals concept fundamental accounting concept that states that income and expenses shown in the profit and loss account should be those that were earned or incurred during the period rather than simply the cash received or paid

Accrual an amount of expense that has been incurred during the period but not yet paid for

Prepayment an amount of expense that has been paid for but relates to the following accounting period

Accrual of income an amount of income that is due for the period but has not yet been received

Prepayment of income an amount of income that has been received but relates to the following accounting period

HOW MUCH HAVE YOU LEARNED?

1 a) Rent paid in advance for the following accounting period would appear as .... in the balance sheet.

b) Motor expenses owing to the local garage would appear as .... in the balance sheet.

2 State what effect each of the following would have in the profit and loss account and the balance sheet of a business with an accounting year end of 31 March 2009:

a) The balance on the heat and light expense account of £670 does not include the latest bill which shows £200 of heat and light expenses for the first three months of the year

b) The rental income account balance of £380 includes £40 of rent received for April 2009

c) The insurance account balance of £1,400 includes £300 for insurance for April to June 2009

d) The commissions received account balance of £180 does not include £20 of commission due for March 2009

3 A business has an accounting year end of 30 June 2008. On that date the motor expenses account shows a balance of £845. This includes £150 of road fund licence for the year from 1 January 2008.

Show the accounting entries required for this using an accruals or prepayments account as relevant.

4 A business has an accounting year end of 31 March 2009. At that date the balance on the electricity account is £470. On 7 April 2009 a further electricity bill is received for January to March 2009 totalling £180. This bill is then paid on 25 April 2009.

a) Show the accounting entries using only the electricity account that are required to show the correct picture at the year end.

b) Show how the payment of the bill on 25 April would be accounted for.

chapter 9: BAD AND DOUBTFUL DEBTS

chapter coverage 

In this chapter we will be considering the debtors balance at the end of the accounting year and any adjustments that might be required. The topics that we shall cover are:

- chasing debts
- accounting treatment of bad debts
- VAT on bad debts
- bad debts that are recovered
- doubtful debts
- accounting for doubtful debts
- types of provisions for doubtful debts
- adjusting the provision for doubtful debts

KNOWLEDGE AND UNDERSTANDING AND PERFORMANCE CRITERIA COVERAGE

knowledge and understanding

- the methods of recording information for the organisational accounts of sole traders and partnerships
- how to make and adjust provisions
- the importance of maintaining the confidentiality of business transactions
- principles of double entry accounting
- the objectives of making provisions for depreciation and other purposes

Performance criteria – element 5.2

- correctly identify, calculate and record appropriate adjustments
- conduct investigations into business transactions with tact and courtesy

student notes

BAD DEBTS

Accruals and prudence

When a sale is made on credit it is recognised immediately in the accounting records by recording it as a sale and setting up a debtor for the amount due – this is in accordance with the accruals concept. In most cases we will expect the debt to be honoured and the amount paid by the debtor. However it is possible that some debts may never be recovered and according to the prudence concept any debts that are not likely to be received should not be shown as an asset in the balance sheet.

A BAD DEBT is one that after every attempt to collect the money the business believes will never be paid.

Chasing debts

If a debt has not been paid by a debtor within a reasonable time it will be necessary for the sales ledger clerk to start chasing the debt. This might begin with a polite telephone call enquiring if there is any query regarding the amount that is due and reminding the customer that the stated credit period has been exceeded. If there is no response within a reasonable time the telephone call should be followed up by a letter requesting payment. Again if there is no response within a reasonable time then a further letter should be sent possibly including the threat of legal action if payment is not received. Finally the matter may be put into the hand's of the business's solicitor if it is the business's policy to try to recover debts in this manner.

At all times when communicating with customers whether it is on the telephone or in a letter the customer should be dealt with with tact and courtesy whilst at the same time getting over a firm message that payment is overdue.

If all attempts at recovering the debt are unsuccessful then the business will have to accept that the debt is bad.

Accounting treatment of bad debts

If a debt is not going to be recovered then according to the prudence concept it should be written out of the business's books and should not be shown as a debtor in the balance sheet. The double entry for this is:

Debit BAD DEBTS EXPENSE ACCOUNT
Credit Debtors control account

This will remove the debt from the debtors balance and creates a further expense, bad debts written off, in the profit and loss account.

If a subsidiary sales ledger is maintained for the individual credit customers, then the debtors account will be called the sales ledger control account, and the debtor's individual account in the subsidiary ledger, the sales ledger, must also have the debt removed from it by a credit entry here as well.

student notes

HOW IT WORKS

At her year end, 31 March 2009, Dawn Fisher finds that the balance on her sales ledger control account is £10,857. She is however very concerned about an amount of £337 owing from K Whistler. The last money received from this customer was in September 2008 and since then Dawn has telephoned and written letters requesting payment. However her latest letter has been returned unopened with a scribbled comment on the envelope 'K Whistler not known at this address'. Dawn has now decided to accept that the debt will never be paid and is to write it off as bad.

Bad debts expense account

Date	Details	£	Date	Details	£
31 Mar	Sales ledger control	337			

Sales ledger control account

Date	Details	£	Date	Details	£
31 Mar	Balance b/d	10,857	31 Mar	Bad debts expense	337
			31 Mar	Balance c/d	10,520
		10,857			10,857
1 Apr	Balance b/d	10,520			

The sales ledger control account now shows the amended balance of £10,520 after having removed K Whistler's debt. The bad debts expense account has a debit balance of £337 which is an expense of the business, one of the risks of making sales on credit, and as such will be charged in the profit and loss account as an expense.

In the subsidiary sales ledger K Whistler's account must also be credited with this bad debt in order to remove it from these records as well:

K Whistler

Date	Details	£	Date	Details	£
31 Mar	Balance b/d	337	31 Mar	Bad debt written off	337

student notes

Activity 1

A business has debtors at the year end of £26,478. Of these it is felt that £976 should be written off as bad.

What is the double entry for the write off of these bad debts?

VAT on bad debts

When the sale was made to the customer, if the business is registered for VAT, then VAT would have been charged and this would have been paid over to HM Revenue and Customs as part of the output tax for the period. If the money is never recovered from the debtor then HM Revenue & Customs do allow VAT registered businesses to recover the VAT on the bad debts written off provided that the debt is more than six months overdue.

Care should be taken with this as the HM Revenue & Customs rule is if the debt is more than six months overdue, not more than six months old. Therefore if the invoice was dated 1 January and the stated credit terms were 60 days then the debt would not be six months overdue until 31 August – the VAT could not be recovered until this date.

Bad debts recovered

Occasionally in practice, and more commonly in assessments and exams, a debt will be received from the customer after it has been written off as bad.

The full double entry for this requires two separate entries:

Debit Bank account
Credit Debtors account

- this records the money being received as if from a normal debtor however the debt has been written off as bad and has therefore been removed from the debtors account – therefore the debt must be reinstated and the bad debts expense cancelled

Debit Debtors account
Credit Bad debts expense account

- as you can see from this double entry there is both a debit and a credit entry to the debtors account which cancel each other out therefore often these entries are left out and the double entry is simplified to:

Debit Bank account
Credit Bad debts expense account

student notes

In some businesses a separate Bad debts recovered account will be kept which will be credited instead of the Bad debts expense account. However as this situation will normally be a fairly rare occurrence it makes more sense to use the bad debts expense account when such a debt is recovered.

Activity 2

A business has written off a debt for £1,000 from one of its customers and then three months later the amount is received.

What is the full double entry for this receipt?

DOUBTFUL DEBTS

We have seen that a bad debt is one that we are fairly sure will never be recovered. However there may be other debts that we are concerned about but are not yet ready to write off as bad. For example if a customer is querying an amount or if there has been no response to initial requests for payment of an overdue debt.

These debts over which there is some concern are known as DOUBTFUL DEBTS.

There is also another scenario with debtors. A business may not necessarily be able to pinpoint specific debts that are doubtful but the sales ledger clerk knows from experience that on average a certain percentage of debts turn out to be problems. In this case by applying the percentage to the total debtors figure will give an indication of the amount of doubtful debts.

Accounting for doubtful debts

Again according to the prudence concept if a business has some debts over which there is doubt as to their recoverability then they should not be shown in the balance sheet as assets. However these debts are not to be removed totally from the debtors account, as with a bad debt. Instead a PROVISION FOR DOUBTFUL DEBTS is set up.

A provision is a credit balance which is netted off against an asset. Remember that the provision for depreciation account balance was deducted from the fixed assets at cost total in order to arrive at the net book value of fixed assets.

In a similar way the provision for doubtful debts is a credit balance which is to be deducted from the debtors account balance to show the net debtors that are thought to be recoverable in the balance sheet. This is less permanent than writing the debt out of the debtors account as with a bad debt.

student notes

The double entry for initially setting up a provision for doubtful debts is:

Debit Doubtful debts expense account
Credit Provision for doubtful debts account

In some businesses the debit entry will in fact be to the bad debts expense account rather than having a separate doubtful debts expense account.

Types of provision for doubtful debts

As we have seen there are potentially two types of doubtful debt – the specific debts that can be pinpointed as doubtful and the more general percentage approach.

This means that there could be two elements to any provision for doubtful debts:

- A SPECIFIC PROVISION
- A GENERAL PROVISION

HOW IT WORKS

Dawn Fisher's balance on her debtors account at her year end, 31 March 2009, after writing off the bad debt from K Whistler is £10,520.

When Dawn considers these debts in detail she decides that she is definitely concerned about the recoverability of one debt for £320. She has also been advised by friends in business that she is likely to have problems on average with about 2% of her debtors.

Therefore Dawn wishes to set up a provision for doubtful debts made up of two elements:

- A specific provision for £320
- A general provision of 2% of the remaining debtors

Firstly we must calculate the total amount of the provision. When applying a percentage to the debtors total to calculate a general provision you should always deduct any bad debts that are to be written off and any debts against which a specific provision is to be made before applying the percentage.

student notes

	£
Debtors balance after writing off bad debts	10,520
Specific provision	(320)
	10,200

General provision 2% x 10,200	204
Specific provision	320
	524

Now we have the total for the provision required it must be entered into the ledger accounts (Dawn is using her bad debts expense account for this rather than setting up a separate doubtful debts expense account).

Bad debts expense account

Date	Details	£	Date	Details	£
31 Mar	Sales ledger control	337	31 Mar	Profit & loss a/c	861
31 Mar	Provision for doubtful debts	524			
		861			861

Provision for doubtful debts

Date	Details	£	Date	Details	£
			31 Mar	Bad debts expense	524

The balance on the bad debts expense account of £861 is made up of the bad debt that has been written off and the setting up of the provision for doubtful debts. The whole of this amount is charged to the profit and loss account as an expense.

When Dawn produces her balance sheet then the debtors balance will have the provision deducted from it to show the net debtors that are truly recoverable:

	£
Debtors	10,520
Less: provision for doubtful debts	(524)
	9,996

Activity 3

A business has debtors of £21,680. Of these one debt of £680 is to be written off as bad and a provision of 3% is to be made against the remainder.

Write up the bad debts expense account, debtors account and provision for doubtful debts account to reflect this.

student notes

Adjustments to the provision for doubtful debts

The double entry that we have seen for the provision for doubtful debts is the double entry required when the provision is first set up. In subsequent years the balance on the provision for doubtful debts account will remain in the ledger accounts as it is a balance sheet account but it may require increasing or decreasing each year.

If the provision for doubtful debts is to be increased the double entry is:

Debit Bad debts expense account
Credit Provision for doubtful debts account

- with the amount of the increase required

If the provision for doubtful debts is to be decreased the double entry is:

Debit Provision for doubtful debts account
Credit Bad debts expense account

- with the amount of the decrease required

HOW IT WORKS

A business has a policy of providing against 4% of its debtors at the year end. Its debtors at 31 December 2006, the first year of trading, were £24,000 after writing off bad debts of £200. The debtors figures at the end of 2007 and 2008 were £30,000 and £26,000 again after writing off bad debts of £400 and £300 respectively.

The provisions required each year are:

2006	£24,000 x 4%	=	£960
2007	£30,000 x 4%	=	£1,200
2008	£26,000 x 4%	=	£1,040

student notes

31 December 2006 – set up the provision for doubtful debts

Bad debts expense account

Date	Details	£	Date	Details	£
2006			2006		
31 Dec	Debtors	200	31 Dec	Profit & loss a/c	1,160
31 Dec	Provision for doubtful debts	960			
		1,160			1,160

Provision for doubtful debts account

Date	Details	£	Date	Details	£
2006			2006		
31 Dec	Balance c/d	960	31 Dec	Bad debts expense	960
			2007		
			1 Jan	Balance b/d	960

The provision has been set up by charging the whole amount to the bad debts expense account. This is then taken to the profit and loss account so no balance remains on that account. In contrast the provision for doubtful debts is a balance sheet account so when the balance has been listed in the balance sheet it still remains as the opening balance for 2006.

31 December 2007 – increase provision to £1,200

Bad debts expense account

Date	Details	£	Date	Details	£
2007			2007		
31 Dec	Debtors	400	31 Dec	Profit & loss a/c	640
31 Dec	Provision for doubtful debts	240			
		640			640

Bad debts expense account

Date	Details	£	Date	Details	£
2006			2006		
31 Dec	Balance c/d	960	31 Dec	Bad debts expense	960
2007			2007		
31 Dec	Balance c/d	1,200	1 Jan	Balance b/d	960
			31 Dec	Bad debts expense	240
		1,200			1,200
			2008		
			1 Jan	Balance b/d	1,200

The bad debts expense account has only been charged with the amount that is necessary to bring the balance on the provision account up to this year's required provision – in this case £240.

student notes

31 December 2008 – decrease provision to £1,040

Bad debts expense account

Date	Details	£	Date	Details	£
2008			2008		
31 Dec	Debtors	300	31 Dec	Provision for doubtful debts	160
		300	31 Dec	Profit & loss a/c	140
					300

Provision for doubtful debts account

Date	Details	£	Date	Details	£
2006			2006		
31 Dec	Balance c/d	960	31 Dec	Bad debts expense	960
2007			2007		
31 Dec	Balance c/d	1,200	1 Jan	Balance b/d	960
			31 Dec	Bad debts expense	240
		1,200			1,200
2008			2008		
31 Dec	Bad debts expense	160	1 Jan	Balance b/d	1,200
31 Dec	Balance c/d	1,040			
		1,200			1,200
			2009		
			1 Jan	Balance b/d	1,040

In this case the provision had to be reduced by £160 therefore the bad debts expense account was credited and the provision account debited in order to bring the provision account balance down to the amount required.

At each year end in the balance sheet the debtors would appear as follows:

	2006	*2007*	*2008*
	£	£	£
Debtors	24,000	30,000	26,000
Less: provision for doubtful debts	960	1,200	1,040
	23,040	28,800	24,960

Activity 4

On 31 December 2007 a business had a balance on its provision for doubtful debts account of £1,500. At the year end of 31 December 2008 its debtors account balance was £60,000. On consideration of these debts it was decided that £2,400 were to be written off as bad debts and that a provision of 3% was to be made against the remainder.

Write up the debtors account, bad debts expense account and provision for doubtful debts account at 31 December 2008.

CHAPTER OVERVIEW

- the accruals concept requires that sales on credit are recognised as soon as they are made rather than waiting until the cash is received from the debtor – the prudence concept however requires that if money from a debtor is unlikely to be received then it should not appear as an asset in the balance sheet
- any debts that are not going to be recovered should be written off as bad debts by debiting the bad debts expense account and crediting the debtors account (called the sales ledger control account when a subsidiary sales ledger is also maintained) – the debtor's individual account in the subsidiary sales ledger must also be credited with the amount of the bad debt
- provided that the bad debt written off is more than six months overdue the VAT on the amount can be recovered
- if a debtor eventually pays a debt that has already been written off as a bad debt then the bank account is debited with the receipt and normally the bad debts expense account will be credited although some businesses may keep a separate bad debts recovered account for the credit entry
- a doubtful debt is one where there is concern about its recoverability – these are dealt with in the accounting records by setting up a provision for doubtful debts
- in some cases the provision will be against specific debts and in other cases a general provision will be required at a percentage of the debtors balance
- once the provision for doubtful debts has initially been set up then each year the balance must be increased or decreased to the amount that is required – this is done by debiting or crediting the bad debts expense account by the amount of the increase or decrease required

KEY WORDS

Bad debt a debt that it is believed will not be recovered

Bad debts expense account the expense account used to record the bad debts that are written off – the balance appears as an expense in the profit and loss account

Doubtful debts amounts over which there is some doubt as to their recoverability

Provision for doubtful debts an amount that will be deducted from the debtors balance in the balance sheet to indicate that there is doubt as to the recoverability of these debts

Specific provision a provision against particular debts that are recognised as doubtful

General provision a provision set up as a percentage of the debtors balance to reflect the fact that on average a certain percentage of debts will be doubtful

HOW MUCH HAVE YOU LEARNED?

1 A business has debtors at 30 April 2008 of £25,673. Of these it was decided that two debts were never going to be recovered, £157 from H Taylor and £288 from C Phelps. These are to be written off as bad.

Write up the main ledger and subsidiary ledger accounts necessary to record these bad debts.

2 In 2007 a business had written off a bad debt from a customer of £250. During 2008 this amount was unexpectedly received from the customer.

Write up the main ledger accounts in full to reflect this receipt.

3 At the end of the first year of trading a business has debtors of £11,650. Of these it is decided that one debt of £350 is to be written off as bad. A provision for doubtful debts is to be made against a further debt of £200 and a general provision is required of 2% of the remainder of the debtors.

a) Calculate the amount of the provision for doubtful debts that is required at the year end

b) Write up the bad debts expense account, debtors account and provision for doubtful debts account at the year end to reflect the position.

4 On 1 January 2007 there is a balance on a business's provision for doubtful debts account of £1,460. At 31 December 2007 the balance on the debtors account is £42,570. Of this it is decided that £370 should be written off as a bad debt and a provision for doubtful debts of 4% is required against the remainder.

At 31 December 2008 the debtors total was £38,400 of which £400 is to be written off as a bad debt. A provision for doubtful debts of 4% of the remainder of the debtors is required.

Write up the bad debts expense account and the provision for doubtful debts account for 2007 and 2008.

chapter 10: CONTROL ACCOUNT RECONCILIATIONS

chapter coverage

In this chapter we will start to consider the checks and controls that a business will have to ensure that the figures that appear in the trial balance and eventually in the final accounts are correct. In this chapter we will consider the balances on the sales ledger and purchases ledger control accounts and the reconciliations that should be prepared on a regular basis with these accounts. The topics that are covered are:

- the accounting system for sales on credit
- the accounting system for purchases on credit
- sales ledger control account
- purchases ledger control account
- contra entries
- errors in control accounts and the subsidiary ledgers
- sales ledger control account reconciliation
- purchases ledger control account reconciliation

KNOWLEDGE AND UNDERSTANDING AND PERFORMANCE CRITERIA COVERAGE

knowledge and understanding

- how to identify and correct different types of error
- principles of double entry accounting

Performance criteria – element 5.2

- correctly prepare reconciliations for the preparation of final accounts
- identify any discrepancies in the reconciliation process and either take steps to rectify them or refer them to the appropriate person

student notes

SALES LEDGER CONTROL ACCOUNT AND THE SUBSIDIARY SALES LEDGER

Before we look at the control account procedures and reconciliations we will firstly run through how the accounting system works for sales on credit.

Accounting system for sales on credit

The process of accounting for sales on credit and debtors goes like this:

- The sales invoices sent to debtors are recorded in the sales day book
- The total of the sales day book is regularly posted to the sales ledger control account
- The individual invoices in the sales day book are posted to the individual debtors' accounts in the subsidiary sales ledger (or subsidiary debtors ledger)
- The receipts of cash/cheques from debtors are recorded in the cash receipts book
- The total of the cash receipts book is regularly posted to the sales ledger control account
- The individual receipts are posted to the individual debtor's accounts in the subsidiary sales ledger (or subsidiary debtors ledger)

HOW IT WORKS

Fred Simpson has recently set up in business and he currently has just three credit customers Bill, John and Karen. His sales day book and cash receipts book for the month of June are given below.

student notes

Sales day book

Date	Customer	Invoice no.	Ref	Gross £	VAT £	Net £
3/06	Bill	0045	SL01	235.00	35.00	200.00
5/06	Karen	0046	SL03	141.00	21.00	120.00
8/06	John	0047	SL02	176.25	26.25	150.00
15/06	Karen	0048	SL03	258.50	38.50	220.00
20/06	John	0049	SL02	117.50	17.50	100.00
28/06	Bill	0050	SL01	211.50	31.50	180.00
				1,139.75	169.75	970.00

These figures must be posted to the sales ledger control account and the individual debtors accounts in the subsidiary ledger:

Main ledger

Sales ledger control account

	£		£
Balance b/d	587.50		
SDB	1,139.75		

Subsidiary sales ledger

Bill SL01

Date	Details	£	Date	Details	£
1/06	Balance b/d	235.00			
3/06	SDB 0045	235.00			
28/06	SDB 0050	211.50			

John SL02

Date	Details	£	Date	Details	£
1/06	Balance b/d	117.50			
8/06	SDB 0047	176.25			
20/06	SDB 0049	117.50			

student notes

Karen SL03

Date	Details	£	Date	Details	£
1/06	Balance b/d	235.00			
5/06	SDB 0046	141.00			
15/06	SDB 0048	258.50			

Can you see how the totals of the opening balances on each individual account in the subsidiary ledger add up to the opening balance on the sales ledger control account?

Opening balances

	£
Bill	235.00
John	117.50
Karen	235.00
Sales ledger control account	587.50

As we will see later this should always be the case if the accounting has been correctly carried out – the totals of the balances at any point in time on the individual accounts in the subsidiary sales ledger should be equal to the balance on the sales ledger control account.

Now we will deal with the receipts from these debtors in the month of June:

Cash receipts book

Date	*Details*	*Ref*	*Total* £	*VAT* £	*Cash sales* £	*Sales ledger* £	*Discounts allowed* £
6/06	John	SL02	117.50			117.50	
10/06	Bill	SL01	225.60			225.60	9.40
13/06	Karen	SL03	200.00			200.00	
20/06	Bill	SL01	225.60			225.60	9.40
28/06	Karen	SL03	100.00			100.00	
30/06	John	SL02	176.25			176.25	
			1,044.95			1,044.95	18.80

These figures must now also be posted to the main ledger and the subsidiary ledger.

student notes

Main ledger

Sales ledger control account

	£		£
Balance b/d	587.50	CRB	1,044.95
SDB	1,139.75	CRB – discounts	18.80

Subsidiary sales ledger

Bill SL01

Date	Details	£	Date	Details	£
1/06	Balance b/d	235.00	10/06	CRB	225.60
3/06	SDB 0045	235.00	10/06	CRB – discount	9.40
28/06	SDB 0050	211.50	20/06	CRB	225.60
			20/06	CRB – discount	9.40

John SL02

Date	Details	£	Date	Details	£
1/06	Balance b/d	117.50	6/06	CRB	117.50
8/06	SDB 0047	176.25	30/06	CRB	176.25
20/06	SDB 0049	117.50			

Karen SL03

Date	Details	£	Date	Details	£
1/06	Balance b/d	235.00	13/06	CRB	200.00
5/06	SDB 0046	141.00	28/06	CRB	100.00
15/06	SDB 0048	258.50			

Finally at the end of June each of the accounts should be balanced.

Main ledger

Sales ledger control account

	£		£
Balance b/d	587.50	CRB	1,044.95
SDB	1,139.75	CRB – discounts	18.80
	1,727.25	Balance c/d	663.50
			1,727.25
Balance b/d	663.50		

student notes

Subsidiary sales ledger

Bill SL01

Date	Details	£	Date	Details	£
1/06	Balance b/d	235.00	10/06	CRB	225.60
3/06	SDB 0045	235.00	10/06	CRB – discount	9.40
28/06	SDB 0050	211.50	20/06	CRB	225.60
			20/06	CRB – discount	9.40
				Balance c/d	211.50
		681.50			681.50
	Balance b/d	211.50			

John SL02

Date	Details	£	Date	Details	£
1/06	Balance b/d	117.50	6/06	CRB	117.50
8/06	SDB 0047	176.25	30/06	CRB	176.25
20/06	SDB 0049	117.50		Balance c/d	117.50
		411.25			411.25
	Balance b/d	117.50			

Karen SL03

Date	Details	£	Date	Details	£
1/06	Balance b/d	235.00	13/06	CRB	200.00
5/06	SDB 0046	141.00	28/06	CRB	100.00
15/06	SDB 0048	258.50		Balance c/d	334.50
		634.50			634.50
	Balance b/d	334.50			

Closing balances

Note how the total of each of the individual debtor balances equals the balance on the sales ledger control account at the end of June:

	£
Bill	211.50
John	117.50
Karen	334.50
Sales ledger control balance	663.50

If the double entry has all been correctly carried out then the total of the list of debtor balances will always equal the balance on the sales ledger control account.

This whole process of accounting for credit sales in the main ledger and in the subsidiary sales ledger can be illustrated in a diagram:

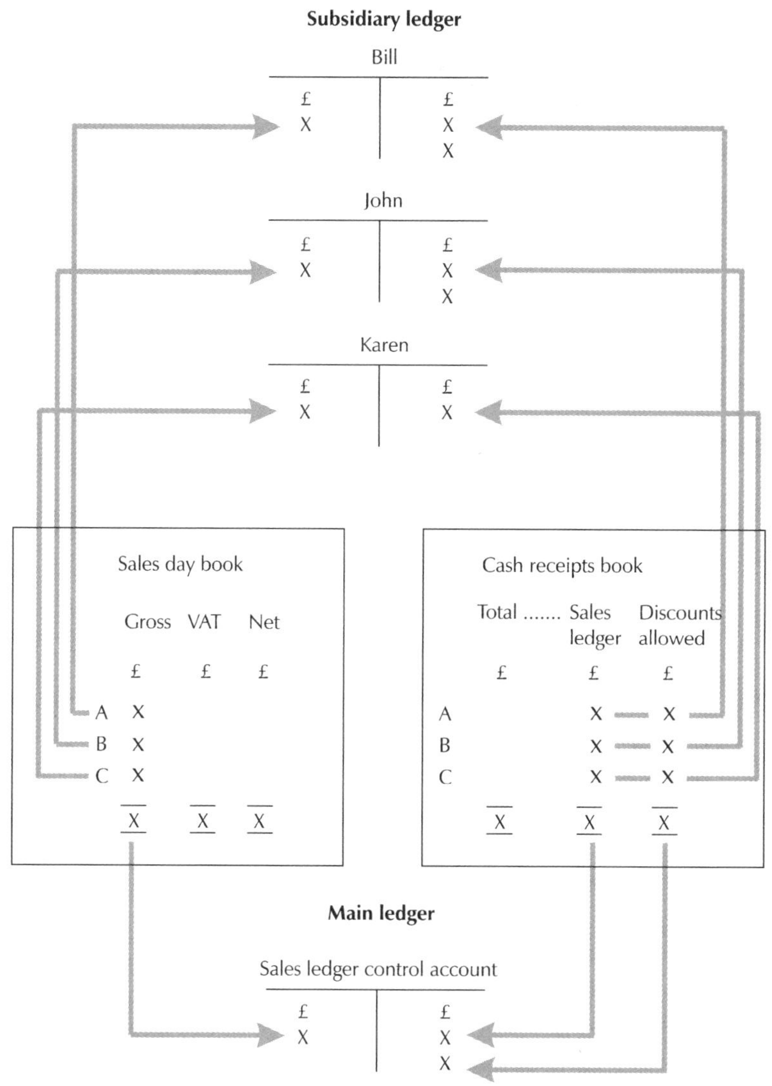

student notes

Activity 1

What is the double entry in the main ledger for sales on credit which include VAT?

student notes

PURCHASES LEDGER CONTROL ACCOUNT AND THE SUBSIDIARY PURCHASES LEDGER

Accounting for credit purchases

The accounting process for credit purchases and creditors is precisely the same as for debtors except that the entries in the accounts are the other way around.

- The purchase invoices received are recorded in the purchases day book
- The total of the purchases day book is regularly posted to the purchase ledger control account
- The individual invoices in the purchases day book are posted to the individual creditors accounts in the subsidiary purchases ledger (or subsidiary creditors ledger)
- The payments to creditors are recorded in the cash payments book
- The total of the cash payments book is regularly posted to the purchases ledger control account
- The individual payments are posted to the individual creditors accounts in the subsidiary purchases ledger (or subsidiary creditors ledger)

Again this can be shown in a diagram:

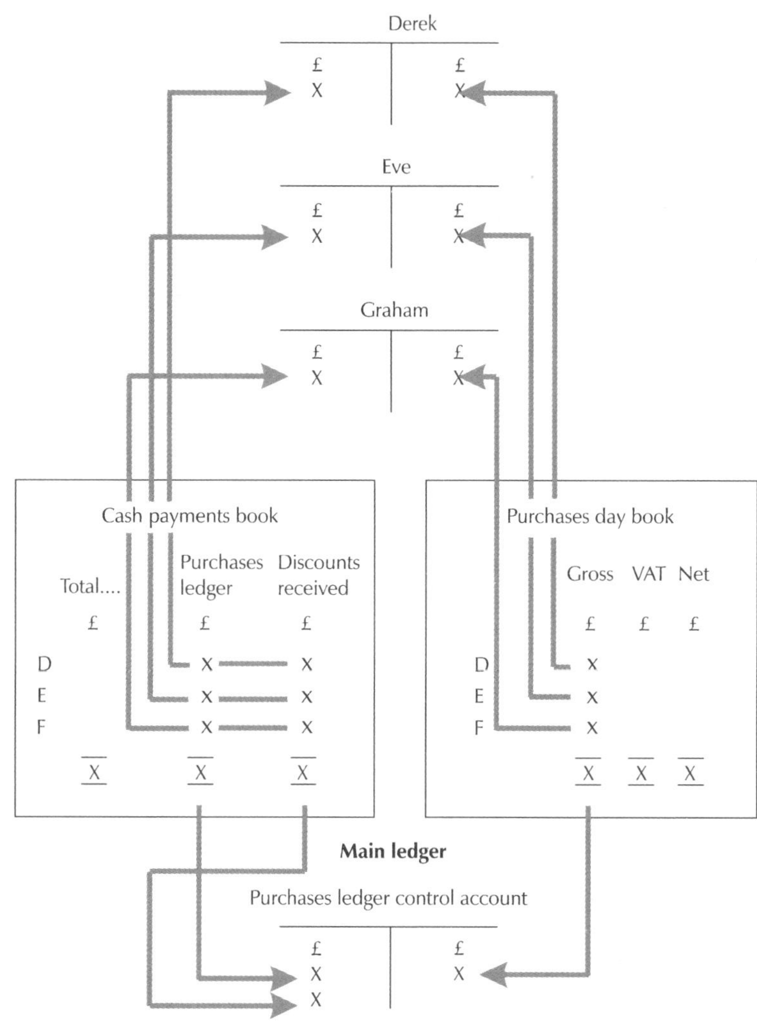

student notes

Closing balances

In just the same way as with the accounting system for debtors, if the double entry has been correctly performed then the closing balances on the individual creditor accounts in the subsidiary ledger should total back to the balance on the purchases ledger control account.

student notes

HOW IT WORKS

If Fred Simpson has three credit suppliers, Derek, Eve and Graham then the final balances on their accounts and the purchases ledger control account should agree:

Subsidiary purchases ledger

Derek

	£		£
		Closing balance	115.60

Eve

	£		£
		Closing balance	220.00

Graham

	£		£
		Closing balance	150.00

Main ledger

Purchases ledger control account

	£		£
		Closing balance	485.60

	£
Derek	115.60
Eve	220.00
Graham	150.00
Purchases ledger control account balance	485.60

student notes

Activity 2

What is the double entry in the main ledger for purchases on credit which include VAT?

CONTROL ACCOUNTS

We will now look in more detail at the figures that are likely to appear in the sales ledger and purchases ledger control accounts as so far we have only considered the basic entries for invoices and cash.

Sales ledger control account

A typical sales ledger control account might have the following entries:

Sales ledger control account

	£		£
Balance b/d	X	Balance b/d	X
Credit sales	X	Sales returns	X
Returned cheques	X	Cash/cheques from debtors	X
		Discounts allowed	X
		Bad debts written off	X
		Contra entry	X
Balance c/d	X	Balance c/d	X
	X		X
Balance b/d	X	Balance b/d	X

These entries need a little more explanation:

Balances b/d The opening balance on the account can potentially be a large debit opening balance and a smaller credit opening balance. Normally a debtor's account will have a debit balance, ie the debtor owes the business money. However in some circumstances a debtor's account may have a credit balance at the start of the period.

Possible reasons for a credit balance might be:

- if the customer paid too much for the goods owing by mistake this would then turn him from being a debtor into being a creditor ie, the business owes the money back to the customer
- if the customer had returned goods after paying for them then again there would be a credit balance on the account as the business owes the cost of the returned goods back to the customer

student notes

There are only likely to be a few credit balances on debtor accounts but they are normally shown separately as the opening balance on the control account rather than being netted off against the debit balances.

Credit sales This is the figure that is posted from the gross column total in the sales day book.

Returned cheques If a customer has paid for goods then the entry to the sales ledger control account would be a credit entry. If the bank then returns the cheque as unpaid ie, the cheque has 'bounced', the entry must be reversed by debiting the control account and crediting the bank account.

Sales returns This is the posting of the total of the gross column in the sales returns day book.

Cash/cheques from debtors This is the posting of the sales ledger (or debtors ledger) column total from the cash receipts book.

Discounts allowed This is the posting from the memorandum discount column in the cash receipts book.

Bad debts written off When a sale is made on credit to a customer it is assumed that the customer will eventually pay the amount due. However on occasion it may become clear that a debtor is not going to pay the amount due, this may be due to the fact that he has gone into liquidation or receivership or simply that he has disappeared. Whatever the reason if it is thought that the debtor will not pay then this is known as a BAD DEBT. This was covered in detail in Chapter 9.

Contra entry A contra entry, sometimes known as a set off, can come about where a debtor of the business is also a creditor ie, we both sell to him and buy from him on credit. The contra entry is an amount owing by the debtor which is set off against the amount we owe to him as a creditor. This will be dealt with in more detail later in the chapter.

Balances c/d and b/d Again as with the opening balances on the account the majority of balances will be debit balances therefore carried down on the credit side and brought down on the debit side. With the brought down balances the large balance will be on the debit side and the small balance on the credit side.

Activity 3

What is the double entry in the main ledger for writing off a bad debt?

student notes

Purchases ledger control account

A typical purchases ledger control account might look like this:

Purchases ledger control account

	£		£
Balance b/d	X	Balance b/d	X
Purchases returns	X	Credit purchases	X
Cash/cheques paid to creditors	X		
Discounts received	X		
Contra entry	X		
Balance c/d	X	Balance c/d	X
	X		X
Balance b/d	X	Balance b/d	X

Balances b/d The large balance brought down will be on the credit side of the account as most creditors accounts will have credit balances. However there may be a small number of debit balances on creditors accounts, for the reasons discussed when considering debtors, and these will be the opening debit balances.

Purchases returns This is the posting from the gross column total of the purchases returns day book.

Cash/cheques paid to creditors This is the posting from the purchases ledger column total from the cash payments book.

Discounts received This is the posting from the memorandum discounts received column total from the cash payments book.

Contra entry This is the other side of the posting from the sales ledger control account – see below for more detail.

Credit purchases This is the posting from the gross column total of the purchases day book.

Balances c/d and b/d Again as with the opening balances there will be a large amount of credit balances and a small amount of debit balances. The credit balances will be carried down on the debit side and brought down on the credit side. The debit balances will be carried down on the credit side and brought down on the debit side.

student notes

Contra entries

It is entirely possible that a person or business can be both a debtor and a creditor of your business at the same time. This would come about if your business makes credit sales to this person and buys goods on credit from the same person. If the business is owed money by this person and also owes money to him then it would make sense to net the two amounts off against each other and only pay or receive the difference. This is what a CONTRA ENTRY reflects.

HOW IT WORKS

Dawn Fisher sells goods on credit to Emma Jones and currently Emma owes Dawn £210. Dawn also sometimes buys goods on credit from Emma and currently Dawn owes Emma £100. The accounts for Emma in Dawn's subsidiary sales ledger and subsidiary purchases ledger appear as follows:

Subsidiary sales ledger

Emma Jones

	£		£
Balance b/d	210		

Subsidiary purchases ledger

Emma Jones

	£		£
		Balance b/d	100

Dawn and Emma have discussed this situation and have agreed that rather than Emma paying Dawn £210 and then Dawn paying Emma £100 it would be easier to net the two amounts off and for Emma simply to pay Dawn the remaining £110 that she owes. This must be reflected in the accounting records by a contra entry for the £100.

This £100 will be debited to Emma's creditor account in the subsidiary purchases ledger and credited to her debtors account in the subsidiary sales ledger.

student notes

Subsidiary sales ledger

Emma Jones

	£		£
Balance b/d	210	Contra	100
		Balance c/d	110
	210		210
Balance b/d	110		

Subsidiary purchases ledger

Emma Jones

	£		£
Contra	100	Balance b/d	100

This leaves Dawn with a balance of £110 on Emma's account in the subsidiary sales ledger reflecting the agreed situation.

However if entries are made in the subsidiary ledgers then they must also be reflected in the main ledger. Therefore the double entry in the main ledger would be:

Debit	Purchases ledger control account	£100
Credit	Sales ledger control account	£100

Main ledger

Sales ledger control account

	£		£
		Contra	100

Purchases ledger control account

	£		£
Contra	100		

Activity 4

A business owes £500 to a creditor and that creditor also owes the business £800. They agree to net these amounts off.

What would be the double entry in the business's main ledger?

student notes✍

CONTROL ACCOUNT RECONCILIATIONS

We have seen that if all of the double entry in the main ledger and entries in the subsidiary ledgers is correctly carried out then the totals of the balances on the subsidiary ledger should be equal to the balance on the control account.

Control account balances

The balances on the sales ledger and purchases ledger control accounts are the figures that will appear in the trial balance for debtors and creditors and eventually in the final accounts. Therefore it is important to ensure that these figures are correct. This is done by carrying out a SALES LEDGER CONTROL ACCOUNT RECONCILIATION and a PURCHASES LEDGER CONTROL ACCOUNT RECONCILIATION.

The purpose of these reconciliations is to compare the balance on the control account to the total of the balances of the individual accounts in the subsidiary ledger. If the two totals do not agree then there have been errors made in either the control account or the subsidiary ledger or both. These errors must be investigated, discovered and corrected.

Some of the errors might have been made in the double entry in the main ledger therefore affecting the control account. Other errors might have been made when posting entries to the individual accounts in the subsidiary ledger or in listing the balances in the subsidiary ledger.

Errors affecting the control account

Typical types of errors that might have been made in the double entry in the main ledger and therefore affecting the control account balance might include the following:

- The primary records may have been undercast (under-totalled) or overcast (over-totalled) therefore meaning that the incorrect total is posted to the control account
- Postings from the primary records may have been made to the wrong side of the control account
- The discounts recorded in the cash book may be incorrectly treated
- A bad debt may not have been entered into the main ledger although it was written off in the subsidiary ledger
- A contra entry may have been made in the subsidiary ledgers but not entered into the main ledger accounts

Errors affecting the list of balances

student notes

Some errors will not affect the double entry in the main ledger but will mean that the individual balances in the subsidiary ledger are not correct or that these balances are listed and totalled incorrectly. Typical of these are the following:

- An entry from the primary records might be posted to the wrong account in the subsidiary ledger
- Entries from the primary records may be posted to the wrong side of the subsidiary ledger account
- An entry from the primary records may be posted as the wrong amount to the subsidiary ledger account
- A balance on an account in the subsidiary ledger may be included in the list of balances as the wrong amount or as the wrong type of balance, eg a debit rather than a credit

Activity 5

If the sales day book total for a week is overcast by £1,000 would this affect the sales ledger control account or the individual debtors' accounts in the subsidiary ledger?

SALES LEDGER CONTROL ACCOUNT RECONCILIATION

A sales ledger control account reconciliation is a comparison of the balance on the sales ledger control account to the total of the list of debtor balances from the subsidiary ledger. This will be carried out on a regular basis, usually monthly.

HOW IT WORKS

Dawn Fisher is carrying out her sales ledger control account reconciliation at the end of December 2008. The balances on the sales ledger control account are debit balances of £12,223 and credit balances of £645. The total of the list of debtors account balances from the subsidiary ledger comes to £11,104.

student notes

Step 1 Check whether the control account total agrees to the total of the subsidiary ledger balances.

	£
Control account total	
Debit balances	12,223
Less: credit balances	(645)
Net balance	11,578

As this does not agree to the total of the list of balances, £11,104 then the difference must be investigated. You do however discover that the figure of £645 for credit balances on debtors accounts is correct.

Step 2 The control account and the individual accounts and balances must be checked and any errors or omissions noted.

In Dawn's case the following errors were noted:

a) A page of the cash receipts book had been undercast by £100

b) The total from the sales day book for a week had been posted as £2,340 instead of £2,430

c) A bad debt of £80 had been written off in the individual debtor's account but not in the main ledger

d) An invoice to G Harper for £250 had been entered into the account of G Draper instead

e) A cash receipt from David Carr had been entered into the debtor's account as £175 instead of the correct figure from the cash receipts book of £157

f) A debit balance of £406 on one debtor's account had been omitted from the list of balances

g) A credit balance of £20 on a debtor's account had been included in the list of balances as a debit balance

Step 3 The sales ledger control account must be adjusted for any errors that affect it:

TC – With decimal place

	£		£
Balance b/d	12,223	Balance b/d	645
		a) Cash receipts books	100
		c) Bad debt	80
b) Sales day book	90		
Balance c/d (known)	645	Balance c/d(bal fig)	12,133
	12,958		12,958
Balance b/d	12,133	Balance b/d	645

student notes

a) The total from the cash receipts book would be credited to the sales ledger control account therefore if it was undercast by £100 the account must be credited with a further £100

b) The total from the sales day book is debited to the sales ledger control account and as the entry was for £90 too little an extra debit entry of £90 is required

c) To write off a bad debt the sales ledger control account must be credited

Therefore the amended net balance on the control account is:

	£
Debit balance	12,133
Less: credit balances	(645)
	11,488

Step 4 Adjust the total of the list of balances by adding or deducting the errors that affect this total.

	£
Original total	11,104
Add: cash receipt adjustment (175 – 157) e)	18
Add: balance omitted f)	406
Less: credit balance included as debit balance g)	(40)
	11,488

d) The two debtors accounts will need to be adjusted to reflect the error but this type of error does not affect the total of the balances on all of the debtor accounts

e) The receipt was recorded at a figure of £18 too much therefore the balance on this debtors account should be £18 higher

f) The balance omitted must be added in to the total of the list of balances

g) The £20 credit balance that was included as a debit balance would reduce debtors if it were correctly included – however twice the amount of the balance must be deducted as the balance has not been omitted but included on the wrong side which must be cancelled out

The amended total of the list of balances now agrees to the amended sales ledger control account total and the main ledger and subsidiary ledger are now reconciled.

student notes

Activity 6

If the total of the discounts allowed column from the cash receipts book of £120 were not posted for a period how would this be adjusted for in the sales ledger control account reconciliation?

PURCHASES LEDGER CONTROL ACCOUNT RECONCILIATION

A purchases ledger control account reconciliation works in exactly the same manner as a sales ledger control account reconciliation with the entries on the opposite sides.

HOW IT WORKS

Dawn Fisher is currently preparing her purchases ledger control account reconciliation at the end of October 2008. The balance on the purchases ledger control account was £9,240 and the total of the list of creditors' balances from the subsidiary purchases ledger was £9,040.

The following errors and omissions were noted:

a) One page of the purchases day book has been undercast by £100

b) An invoice has been posted to an individual creditor's account in the subsidiary ledger as £863 instead of the correct figure from the purchases day book of £683

c) The total of discounts received of £160 was credited to the purchases ledger control account

d) One of the balances in the subsidiary ledger was included in the total at a figure of £235 instead of £325.

e) A contra entry for £70 had been made in the subsidiary purchases ledger but not in the main ledger

Step 1 Amend the control account balance for any errors that affect it.

Purchases ledger control account

	£		£
		Balance b/d	9,240
c) Discounts	320	a) Purchases day book	100
e) Contra	70		
Balance c/d (bal fig)	8,950		
	9,340		9,340
		Balance b/d	8,950

student notes

a) The total from the purchases day book is credited to the purchases ledger control account and therefore if it was undercast by £100 then the account must be credited with £100

c) The discounts received should have been debited to the purchases ledger control account – instead they were credited and therefore not only should there be one debit of £160 but two, one to cancel out the credit and one to put the debit entry in, therefore a debit of £320

e) The contra entry must be put into the purchases ledger control account as a debit of £70

Step 2 Amend the total of the list of balances to adjust for any errors that affect the individual balances or their total.

	£
Original total	9,040
Less: invoice misposting (863 – 683) b)	(180)
Add: balance misstated e)	90
	8,950

b) An invoice would be posted to the credit side of the creditor's account – in this case it was posted at a figure £180 too high and therefore the creditors' balances would be reduced when the account was amended

d) The balance that was misstated was shown as £90 too small – therefore the balances need to be increased by £90.

Now the amended balance on the purchases ledger control account of £8,950 agrees with the amended list of balances in the subsidiary purchases ledger. This figure of £8,950 can now be used as the creditors figure in the trial balance.

Activity 7

An invoice for £350 was entered into the individual creditor's account in the subsidiary ledger on the wrong side of the account. How should this be adjusted for in the purchases ledger control account reconciliation?

CHAPTER OVERVIEW

- the sales ledger control account is debited with the sales invoices from the sales day book and credited with cash receipts and discounts from the cash receipts book
- the individual accounts for each debtor in the subsidiary sales ledger are also debited with each invoice total and credited with the cash and discounts
- if all of the entries are correctly carried out then the total of the closing balances on the individual debtors accounts from the subsidiary ledger should agree to the balance on the sales ledger control account

KEY WORDS

Sales ledger control account reconciliation an exercise which agrees the balance on the sales ledger control account to the total of the list of balances in the subsidiary sales ledger

Purchases ledger control account reconciliation an exercise which agrees the balance on the purchases ledger control account to the total of the list of balances in the subsidiary purchases ledger

- the same system applies to accounting for creditors although the entries are all on the opposite sides
- the sales ledger control account will also potentially have entries for sales returns, returned cheques, bad debts written off and contra entries as well as the basic entries for invoices, cash and discounts
- the purchases ledger control account will also potentially have entries for purchases returns and a contra entry as well as the basic entries for invoices, cash and discounts
- a contra entry is caused by netting off a debtor and creditor balance with the same party – in the main ledger this is done by debiting the purchases ledger control account and crediting the sales ledger control account – in the subsidiary ledgers the debtor's account will be credited and the creditor's account debited
- if all of the entries in the main ledger and subsidiary ledger have not been properly performed then the subsidiary ledger balances total will not agree to the balance on the control account – in which case the causes of the difference must be discovered
- a sales ledger control account reconciliation compares the balance on the sales ledger control account to the total of the debtors account balances in the subsidiary ledger – both are amended for any errors that have been made and the total and balance should agree after putting through the amendments
- a purchases ledger control account reconciliation works in exactly the same way as the sales ledger reconciliation although all of the entries and balances are on the opposite sides

HOW MUCH HAVE YOU LEARNED?

1 DP Printing is a small company that has currently only four credit customers. The opening balances on their debtor's account in DP's subsidiary sales ledger at the start of May were as follows:

	£
Virgo Partners	227.58
McGowan & Sons	552.73
J J Westrope	317.59
Jacks Ltd	118.36

The opening balance on the sales ledger control account at the start of May was £1,216.26.

The sales day book and cash receipts book for May are given below:

Sales day book

Date	*Customer*	*Gross* £	*VAT* £	*Net* £
3 May	J J Westrope	163.90	24.41	139.49
10 May	Virgo Partners	94.70	14.10	80.60
12 May	Jacks Ltd	105.47	15.70	89.77
15 May	JJ Westrope	271.57	40.44	231.13
20 May	McGowan & Sons	582.69	86.78	495.91
23 May	Jacks Ltd	173.99	25.91	148.08
30 May	Virgo Partners	210.00	31.27	178.73
		1,602.32	238.61	1,363.71

Cash receipts book

Date	*Details*	*Total* £	*VAT* £	*Cash sales* £	*Sales ledger* £	*Discounts allowed* £
3 May	Cash sales	476.90	71.02	405.88		
4 May	Virgo Partners	117.38			117.38	
10 May	Cash sales	442.38	65.88	376.50		
12 May	J J Westrope	308.86			308.86	8.73
15 May	McGowan & Sons	552.73			552.73	
17 May	Cash sales	501.67	74.71	426.96		
20 May	Jacks Ltd	100.00			100.00	
30 May	Cash sales	570.15	84.91	485.24		
		3,070.07	296.52	1,694.58	1,078.97	8.73

Write up the sales ledger control account for the month and the individual debtors' accounts in the subsidiary sales ledger. Agree the control account balance to the total of the subsidiary account balances at the end of the month.

2 DP Printing has three credit suppliers and the opening balances on their creditor accounts in the subsidiary ledger for creditors at the start of May were:

	£
Jenkins Supplies	441.56
Kilnfarm Paper	150.00
Barnfield Ltd	247.90

The opening balance on the purchases ledger control account at the start of May was £839.46.

The purchases day book and cash payments book for the period are given below:

Purchases day book

Date	*Supplier*	*Gross* £	*VAT* £	*Net* £
5 May	Kilnfarm Paper	150.00	22.34	127.66
10 May	Jenkins Supplies	215.47	32.09	183.38
12 May	Barnfield Ltd	310.58	46.25	264.33
20 May	Kilnfarm Paper	150.00	22.34	127.66
27 May	Jenkins Supplies	441.90	65.81	376.09
30 May	Barnfield Ltd	305.77	45.54	260.23
		1,573.72	234.37	1,339.35

Cash payments book

Date	*Details*	*Total* £	*VAT* £	*Cash purchases* £	*Purchases ledger* £	*Discounts received* £
5 May	Cash purchases	225.68	33.61	192.07		
10 May	Jenkins Supplies	423.89			423.89	17.67
12 May	Kilnfarm Paper	150.00			150.00	
15 May	Cash purchases	315.22	46.94	268.28		
20 May	Barnfield Ltd	235.50			235.50	12.40
27 May	Kilnfarm Paper	150.00			150.00	
30 May	Cash purchases	210.44	31.34	179.10		
		1,710.73	111.89	639.45	959.39	30.07

Write up the purchases ledger control account for May and the individual creditors' accounts in the subsidiary ledger. Agree the control account balance at the end of May to the total of the list of individual balances in the subsidiary purchases ledger.

3 Write up the sales ledger control account for the month of July from the following information:

	£
Opening balance 1 July	16,339
Credit sales for the month	50,926
Cash sales for the month	12,776
Sales returns (all for credit sales) for the month	3,446
Cash received from debtors in the month	47,612
Settlement discounts allowed to debtors in the month	1,658
Bad debt to be written off	500
Cheque returned by the bank 'refer to drawer'	366

4 Write up the purchases ledger control account for the month of July from the following information:

	£
Opening balance 1 July	12,587
Cash purchases for the month	15,600
Credit purchases for the month	40,827
Purchases returns (all for purchases on credit)	2,568
Cheques paid to creditors in the month	38,227
Settlement discounts received from suppliers in the month	998

5 The balance on a business's sales ledger control account at the end of June was £41,774 and the total of the list of debtor balances from the subsidiary ledger came to £41,586.

The following errors were discovered:

a) The sales day book was undercast by £100 on one page

b) A page from the sales returns day book with a total of £450 had not been posted to the control account although the individual returns had been recorded in the subsidiary ledger

c) An invoice from the sales day book had been posted to the individual account of the debtor as £769 instead of the correct figure of £679

d) A discount allowed to one customer of £16 had been posted to the wrong side of the customer's account in the subsidiary ledger

e) A bad debt of £210 had been written off in the debtor's individual account in the subsidiary ledger but not in the main ledger

f) A credit balance in the subsidiary ledger of £125 had been included in the list of balances as a debit balance

Reconcile the sales ledger control account to the total of the list of balances from the subsidiary ledger after taking account of the errors noted.

6 The balance on a business's purchases ledger control account at the end of June is £38,694 and the total of the list of balances in the subsidiary purchases ledger came to £39,741.

The following errors were noted for the month:

a) A page in the purchases returns day book was overcast by £300

b) A total from the cash payments book of £3,145 was posted in the main ledger as £3,415

c) Settlement discounts received from suppliers of £267 were omitted from both the main ledger and the subsidiary ledger

d) A credit note from a supplier for £210 was entered into the supplier's account in the subsidiary ledger as £120

e) A debit balance on a creditor's account in the subsidiary ledger of £187 was omitted from the list of balances

f) A credit balance in the subsidiary ledger should have been included in the list as £570 but instead was recorded as £770

Reconcile the balance on the purchases ledger control account to the total of the list of balances in the subsidiary purchases ledger after taking account of these errors.

chapter 11: ERRORS AND THE SUSPENSE ACCOUNT

chapter coverage

In the previous chapters we have considered methods of accounting for transactions and adjustments and the processes and procedures that would be carried out in order to ensure that the figures that go into the trial balance are as correct as possible. In this chapter we will now move on to preparing the trial balance and dealing with any further errors in the accounting records that come to light when we prepare the trial balance. The topics that we shall cover are:

- preparing the trial balance
- errors that cause an imbalance in the trial balance
- errors that do not cause an imbalance in the trial balance
- setting up a suspense account from the trial balance
- clearing the suspense account
- setting up a suspense account with an unknown double entry
- journal entries

KNOWLEDGE AND UNDERSTANDING AND PERFORMANCE CRITERIA COVERAGE

knowledge and understanding

- how to use the transfer journal
- how to identify and correct different types of error
- the principles of double entry accounting
- the function and form of a trial balance and an extended trial balance

Performance criteria – element 5.2

- accurately prepare a trial balance and open a suspense account to record any imbalance
- establish the reasons for any imbalance and clear the suspense account by correcting the errors, or reduce them and refer outstanding items to the appropriate person.

student notes

PREPARING A TRIAL BALANCE

At regular intervals, normally each month, when all of the transactions for the period have been recorded and the bank, sales ledger and purchase ledger reconciliations have been carried out most businesses will prepare a trial balance. The trial balance is a further method of checking whether there are any errors in the accounting records.

If the trial balance balances, ie the total debits equal the total credits, this is a good indication that the ledger accounts have been correctly prepared – although as we will see later in the chapter there are types of error that will not be found by preparing a trial balance. If the trial balance does not balance then this must be investigated and the reasons for it not balancing discovered and rectified. The preparation of a trial balance from the brought down balances on the ledger accounts was covered in detail in Chapter 2. Refer back to that chapter if you need a reminder before we move on!

TYPES OF ERROR

In a manual accounting system there are a variety of types of error that can be made when making entries to the ledger accounts. Some errors will be picked up when the bank reconciliation and control account reconciliations are prepared as we have seen in earlier chapters. Some further errors will be identified when a trial balance is extracted but a number of types of error can take place and the trial balance will still balance – they will not be shown up by an imbalance on the trial balance.

Errors leading to an imbalance on the trial balance

There are a number of types of errors that will mean that the total of the debit balances on the trial balance will not equal the total of the credit balances.

Single entry – if only one side of the double entry has been made in the ledger accounts, eg, the debit and not the credit, then the trial balance will not balance.

Double sided entry – this is where a transaction is entered into the correct accounts but two debit entries are made or two credit entries, rather than a debit and a credit entry.

Transposition error – a transposition error is where the digits in a number are transposed, eg, a transaction for £650 is recorded correctly as a debit but is recorded as a credit of £560. It is also possible for the balance on an account to be transposed when it is taken to the trial balance eg, a balance of £980 is recorded in the trial balance as £890. This will also mean that the trial balance will not balance.

student notes

If a transposition error has been made and is the only error then the difference between the debits and the credits will be divisible by 9. This is often useful when trying to track down errors made.

Balancing error – if a ledger account has not been correctly balanced and the incorrect balance has been included in the trial balance then again the trial balance will not balance.

Balance omission – if a balance on a ledger account is omitted from the trial balance then again this means that the debits will not equal the credits.

Activity 1

A sales invoice recorded in the sales day book at £1,432 has been correctly recorded in the debtors account but has been entered into the sales account as £1,342. What type of error is this?

Errors which do not cause an imbalance on the trial balance

Unfortunately there are also a variety of types of error that will not cause a difference on the trial balance and therefore cannot be shown up through the trial balance process.

Error of original entry – here both entries into the main ledger, debit and credit, have been made using the wrong amount. This may be due to the fact that the transaction was recorded in the primary record at the incorrect amount or that the wrong figure was picked up from the primary record (eg a transposition error) and this incorrect figure was used for both the debit and the credit entry. However as long as both the debit and the credit entry are equal this error will not cause an imbalance in the trial balance.

Error of omission – an entry is completely omitted from the ledger accounts. If the transaction is not recorded as either a debit or a credit then it will not affect the trial balance.

Error of reversal – this type of error is where the correct figure has been used and a debit and a credit entry made but the debit and the credit are on the wrong side of the respective accounts. The trial balance will still balance but the two accounts will have incorrect balances.

Error of commission – the double entry is arithmetically correct but a wrong account of the same type has been used. For example if the telephone bill is paid the bank account will be credited and an expense account, the telephone account, should be debited. If instead the electricity account is debited this is an error of commission. It does not

student notes

affect the trial balance but it does mean that both the telephone accoun and electricity account show the wrong balance.

Error of principle – an error of principle is similar to an error o commission in that the double entry is arithmetically correct but with ar error of principle the wrong type of account has been used. For exampl if computer discs are purchased the bank account should be credited anc the computer expenses or office expenses account debited. If instead the cost of the discs is debited to the computer fixed asset account then thi is an error of principle but again will not affect the balancing of the tria balance.

Compensating errors – these are probably rare in practice but it is where two errors are made which exactly cancel each other out. For example i the sales ledger control account is entered at £100 too high an amoun (a debit balance) and the purchases returns (a credit balance) is also entered at £100 too high an amount, the two errors will cancel each othe out. The errors are unrelated but the fact that they both occurred wil mean that there is no imbalance in the trial balance.

Activity 2

A sales invoice to P Tracy was recorded in the subsidiary sales ledger in the account of Tracy Brothers. What type of error is this?

IMBALANCE ON THE TRIAL BALANCE

If the trial balance does not balance then the reason or reasons for this hav to be discovered. However while the errors that have caused the imbalanc are being discovered an extra account is set up in the trial balance to recorc the difference – this is known as the SUSPENSE ACCOUNT. It is not permanent account and is only set up to allow preparation of the fina accounts whilst the errors are being discovered.

HOW IT WORKS

student notes

When Dawn Fisher was preparing her trial balance at her year end, 31 March 2009, the total of the debits and credits in the trial balance were:

	Debits	*Credits*
	£	£
	190,467	191,996

In order to carry on with the final accounts preparation while searching for the errors that have caused this difference a suspense account is created to make the debits and credits equal.

	Debits	*Credits*
	£	£
	190,467	191,996
Suspense account	1,529	
	191,996	191,996

This debit balance on the suspense account will need to be cleared when the errors that have caused it are discovered.

Activity 3

A business has a total of debit balances in its trial balance of £125,366 and the total of credit balances is £123,557.

How much is the balance on the suspense account that is set up and is it a debit or a credit balance?

Finding the error or errors

As we have seen in earlier paragraphs there are many types of error that could cause the total of the debits not to equal the total of the credits. Rather than going back to each ledger account and checking each entry to find the cause of the imbalance it makes sense, both in practice and in assessments and exams, to take a logical approach to finding the causes of any imbalance.

The problem might be arithmetical or to do with the double entry but it makes sense to check the more obvious and simple errors before getting involved with detailed checking of the ledger accounts.

student notes

Procedure for finding the error/errors

Step 1 Check the totalling of the debit column and the credit column. It is very easy to make an error when totalling a large column of figures. Therefore this is an obvious place to start.

Step 2 Calculate the difference between the debit and credit total as this may come in useful later in the checking exercise if the difference cannot be found easily.

Step 3 Check that each balance in the trial balance has been correctly copied into the trial balance and that each has been included on the correct side, debit or credit.

Step 4 Check that all of the balances in the main ledger have been included in the trial balance. In particular ensure that the bank balance and petty cash balances have been included as these are generally kept physically separate from the main ledger.

Step 5 Check that the calculation of the balance on each ledger account is correct.

Step 6 Look in the ledger accounts for any entry that is for the same amount as the difference on the trial balance and, if it is found, check that the double entry for this transaction has been correctly carried out.

Step 7 Look in the ledger accounts for any entry that is for half the amount of the difference on the trial balance and if it is found check that the double entry for this transaction has been correctly carried out.

If all else fails resort to:

Step 8 Check all of the bookkeeping entries since the date of the last trial balance. This will entail following through each transaction from the primary records to the ledger accounts.

Number tricks to look out for

If the difference on the trial balance is divisible exactly by nine then the error is likely to be a transposition error. This means that two digits in a figure have been reversed, eg £654 is entered as £564 – the difference of £90 is exactly divisible by 9.

If the difference on the trial balance is a round number eg £10,£100,£1,000 etc then it is likely that the error that has been made is arithmetical rather than a double entry error. Therefore take great care when checking account balance calculations.

student notes

CLEARING THE SUSPENSE ACCOUNT

Once the errors in the accounts have been discovered then they must be dealt with by double entry that corrects the error. Sometimes this will involve an entry to the suspense account but not on all occasions. In some cases the error has had no effect on the balancing of the trial balance and therefore there will be no entry required in the suspense account.

Often determining the correcting double entry can be tricky. The easiest method is to decide what has been done that is incorrect and to write this down in working ledger accounts, then to determine what the correct double entry should have been – then finally to decide what double entry will take you from the incorrect entry to the correct position.

HOW IT WORKS

Dawn Fisher has a debit balance on her suspense account of £1,529. She has now discovered the following errors:

a) Payment for motor expenses of £350 was correctly recorded in the cash payments book but was credited to the motor expenses account

b) Payment for postage costs of £67 was correctly recorded in the cash payments book but was entered into the postage costs account as £76

c) An invoice for £470 including VAT was omitted from the sales day book

d) When the discounts allowed account was balanced the balance was undercast by £100

e) Cleaning costs of £240 were included in the cash payments book but were not posted to the cleaning costs account

f) The balance on the miscellaneous expenses account of £498 was omitted from the trial balance

The errors must now be corrected and the suspense account cleared.

First of all set up the suspense account with its debit balance:

Suspense account

	£		£
Balance	1,529		

student notes

Then deal with each of the errors in turn:

a) Payment for motor expenses of £350 was correctly recorded in the cash payments book but was credited to the motor expenses account

The double entry that has taken place is:

Credit	Bank account	£350
Credit	Motor expenses account	£350

The motor expenses account should have been debited with £350 although the entry to the bank account is correct. In order to correct this the motor expenses account needs to be debited with £700 in order to cancel the incorrect credit and to enter the correct debit – there is no other entry required. Therefore the other side of the entry must be to the suspense account. The correcting entry required is:

Debit	Motor expenses account	£700
Credit	Suspense account	£700

Suspense account

	£		£
Balance	1,529	Motor expenses	700

b) Payment for postage costs of £67 was correctly recorded in the cash payments book but was entered into the postage costs account as £76

The debit entry in the postage costs account should have been £67 not £76. Therefore the postage costs account must be credited with £9 and as no other account is incorrect the debit entry is to the suspense account. The correcting entry is:

Debit	Suspense account	£9
Credit	Postage costs account	£9

Suspense account

	£		£
Balance	1,529	Motor expenses	700
Postage costs	9		

c) An invoice for £470 including VAT was omitted from the sales day book

As this invoice was omitted from the sales day book then it has never been entered into the accounting records. Therefore the entry required is:

Debit	Debtors account	£470
Credit	Sales account	£400
Credit	VAT account	£70

There is no entry required to the suspense account

d) When the discounts allowed account was balanced the balance was undercast by £100

The balance on the discounts allowed account is a debit balance and it is £100 too small. Therefore this account must be debited in the trial balance and as no other account is incorrect then the credit entry is to the suspense account. The correcting entry is:

Debit	Discounts allowed balance	£100
Credit	Suspense account	£100

Suspense account

	£		£
Balance	1,529	Motor expenses	700
Postage costs	9	Discounts allowed	100

e) Cleaning costs of £240 were included in the cash payments book but were not posted to the cleaning costs account

The entry to the cleaning costs account has been omitted but the entry in the bank account is correct. Therefore the cleaning costs account must be debited but no other account is incorrect so the credit entry is to the suspense account. The correcting entry is:

Debit	Cleaning costs account	£240
Credit	Suspense account	£240

Suspense account

	£		£
Balance	1,529	Motor expenses	700
Postage costs	9	Discounts allowed	100
		Cleaning costs	240

student notes

student notes

f) The balance on the miscellaneous expenses account of £498 was omitted from the trial balance.

The miscellaneous expenses account should have been a debit balance in the trial balance. In order to correct this the trial balance must have a further debit balance and as no other account is incorrect the other side of the entry is to the suspense account. The correcting entry is:

Debit	Miscellaneous account	£498
Credit	Suspense account	£498

Suspense account

	£		£
Balance	1,529	Motor expenses	700
Postage costs	9	Discounts allowed	100
		Cleaning costs	240
		Miscellaneous expenses	498
	1,538		1,538

You will now see that there is no balance on the suspense account – the suspense account has been cleared by the correction of the errors.

Activity 4

A business has a suspense account after discovering a difference in the trial balance. The following errors were identified:

a) A telephone bill which was paid for £330 was posted to the electricity account

b) The balance for discounts received of £400 was entered as a debit balance in the trial balance

What is the double entry required to correct each of these errors?

student notes

Unknown double entry

A suspense account is sometimes set up deliberately by the bookkeeper as he does not know what the other side of a double entry should be – therefore instead the unknown entry is made in the suspense account.

HOW IT WORKS

In January 2009 Dawn Fisher sold a sewing machine that she no longer required for £100. She did not know how to account for this and therefore debited the bank account (the cash receipts book) and credited a suspense account.

The machine had originally cost £250 and had accumulated depreciation of £120. After advice from an accountant friend Dawn now understands how to account for this and is to clear the suspense account.

Suspense account

	£		£
		Balance	100

The double entry required is:

Debit	Accumulated depreciation account	£120	
Debit	Disposal account	£250	
Credit	Fixed asset at cost account		£250
Credit	Disposal account		£120
Debit	Suspense account	£100	
Credit	Disposal account		£100
Debit	Profit and loss account	£30	
Credit	Disposal account		£30

There is a loss on disposal of £30 as the net book value of the asset is £130 and the proceeds were only £100. Therefore the entries not only reflect the clearing out of the fixed asset at cost account and the accumulated depreciation but also the entry of the proceeds to the disposal account and the accounting for the loss in the disposal account and the profit and loss account.

The suspense account is now cleared:

Suspense account

	£		£
Disposal account	100	Balance	100

student notes

JOURNAL ENTRIES

We have seen the double entry for dealing with errors in the accounting system. However there has to be a system for entering these corrections into the ledger accounts. This is done using a JOURNAL ENTRY.

The journal is an instruction to the bookkeeper to post a double entry to the ledger accounts.

A typical journal entry is given below:

Journal number: 0225

Date: 5 April 2009

Authorised by: D Fisher

Account	*Reference*	*Debit*	*Credit*
		£	£
Motor expenses	ML23	700	
Suspense account	ML100		700

Being correction of credit entry to motor expenses account

The key points to be noted about the journal entry are:

- each journal has a sequential number to ensure that all are entered into the ledger accounts
- each journal must be dated and authorised – the authorisation is vital as this is an adjustment to the accounts
- the accounts that are to be debited and credited are named, coded and the amounts shown
- a narrative is included in order to determine what the journal entry is for

In assessments and exams you are sometimes instructed not to include a narrative, therefore read the instructions carefully.

student notes

Activity 5

The following errors have been identified on 7 January 2009 when trying to clear a suspense account balance. The last journal number to be used was 01275.

a) A telephone bill which was paid for £330 was posted to the electricity account

b) The balance for discounts received of £400 was entered as a debit balance in the trial balance

Prepare the journal entry for each of these errors.

Other uses of the journal

Journal entries are not only used to correct errors but also to record non-regular entries in the accounting records that do not appear in the other primary records.

Examples of such entries that require a journal are:

- writing off bad debts
- accounting for provisions for doubtful debts
- accounting for contra entries
- accounting for provisions for depreciation
- accounting for accruals and prepayments

Each of these have been dealt with in earlier chapters in detail.

HOW IT WORKS

At 31 March 2009 Dawn Fisher has to write off a debt of £337 and provide an initial provision for doubtful debts of £524. The last journal entry number that Dawn used was 0011.

student notes

The journal entries for these transactions are:

Journal number: 0012

Date: 31 March 2009

Authorised by: D Fisher

Account	*Reference*	*Debit*	*Credit*
		£	£
Bad debts expense		337	
Debtors			337

Being write off of a bad debt from K Whistler

Journal number: 0013

Date: 31 March 2009

Authorised by: D Fisher

Account	*Reference*	*Debit*	*Credit*
		£	£
Bad debts expense		524	
Provision for doubtful debts			524

Being initial set up of provision for doubtful debts

Activity 6

A business is to charge depreciation of £2,450 for the year on its machinery.

Write up the journal entry number 1245 dated 31 January 2009 to record this.

CHAPTER OVERVIEW

- once the bank, sales ledger and purchases ledger reconciliations have been prepared the initial trial balance will be drawn up
- some errors in the accounting records will result in an imbalance on the trial balance – these include single entry rather than double entry, a transposition error, a balancing error and a balance being omitted from the trial balance
- there are other errors in the accounting records which will not cause an imbalance on the trial balance – error of original entry, error of omission, error of reversal, error of commission, error of principle, compensating error
- if the trial balance does not initially balance a suspense account will be set up in order to make the trial balance add up – the suspense account is not permanent and the errors must be discovered and the suspense account cleared
- in order to find the error or errors if the debit total does not agree with the credit total carry out some basic arithmetical checks before checking the detailed double entry
- calculate the difference on the trial balance and look for this amount or half of this amount in the ledger accounts and check the double entry of this transaction
- once the errors have been discovered they must be corrected – in some cases this will require an entry to the suspense account but not in all cases
- a further way in which a suspense account appears in an organisation is if the other side of a double entry is not known and it is put into the suspense account for the short term
- the correction of errors in the accounting records is done by filling out a journal entry
- the journal is also used to record other non-regular entries in the accounting records such as bad debt write offs, provisions for doubtful debts and depreciation etc

KEY WORDS

Transposition error where two figures in an amount are reversed

Error of original entry both the debit and credit entries in the ledgers have been made at the wrong amount

Error of omission both the debit and credit have been omitted from the ledger accounts

Error of reversal the debit and credit entries have been reversed in the ledger accounts

Error of commission the double entry is largely correct but one of the entries has been made to the wrong account but an account of the correct type

Error of principle the double entry is largely correct but one of the entries has been to the wrong type of account

Compensating error two separate errors that completely cancel each other out

Suspense account an account set up when the trial balance does not balance in order to make it add up or an account that is purposely set up when one side of the double entry is not known

Journal entry an instruction to the bookkeeper to put through a double entry in order to correct an error or enter a non-regular transaction into the accounting records

HOW MUCH HAVE YOU LEARNED?

1 Consider the account below and note any errors that you can find.

Purchase ledger control account

	£		£
Purchases returns	2,456	Opening balance	13,476
Cash paid	11,335	Purchases	15,778
Balance c/d	15,890	Discounts received	1,427
	30,681		30,681

2 A payment for rent of £4,300 has been entered into the cash payments book and the rent account as £3,400. What type of error is this?

3 The sales returns for a period of £1,276 have been entered into the ledger accounts as:

DR Sales ledger control
CR Sales returns

Is this correct? If not what type of error has taken place?

4 A credit note from supplier Hamish & Co has been debited to the account of C Hamish. What type of error is this?

5 The total of the debit balances on a trial balance is £325,778 and the total of the credit balances is £326,048.

a) What would be one of the first types of error that you might look for?

b) How much would the balance on the suspense account be and would it be a debit or a credit balance?

6 When the trial balance of a business is completed it is found that the debit balances total £95,600 and the credit balances total £95,890.

The following errors have been discovered:

a) The rental income of £420 for a month has been correctly entered into the cash receipts book but was recorded as £240 in the rental income account

b) The balance for sales returns of £170 had been omitted from the trial balance

c) The balance for telephone expenses of £150 had been entered as a credit balance on the trial balance

Show the suspense account balance that is set up when the trial balance is totalled and then show how the suspense account is cleared.

7 A business has a debit balance on its suspense account of £1,800.

The following errors have been discovered:

a) The electricity cost for a period of £400 has been correctly entered into the cash payments book but no entry has been made for the expense

b) The sales account balance has been overcast by £1,000

c) A receipt for commissions of £140 has been correctly entered into the cash receipts book but also debited to the commissions income account

d) A payment for cleaning costs of £100 has been debited to the wages account instead of the cleaning costs account

e) Discounts allowed of £340 have been entered on the wrong side of the trial balance

Show the double entry required to correct each of these errors and show how the suspense account balance is cleared.

chapter 12: STOCK

chapter coverage

One important and significant asset that almost all businesses will have is stock. SSAP 9 gives us detailed rules as to how the stock of a business should be valued and these will be considered in this chapter together with methods of valuing the stocks and the accounting treatment of stocks. The topics we shall cover are:

- the stock count
- the closing stock reconciliation
- SSAP 9 requirements for the valuation of stock
- methods of valuing stock
- accounting for stock in the ledger accounts

KNOWLEDGE AND UNDERSTANDING AND PERFORMANCE CRITERIA COVERAGE

knowledge and understanding

- the main requirements of relevant SSAPs and FRSs
- the basic principles of stock valuation including those relating to cost or net realisable value and to what is included in cost

Performance criteria – element 5.2

- correctly prepare reconciliations for the preparation of final accounts
- identify any discrepancies in the reconciliation process and either take steps to rectify them or refer them to the appropriate person
- correctly identify, calculate and record appropriate adjustments

student notes

VALUATION OF CLOSING STOCK

Whenever purchases of goods for resale are made either for cash or on credit the debit entry is always made to the purchases account. A stock account is never debited with these purchases. The only time that a stock account is used is at the end of the accounting period when the stock of the business must be counted and valued.

When purchases of goods or materials for manufacture are made the quantity of the purchase will normally be recorded in the stores records as well as the amount of the purchase being recorded in the ledger accounts. The stores records are sometimes called bin cards. Whatever form the stores records take, for each type of goods that a business purchases there will be a stores record which shows the quantity purchased each time a delivery arrives, the quantity issued as sales or to the factory for manufacture and the quantity on hand.

HOW IT WORKS

Dawn Fisher buys a variety of different coloured T shirts to decorate in a variety of sizes. The stores record for March 2009 for the extra small white T shirts is given below:

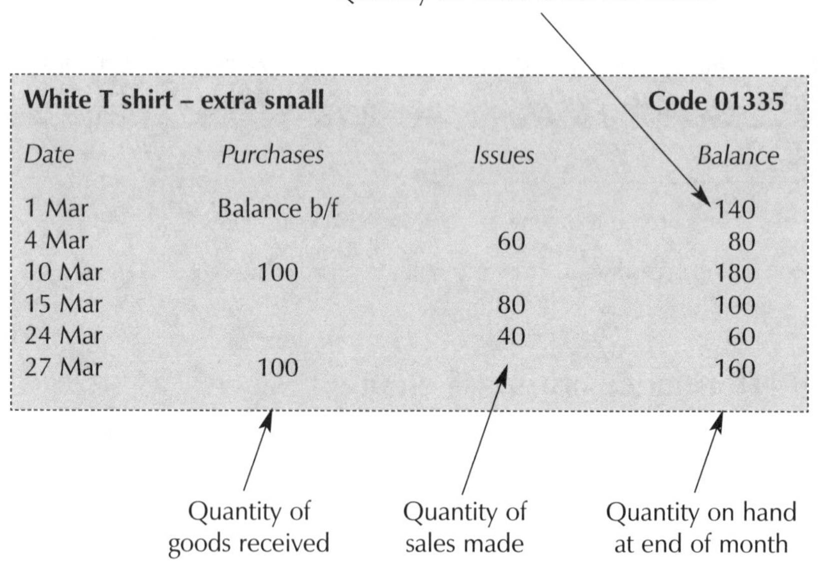

White T shirt – extra small **Code 01335**

Date	*Purchases*	*Issues*	*Balance*
1 Mar	Balance b/f		140
4 Mar		60	80
10 Mar	100		180
15 Mar		80	100
24 Mar		40	60
27 Mar	100		160

student notes

Stock count

At the end of the accounting period each item of actual stock must be counted and listed and the amount counted is then compared to the stores records. If there is a difference between the actual amount of stock counted and the balance on the stores record then this must be investigated. The difference will normally be due to errors in the recording of purchases or issues of the stock. However if there is less stock than according to the records care should be taken to ensure that stock has not been stolen.

This process is known as the STOCK COUNT and will often take place at other times of the year as well as at the year end in order to keep control over the stock. However the year end stock count is the most important as this is the one which will provide the figure for stock that will appear in the final accounts.

Before the stock can be valued the physical amount of stock held must be checked to the stores records and any discrepancies investigated. This is done in the form of a CLOSING STOCK RECONCILIATION.

HOW IT WORKS

At 31 March 2009 Dawn Fisher carried out a stock count and compared the quantity of each line of stock to the stock records. In most cases the stock quantity agreed with the stores records but for two lines of stock Dawn found differences.

	Green T – large	*Blue T – medium*
Quantity counted	48	150
Stock record quantity	54	126

Dawn checked the stock records and documentation carefully and discovered the following:

- On 26 March 6 large green T shirts had been returned to the supplier as they were damaged. A credit note has not yet been received and the despatch note had not been recorded in the stock records
- On 30 March a goods received note showed that 40 blue T shirts in medium size had arrived from a supplier but this had not yet been entered in the stock records
- On 28 March Dawn had taken 16 blue medium T shirts out of stock in order to process a rush order and had forgotten to update the stock record

Using these facts Dawn now prepares her closing stock reconciliation.

student notes

Closing stock reconciliation – 31 March 2009

Green T – large	Quantity
Stock record	54
Less: returned to supplier	(6)
Counted	48

Blue T – medium	Quantity
Stock record	126
Add: GRN note recorded	40
Less: materials requisition	(16)
Counted	150

Dawn can now use her closing stock count quantities to prepare her closing stock valuation.

Valuation of stock

Once each line of stock has been counted and checked and the quantity recorded then each line of stock will be valued:

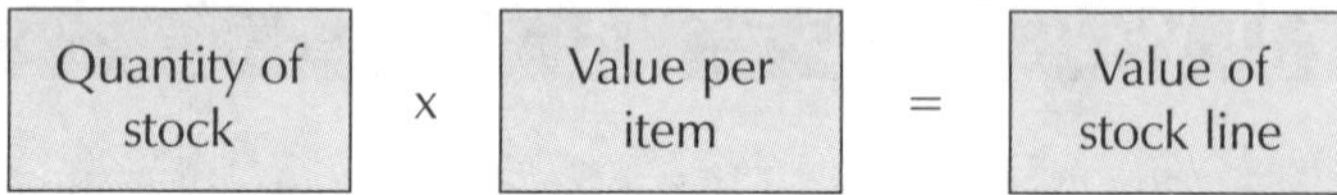

The rules for valuing stock come from SSAP 9, Stocks and long-term contracts. The basic rule for stock valuation is:

Stock should be valued at the lower of COST and NET REALISABLE VALUE.

Before we look at what is included in these two figures we will consider the purpose of this rule from SSAP 9.

It is based upon the accounting concept of prudence. The normal situation is that an item will be purchased for say £30 and then resold for £40. In this case the stock will be valued at cost of £30. However if the items could only be sold for £25 then if they are valued as an asset at £30 we would be overstating the value of the asset – the prudence concept does not allow this therefore the stock must be valued at their selling price of £25.

So what are cost and net realisable value?

- Cost is defined by SSAP 9 as the cost of getting the stock into the current position – therefore this will include delivery charges
- Net realisable value is the expected selling price of the stock, less any further costs to be incurred such as selling or distribution costs

Note that one possible way of determining the cost of the closing stock that could be used by a retailer would be to inspect the selling price of the stocks and then deduct the known profit mark-up included in the selling price. For example, if Ahmed has a policy of setting his selling prices at double what the

student notes

stock cost, then he could determine the cost of his closing stocks by going round his shop and totalling the sales prices of all the goods he has. Halving this total would give the cost price required to be used in the closing stock valuation.

Activity 1

A product that a business sells costs £13.80 to buy. Due to a fall in demand for this product it will only sell for £14.00 and in order to sell at this price it must be delivered to the customer at a cost of 50 pence per unit.

How should stock of this product be valued for accounting purposes?

HOW IT WORKS

A small business has just three lines of stock A, B and C. The total cost and total net realisable value (NRV) of each line of stock is given below:

	Cost	*NRV*
	£	£
A	1,250	2,000
B	1,400	1,200
C	1,100	1,900
	3,750	5,100

Although the total cost of £3,750 is lower than the total net realisable value of £5,100 this is not the value of the closing stock of the business. The cost and net realisable value must be compared for each individual line of stock as follows:

	Cost	*NRV*	*Stock value*
	£	£	£
A	1,250	2,000	1,250
B	1,400	1,200	1,200
C	1,100	1,900	1,100
	3,750	5,100	3,550

The stock should be valued at £3,550 which is the total of the lower of cost and net realisable value for each line of stock.

Methods of valuing closing stock

We have seen that each stock line must be valued at the lower of cost and net realisable value. The next problem that must be faced however is

student notes

determining the actual cost price of the goods that are in stock. If a business has deliveries of an item of stock on a regular basis and issues the stock items as sale items on a regular basis then it will be difficult if not impossible to determine precisely which stock items have been sold and which remain in stock as the closing stock. If the prices at which each batch of the stock was purchased differ then it becomes important that we know which purchases remain in stock at the end of the accounting period.

The time and effort involved in determining exactly which stock item has been sold and exactly which one remains in stock will usually not be worthwhile for a business. Therefore the cost of the closing stock will be determined on one of a number of assumptions. These assumptions are the various methods of estimating the cost of the stock that remains at the year end.

The most commonly used methods or assumptions when valuing stocks are:

FIFO (FIRST IN FIRST OUT) the assumption here is that the stocks that are issued for sale or manufacture are the earliest purchases – therefore the stocks on hand are the most recent purchases.

LIFO (LAST IN FIRST OUT) the assumption here is that the stocks that are issued are the most recent purchases – therefore the stocks on hand are the earliest purchases. SSAP 9 discourages the use of LIFO. It is not generally used for financial accounts.

AVCO (AVERAGE COST) under this method after each new purchase the weighted average cost of the stock is calculated – this is the total cost of the stock in hand divided by the number of units of stock in hand – the closing stock is valued at this weighted average at the end of the period.

HOW IT WORKS

Dawn Fisher's stores record for the extra small white T shirts is shown below.

White T shirt – extra small **Code 01335**

Date	*Purchases*	*Issues*	*Balance*
1 Mar	Balance b/f		140
4 Mar		60	80
10 Mar	100		180
15 Mar		80	100
24 Mar		40	60
27 Mar	100		160

The opening balance of stock was all purchased at a price of £7 per unit, the purchase on 10 March was at £7.50 per unit and the purchase on 27 March at £8.00 per unit.

The value of the 160 units remaining in stock at the end of the month will be calculated on the FIFO, LIFO and AVCO basis.

student notes

FIFO – First in first out

Date	Purchases units	Cost/ unit £	Issues units	Cost/ unit £	Stock units	Balance Cost/ Units £	Total cost £
1 Mar (b/f)				7.00	140	7.00	980.00
4 Mar			(60)	7.00	80	7.00	560.00
10 Mar	100	7.50			100	7.50	750.00
					180		1,310.00
15 Mar			(80)	7.00	100	7.50	750.00
24 Mar			(40)	7.50	60	7.50	450.00
27 Mar	100	8.00			100	8.00	800.00
					160		1,250.00

LIFO – Last in first out

Date	Purchases units	Cost/ unit £	Issues units	Cost/ unit £	Stock units	Balance Cost/ Units £	Total cost £
1 Mar (b/f)					140	7.00	980.00
4 Mar			(60)	7.00	80	7.00	560.00
10 Mar	100	7.50			100	7.50	750.00
					180		1,310.00
15 Mar			(80)	7.50	80	7.00	560.00
					20	7.50	150.00
					100		710.00
24 Mar			(20)	7.50	60	7.00	420.00
			(20)	7.00			
			(40)				
27 Mar	100	8.00			100	8.00	800.00
					160		1,220.00

AVCO – Average cost

Date	Purchases quantity	Cost per unit £	Issues	Cost per unit £	Balance Units	Balance £
1 Mar Bal b/f	140	7.00			140	980.00
4 Mar			60	7.00	(60)	(420.00)
					80	560.00
10 Mar	100	7.50			100	750.00
				7.28	180	1,310.00
15 Mar			80	7.28	(80)	(582.40)
					100	727.60
24 Mar			40	7.28	(40)	(291.20)
					60	436.40
27 Mar	100	8.00			100	800.00
				7.73	160	1,236.40

student notes

As you can see the values of the closing stock under the different methods vary:

	£
FIFO	1,250.00
LIFO	1,220.00
AVCO	1,236.40

Activity 2

A business buys 100 units of a product for £3.50 per unit on 1 May. A further 100 units are purchased on 20 May for £4.00 per unit. The sales for the month were 70 units on 12 May and 80 units on 30 May.

Determine the value of the closing stock using the FIFO method.

LEDGER ACCOUNTING FOR STOCK

As we have already mentioned whenever goods are purchased they must be debited to a purchases account never a stock account. The stock account is only used at the end of the accounting period in order to record the closing stock of the business.

HOW IT WORKS

Dawn Fisher has counted and valued all of her stock at her year end 31 March 2009 and it totals £6,450.

This figure is entered into the ledger accounts by a debit and a credit entry to two different stock accounts:

Debit	Stock account – balance sheet
Credit	Stock account – profit and loss account

Stock account – balance sheet

	£		£
31 Mar	6,450		

Stock account – profit and loss account

	£		£
		31 Mar	6,450

student notes

The balance sheet account balance, a debit balance, is the asset of closing stock that will be listed in the balance sheet as a current asset.

The profit and loss account stock account is cleared out to the profit and loss account at the end of the year to be shown as a deduction from purchases to give the cost of sales figure.

Stock account – profit and loss account

	£		£
31 Mar 2009 Profit and loss account	6,450	31 Mar 2009	6,450

Dawn's purchases account at the end of the year shows a debit balance of £76,850. This and the 'stock account – profit and loss account' balance are cleared to the profit and loss account for the year to be shown as:

	£
Cost of sales:	
Purchases	76,850
Less: closing stock	(6,450)
	70,400

This is Dawn's first year of trading so there is no opening stock.

The only stock account that remains in Dawn's books now is the balance sheet stock account. This remains in the ledger accounts without any further entries to it as the opening stock balance until the end of the following accounting period, 31 March 2010. At this date the closing stock is valued at £7,200 and the purchases for the year were £80,900.

The first step is to clear the balance on the stock account, the opening stock, to the profit and loss account.

Stock account – balance sheet

	£		£
Opening stock	6,450	31 Mar 2010 Profit and loss account	6,450

student notes

Next the closing stock valuation at 31 March 2010 must be entered into the two stock accounts:

Stock account – balance sheet

	£		£
Opening stock	6,450	31 Mar 2010 Profit and loss account	6,450
31 Mar 2009	7,200		

Stock account – profit and loss account

	£		£
		31 Mar 2010	7,200

Finally the profit and loss account stock account must be cleared to the profit and loss account as the closing stock:

Stock account – profit and loss account

	£		£
31 Mar 2010 Profit and loss account	7,200	31 Mar 2010	7,200

The cost of sales in the profit and loss account for the year ended 31 March 2010 will then look like this:

	£
Cost of sales:	
Opening stock	6,450
Purchases	80,900
	87,350
Less: closing stock	(7,200)
	80,150

To summarise:

Profit and loss account – debit with opening stock
credit with closing stock

Balance sheet – show closing stock as a current asset

This may seem complicated now but when we start dealing with the extended trial balance it will become second nature!

Activity 3

Where does closing stock appear in the balance sheet?

CHAPTER OVERVIEW

- when purchases of goods for resale or materials to be used in manufacturing are made they are always debited to a purchases account and never to the stock account

- at the end of the year, and often at other times during the year, the stock must be counted and the quantity of each line of stock listed – this will then be compared to the stores records of the amount of that line of stock that should exist – a stock reconciliation will be carried out.

- once the quantity of each line of stock is known then it must be valued – SSAP 9 states that each line of stock should be valued at the lower of cost and net realisable value

- in order to determine the cost of stocks a method has to be chosen – the most common methods are FIFO, LIFO and average cost

- when the closing stock has been valued it must be included in the final accounts as a current asset in the balance sheet and as a deduction from purchases to give cost of sales in the profit and loss account

KEY WORDS

Stock count the regular and year end process of counting each line of stock and comparing the quantity to the quantity that should exist according to the stores records

Closing stock reconciliation comparison of stock record quantity to quantity actually counted.

Cost the SSAP 9 definition of cost for stock is the cost of getting the stock to its current position which will include delivery costs

Net realisable value the expected selling price of the item less any further costs to be incurred such as selling or distribution expenses

FIFO – first in first out method of stock valuation that assumes that the stocks issued are the earliest purchases leaving the closing stock as the most recent purchases

LIFO – last in first out method of stock valuation that assumes that the stocks issued are the most recent purchases leaving the closing stock as the earliest purchases

AVCO – average cost method of stock valuation that operates by calculating a weighted average price for the stock after each new purchase

HOW MUCH HAVE YOU LEARNED?

1 A business has 120 units of an item of stock at the year end which cost £25.80 plus delivery charges of £1.00 per unit. This item can be sold for £28.00 per unit but must be delivered to the customer at a further cost of £1.10 per unit.

a) What is the cost and the net realisable value of each item of stock?
b) At what value would these 120 units appear in the final accounts?

2 A business has four different stock lines, details of which are given below:

Stock line	*Units in stock*	*Cost per unit*	*Selling price per unit*	*Selling costs per unit*
		£	£	£
A	80	12.90	20.30	0.30
B	65	14.60	15.00	0.80
C	90	19.80	30.20	0.90
D	30	17.50	18.20	1.00

What is the value of the closing stock in accordance with SSAP 9?

3 A business has the following purchases and sales of one of its products during April 2008:

3 April	Purchase 80 units @ £5.20
9 April	Sale 50 units @ £8.50
10 April	Purchase 100 units @ £5.50
15 April	Sale 50 units @ £8.50
17 April	Sale 60 units @ £8.80
20 April	Purchase 100 units @ £5.80
28 April	Sale 70 units @ £8.80

Show the value of the closing stock using the following valuation methods:

a) FIFO
b) LIFO
c) AVCO

chapter 13: FROM TRIAL BALANCE TO FINAL ACCOUNTS – SOLE TRADER

chapter coverage

So far in this Course Companion we have seen how to perform double entry accounting, how to prepare a simple trial balance and how to account for adjustments such as depreciation, accruals and prepayments, bad and doubtful debts and closing stock. We have also looked at various reconciliations that are prepared at the end of an accounting period and how to deal with suspense accounts and errors. We will now bring all of this together in preparing a set of final accounts for a sole trader from a trial balance.

We shall start this chapter with an introduction to one element of a sole trader's accounts which we have not yet covered, his capital, profit and drawings. Then the chapter will work through an example showing how to go from the year end balances for a sole trader to his final accounts via an initial trial balance and various accounting adjustments. The topics that we shall cover are:

- sole traders' capital
- preparing the initial trial balance
- setting up a suspense account
- clearing the suspense account
- journal entries for adjustments
- preparing an amended trial balance
- preparing the profit and loss account and balance sheet

KNOWLEDGE AND UNDERSTANDING AND PERFORMANCE CRITERIA COVERAGE

knowledge and understanding

- the methods of recording information for the organisational accounts of sole traders and partnerships
- the structure of organisational accounts of sole traders and partnerships
- the need to present accounts in the correct form
- the form of final accounts of sole traders and partnerships
- the importance of maintaining the confidentiality of business transactions
- how to use the transfer journal
- the methods of analysing income and expenditure
- how to draft year end final accounts of sole traders and partnerships
- the function and form of a trial balance and an extended trial balance
- the function and form of a profit and loss account and balance sheet for sole traders and partnerships

Performance criteria – element 5.2

- accurately prepare a trial balance and open a suspense account to record any imbalance
- establish the reasons for any imbalance and clear the suspense account by correcting the errors, or reduce them and refer outstanding items to the appropriate person
- correctly identify and record appropriate adjustments
- make the relevant journal entries to close off the revenue accounts in preparation for the transfer of balances to the final accounts
- ensure that the organisation's policies, regulations, procedures and timescales relating to preparing final accounts are observed

Performance criteria – element 5.3

- prepare final accounts of sole traders in proper form, from the trial balance
- observe the organisation's policies, regulations, procedures and timescales in relation to preparing final accounts of sole traders and partnerships
- identify and resolve or refer to the appropriate person discrepancies, unusual features or queries

THE RECORDS AND ACCOUNTS OF A SOLE TRADER

student notes

So far in this Course Companion we have considered the entries in the primary records and ledger accounts of a sole trader. A sole trader has a profit and loss account which shows the income and expenses of the accounting period and a balance sheet which lists the assets and liabilities of the sole trader on the last day of the accounting period.

The bottom section of the balance sheet is the financing element of the balance sheet and shows the amount of capital the sole trader has paid into the business, the net profit that has been earned in this accounting year and the drawings that the sole trader has taken out of the business in the year.

HOW IT WORKS

On 1 April 2008 Dawn Fisher set up her T shirt design business by paying £60,000 of capital into a business bank account. During the year ending 31 March 2009 Dawn's business made a net profit of £11,570 and Dawn withdrew £10,715 from the business for living expenses.

In Dawn's balance sheet this would be shown as:

	£
Capital at 1 April 2008	60,000
Profit for the year	11,570
	71,570
Less: drawings for the year	(10,715)
Capital at 31 March 2009	60,855

All of the profit of the business is due back to Dawn by the business and she can withdraw as much or as little in drawings as she considers appropriate.

Activity 1

A sole trader has opening capital of £23,400, earns a profit for the year of £14,500 and takes out £12,200 of drawings.

What is the capital of the business at the end of the year?

student notes

Drawings

DRAWINGS are cash and goods that the owner of a business takes out of the business for his/her own use. In an earlier chapter we saw how to account for the drawings that an owner of a business takes in cash:

Debit Drawings account
Credit Bank account

In some cases however the owner of a business may take goods out of the business. For example the owner of a food shop may take food off the shelves for her own meals.

The most common double entry for this is:

Debit Drawings account
Credit Purchases account

with the cost to the business of these goods.

An alternative method is to:

Debit Drawings account
Credit Sales account

with the selling price of the goods.

Either method is acceptable although the 'Purchases account' method is the most common.

Activity 2

The owner of a business takes goods which had cost the business £400 for his own use.

What is the double entry for this?

PREPARING FINAL ACCOUNTS

Having considered how the capital, profit and drawings of a sole trader are shown in the balance sheet we now work through a comprehensive example which will take you from ledger account balances through to a profit and loss account and balance sheet for a sole trader.

HOW IT WORKS

student notes

Given below are the brought down balances on the ledger accounts at the end of the day on 31 March 2009 for John Thompson, a sole trader whose year end is 31 March.

Building at cost

		£			£
31 Mar	Balance b/d	100,000			

Fixtures and fittings at cost

		£			£
31 Mar	Balance b/d	4,800			

Motor vehicles at cost

		£			£
31 Mar	Balance b/d	32,700			

Computer at cost

		£			£
31 Mar	Balance b/d	2,850			

Provision for depreciation – building

		£			£
			31 Mar	Balance b/d	4,000

Provision for depreciation – fixtures and fittings

		£			£
			31 Mar	Balance b/d	1,920

Provision for depreciation – motor vehicles

		£			£
			31 Mar	Balance b/d	7,850

student notes

Provision for depreciation – computer

		£			£
			31 Mar	Balance b/d	950

Stock

		£			£
31 Mar	Balance b/d	4,400			

Bank

		£			£
31 Mar	Balance b/d	3,960			

Petty cash

		£			£
31 Mar	Balance b/d	100			

Sales ledger control

		£			£
31 Mar	Balance b/d	15,240			

Purchases ledger control

		£			£
			31 Mar	Balance b/d	5,010

Capital

		£			£
			31 Mar	Balance b/d	130,000

Sales

		£			£
			31 Mar	Balance b/d	155,020

student notes

Sales returns

		£			£
31 Mar	Balance b/d	2,100			

Purchases

		£			£
31 Mar	Balance b/d	80,200			

Purchases returns

		£			£
			31 Mar	Balance b/d	1,400

Bank charges

		£			£
31 Mar	Balance b/d	200			

Discounts allowed

		£			£
31 Mar	Balance b/d	890			

Discounts received

		£			£
			31 Mar	Balance b/d	1,260

Wages

		£			£
31 Mar	Balance b/d	32,780			

Rates

		£			£
31 Mar	Balance b/d	5,500			

student notes

Telephone

		£			£
31 Mar	Balance b/d	1,140			

Electricity

		£			£
31 Mar	Balance b/d	1,480			

Insurance

		£			£
31 Mar	Balance b/d	1,500			

Motor expenses

		£			£
31 Mar	Balance b/d	1,580			

Office expenses

		£			£
31 Mar	Balance b/d	960			

Provision for doubtful debts

		£			£
			31 Mar	Balance b/d	220

VAT

		£			£
			31 Mar	Balance b/d	820

Drawings

		£			£
31 Mar	Balance b/d	15,800			

The first stage is to transfer all of the closing balances on the ledger accounts to the trial balance, add it up and check that it balances. If it does not balance, first check your additions and if this doesn't clear it, then open up a suspense account to make the debits and credits equal.

Draft trial balance as at 31 March 2009

student notes

	£	£
Buildings at cost	100,000	
Fixtures and fittings at cost	4,800	
Motor vehicles at cost	32,700	
Computer at cost	2,850	
Provision for depreciation – buildings		4,000
Provision for depreciation – fixtures and fittings		1,920
Provision for depreciation – motor vehicles		7,850
Provision for depreciation – computer		950
Stock	4,400	
Bank	3,960	
Petty cash	100	
Sales ledger control	15,240	
Purchases ledger control		5,010
Capital		130,000
Sales		155,020
Sales returns	2,100	
Purchases	80,200	
Purchases returns		1,400
Bank charges	200	
Discounts allowed	890	
Discounts received		1,260
Wages	32,780	
Rates	5,500	
Telephone	1,140	
Electricity	1,480	
Insurance	1,500	
Motor expenses	1,580	
Office expenses	960	
Provision for doubtful debts		220
VAT		820
Drawings	15,800	
Suspense	270	
	308,450	308,450

Suspense account

In this case the credit total was £270 larger than the debit total and so a suspense account was opened for the difference. The suspense account must of course be cleared and the errors that were discovered are given below:

a) The purchases returns account was overcast by £100

b) £200 of office expenses has been charged to the motor expenses account

student notes

c) Discounts allowed of £170 had been correctly accounted for in the sales ledger control account but omitted from the discounts allowed account

We must now prepare journal entries to correct these errors and to clear the suspense account.

Journal entries

a) As purchase returns are a credit balance if the account has been overstated then the purchases returns account must be debited and the suspense account credited.

	Debit	*Credit*
	£	£
Purchases returns	100	
Suspense		100

b) As the motor expenses account has been wrongly debited with office expenses then the motor expenses account must be credited and office expenses debited.

	Debit	*Credit*
	£	£
Office expenses	200	
Motor expenses		200

c) The correct double entry for discounts allowed is a debit to the discounts allowed account and a credit to sales ledger control. The credit has been done but the debit is missing. Therefore debit discounts allowed and credit the suspense account.

	Debit	*Credit*
	£	£
Discounts allowed	170	
Suspense		170

Year end adjustments

You are also given information about the following year end adjustments that must be made:

a) Depreciation is to be provided for the year on the following basis:

- Building – 2% on cost
- Fixtures and fittings – 20% on cost
- Motor vehicles – 30% on the reducing balance
- Computer – 33 1/3% on cost

b) Rates of £500 are to be accrued

c) The insurance account includes an amount of £300 prepaid

student notes

d) A bad debt of £240 is to be written off

e) A provision for 2% of the remaining debtors is to be made

We must now prepare the journal entries that will complete these adjustments and close off the accounts for the period.

Journal entries

a) The provision for depreciation accounts in the trial balance are the provisions at the beginning of the year as the annual depreciation charge has yet to be accounted for. In each case the double entry is to debit a depreciation expense account and to credit the relevant provision account.

	Debit	*Credit*
	£	£
Depreciation expense – building		
(100,000 x 2%)	2,000	
Provision for depreciation – building		2,000
Depreciation expense – fixtures and fittings		
(4,800 x 20%)	960	
Provision for depreciation – fixtures and fittings		960
Depreciation expense – motor vehicles		
((32,700 – 7,850) x 30%)	7,455	
Provision for depreciation – motor vehicles		7,455
Depreciation expense – computer		
(2,850 x 33 1/3%)	950	
Provision for depreciation – computer		950

b) Rates of £500 are to be accrued.

	Debit	*Credit*
	£	£
Rates	500	
Accruals		500

c) Insurance has been prepaid by £300.

	Debit	*Credit*
	£	£
Prepayments	300	
Insurance		300

d) A bad debt of £240 is to be written off.

	Debit	*Credit*
	£	£
Bad debts expense	240	
Sales ledger control (ie, debtors)		240

student notes

e) Provision for doubtful debts of 2% of debtors is required.

	£
Provision required = (15,240 – 240) x 2%	300
Current level of provision	220
Increase in provision	80

	Debit	*Credit*
	£	£
Bad debts expense	80	
Provision for doubtful debts		80

Closing stock

The closing stock has been counted and valued at £5,200.

The stock figure in the draft trial balance is the opening stock which will eventually be debited to the profit and loss account as part of cost of sales. The closing stock must now be entered into the accounts with a journal entry.

Journal entry

	Debit	*Credit*
	£	£
Stock – balance sheet	5,200	
Stock – profit and loss account		5,200

Updating ledger accounts

All of the journal entries have now been made for the correction of errors, adjustments and closing stock. These journals must now be entered into the ledger accounts and the ledger accounts balanced to give their amended closing balances. This may mean that a number of new ledger accounts have to be opened.

Errors

student notes

a)

Purchases returns

		£			£
31 March	Journal	100	31 March	Balance b/d	1,400
31 March	Balance c/d	1,300			
		1,400			1,400
			31 March	Balance b/d	1,300

Suspense account

		£			£
31 March	Balance b/d	270	31 March	Journal	100

b)

Office expenses

		£			£
31 March	Balance b/d	960			
31 March	Journal	200	31 March	Balance c/d	1,160
		1,160			1,160
31 March	Balance b/d	1,160			

Motor expenses

		£			£
31 March	Balance b/d	1,580	31 March	Journal	200
			31 March	Balance c/d	1,380
		1,580			1,580
31 March	Balance b/d	1,380			

c)

Discounts allowed

		£			£
31 March	Balance b/d	890			
31 March	Journal	170	31 March	Balance c/d	1,060
		1,060			1,060
31 March	Balance b/d	1,060			

student notes

Year end adjustments

a) Depreciation charges for the year

Depreciation expense – building

		£			£
31 March	Journal	2,000			

Provision for depreciation – building

		£			£
			31 March	Balance b/d	4,000
31 March	Balance c/d	6,000	31 March	Journal	2,000
		6,000			6,000
			31 March	Balance b/d	6,000

Depreciation expense – fixtures and fittings

		£			£
31 March	Journal	960			

Provision for depreciation – fixtures and fittings

		£			£
			31 March	Balance b/d	1,920
31 March	Balance c/d	2,880	31 March	Journal	960
		2,880			2,880
			31 March	Balance b/d	2,880

Depreciation expense – motor vehicles

		£			£
31 March	Journal	7,455			

Provision for depreciation – motor vehicles

		£			£
			31 March	Balance b/d	7,850
31 March	Balance c/d	15,305	31 March	Journal	7,455
		15,305			15,305
			31 March	Balance b/d	15,305

Depreciation expense – computer

		£			£
31 March	Journal	950			

student notes

Provision for depreciation – computer

		£			£
			31 March	Balance b/d	950
31 March	Balance c/d	1,900	31 March	Journal	950
		1,900			1,900
			31 March	Balance b/d	1,900

b) Rates accrual

Rates

		£			£
31 March	Balance b/d	5,500			
31 March	Journal	500	31 March	Balance c/d	6,000
		6,000			6,000
31 March	Balance b/d	6,000			

Accruals

		£			£
			31 March	Journal	500

c) Insurance prepaid

Insurance

		£			£
31 March	Balance b/d	1,500	31 March	Journal	300
			31 March	Balance c/d	1,200
		1,500			1,500
31 March	Balance b/d	1,200			

Prepayments

		£			£
31 March	Journal	300			

d) Bad debt write off

Bad debts expense

		£			£
31 March	Journal	240			

Sales ledger control

		£			£
31 March	Balance b/d	15,240	31 March	Journal	240
			31 March	Balance c/d	15,000
		15,240			15,240
31 March	Balance b/d	15,000			

student notes

e) Provision for doubtful debts

Bad debts expense

		£			£
31 March	Journal	240			
31 March	Journal	80	31 March	Balance c/d	320
		320			320
31 March	Balance b/d	320			

Provision for doubtful debts

		£			£
			31 March	Balance b/d	220
31 March	Balance c/d	300	31 March	Journal	80
		300			300
			31 March	Balance b/d	300

Closing stock

Stock – balance sheet

		£			£
31 March	Journal	5,200			

Stock – profit and loss account

		£			£
			31 March	Journal	5,200

Once all of the ledger accounts have been updated for the journal adjustments then a new final trial balance is drawn up which reflects all of the error corrections and adjustments. This is the one that will be used to prepare the final accounts so take great care to ensure to include all of the updated balances and in particular all of the new balances that have come from the adjustments.

You will find that you have three stock account balances but do not worry about this at the moment as it will be explained when we prepare the final accounts.

student notes

Final trial balance as at 31 March 2009

	£	£
Buildings at cost	100,000	
Fixtures and fittings at cost	4,800	
Motor vehicles at cost	32,700	
Computer at cost	2,850	
Provision for depreciation – buildings		6,000
Provision for depreciation – fixtures and fittings		2,880
Provision for depreciation – motor vehicles		15,305
Provision for depreciation – computer		1,900
Stock	4,400	
Bank	3,960	
Petty cash	100	
Sales ledger control	15,000	
Purchases ledger control		5,010
Capital		130,000
Sales		155,020
Sales returns	2,100	
Purchases	80,200	
Purchases returns		1,300
Bank charges	200	
Discounts allowed	1,060	
Discounts received		1,260
Wages	32,780	
Rates	6,000	
Telephone	1,140	
Electricity	1,480	
Insurance	1,200	
Motor expenses	1,380	
Office expenses	1,160	
Provision for doubtful debts		300
VAT		820
Drawings	15,800	
Suspense	–	
Depreciation expense – building	2,000	
Depreciation expense – fixtures and fittings	960	
Depreciation expense – motor vehicles	7,455	
Depreciation expense – computer	950	
Accruals		500
Prepayments	300	
Bad debts expense	320	
Stock – balance sheet	5,200	
Stock – profit and loss account		5,200
	325,495	325,495

Preparing the final accounts

The next stage is to determine which of the balances in the final trial balance are profit and loss account balances and which are balance sheet balances. This was covered in Chapter 3 and we will just list each balance as either P&L or BS in this exercise.

student notes

Final trial balance as at 31 March 2009

	£	£	*P&L or BS*
Buildings at cost	100,000		BS
Fixtures and fittings at cost	4,800		BS
Motor vehicles at cost	32,700		BS
Computer at cost	2,850		BS
Provision for depreciation – buildings		6,000	BS
Provision for depreciation – fixtures and fittings		2,880	BS
Provision for depreciation – motor vehicles		15,305	BS
Provision for depreciation – computer		1,900	BS
Stock	4,400		P&L
Bank	3,960		BS
Petty cash	100		BS
Sales ledger control	15,000		BS
Purchases ledger control		5,010	BS
Capital		130,000	BS
Sales		155,020	P&L
Sales returns	2,100		P&L
Purchases	80,200		P&L
Purchases returns		1,300	P&L
Bank charges	200		P&L
Discounts allowed	1,060		P&L
Discounts received		1,260	P&L
Wages	32,780		P&L
Rates	6,000		P&L
Telephone	1,140		P&L
Electricity	1,480		P&L
Insurance	1,200		P&L
Motor expenses	1,380		P&L
Office expenses	1,160		P&L
Provision for doubtful debts		300	BS
VAT		820	BS
Drawings	15,800		BS
Suspense	–		–
Depn. expense – building	2,000		P&L
Depn. expense – fixtures & fittings	960		P&L
Depn. expense – motor vehicles	7,455		P&L
Depn. expense – computer	950		P&L
Accruals		500	BS
Prepayments	300		BS
Bad debts expense	320		P&L
Stock – balance sheet	5,200		BS
Stock – profit and loss account		5,200	P&L
	325,495	325,495	

student notes

Final accounts

The final stage is now to take each of the ledger balances and present them in the correct place in the final accounts.

John Thompson
Profit and loss account for the year ending 31 March 2009

	£	£
Sales		155,020
Less: sales returns		(2,100)
		152,920
Cost of sales		
Opening stock	4,400	
Purchases	80,200	
Less: purchases returns	(1,300)	
	83,300	
Less: closing stock	(5,200)	
		(78,100)
Gross profit		74,820
Discount received		1,260
		76,080
Less: expenses		
Bank charges	200	
Discounts allowed	1,060	
Wages	32,780	
Rates	6,000	
Telephone	1,140	
Electricity	1,480	
Insurance	1,200	
Motor expenses	1,380	
Office expenses	1,160	
Depreciation – building	2,000	
fixtures and fittings	960	
motor vehicles	7,455	
computer	950	
Bad debts	320	
		(58,085)
Net profit		17,995

Note how the sales returns and purchases returns have been netted off from the sales and purchases respectively. Note also that here the discount received has been shown as miscellaneous income under gross profit but it could also be shown in the list of expenses as a negative expense (with brackets round it).

student notes

Balance sheet as at 31 March 2009

	Cost	Provision for depreciation	Net book value
	£	£	£
Fixed assets			
Building	100,000	6,000	94,000
Fixtures and fittings	4,800	2,880	1,920
Motor vehicles	32,700	15,305	17,395
Computer	2,850	1,900	950
	140,350	26,085	114,265
Current assets			
Stock		5,200	
Debtors	15,000		
Less: provision	(300)		
		14,700	
Prepayments		300	
Bank		3,960	
Cash		100	
		24,260	
Current liabilities			
Creditors	5,010		
VAT	820		
Accruals	500		
		(6,330)	
Net current assets			17,930
			132,195
Capital at 1 April 2008			130,000
Net profit for the year			17,995
			147,995
Less: drawings			(15,800)
Capital at 31 March 2009			132,195

Activity 3

Why do drawings appear in the balance sheet and not as an expense in the profit and loss account?

Final ledger account adjustments

student notes

Once the balances on the trial balance have been taken to the profit and loss account and balance sheet there is one final set of adjustments that must be done to the some of the ledger accounts.

The income and expense ledger accounts must be closed off as the balances are no longer required in the ledger. This is done by taking the balances on each individual income and expense ledger account to a new ledger account known as the profit and loss ledger account.

How it works

The final balances on the sales account, purchases account and wages account are shown below.

Sales

	£		£
		Balance b/d	155,020

Purchases

	£		£
Balance b/d	80,200		

Wages

	£		£
Balance b/d	32,780		

These accounts must now be closed off ready to start with a clean sheet at the start of the next accounting period. This is done by transferring the balances remaining to a profit and loss ledger account.

Sales

	£		£
Profit and loss account	155,020	Balance b/d	155,020

Purchases

	£		£
Balance b/d	80,200	Profit and loss account	80,200

student notes

Wages

	£		£
Balance b/d	32,780	Profit and loss account	32,780

Profit and loss account

	£		£
Purchases	80,200	Sales	155,020
Wages	32,780		

This will be done for all profit and loss account balances and there will need to be journal entries for each of these final adjustments. Therefore the final set of journal entries in full will be as follows.

Journal entries

Opening stock

	Debit	*Credit*
Profit and loss account	4,400	
Stock		4,400
Sales		
Sales	155,020	
Profit and loss account		155,020
Sales returns		
Profit and loss account	2,100	
Sales returns		2,100
Purchases		
Profit and loss account	80,200	
Purchases		80,200
Purchases returns		
Purchases returns	1,300	
Profit and loss account		1,300
Bank charges		
Profit and loss account	200	
Bank charges		200
Discounts allowed		
Profit and loss account	1,060	
Discounts allowed		1,060
Discounts received		
Discounts received	1,260	
Profit and loss account		1,260

	Debit	Credit
Wages		
Profit and loss account	32,780	
Wages		32,780
Rates		
Profit and loss account	6,000	
Rates		6,000
Telephone		
Profit and loss account	1,140	
Telephone		1,140
Electricity		
Profit and loss account	1,480	
Electricity		1,480
Insurance		
Profit and loss account	1,200	
Insurance		1,200
Motor expenses		
Profit and loss account	1,380	
Motor expenses		1,380
Depreciation expense – buildings		
Profit and loss account	2,000	
Depr'n expense – buildings		2,000
Depreciation expense – fixtures and fittings		
Profit and loss account	960	
Depr'n expense – fixtures and fittings		960
Depreciation expense – motor vehicles		
Profit and loss account	7,455	
Depr'n expense – motor vehicles		7,455
Depreciation expense – computer		
Profit and loss account	950	
Depr'n expense – computer		950
Bad debt expense		
Profit and loss account	350	
Bad debt expense		350
Stock – profit and loss account		
Stock – profit and loss account	5,200	
Profit and loss account		5,200

student notes

student notes

Balance sheet ledger account balances

There is no need to do any similar adjustments to balance sheet item ledger accounts ie assets and liabilities. This is due to the fact that they remain as opening balances for the following accounting period in the ledger account. For example the closing balance on the Buildings at cost account is £100,000 and this remains as the opening balance for the buildings at the start of the next accounting period.

Activity 4

What are the year-end journal entries required to clear the following accounts:

a) purchases returns account
b) insurance account
c) sales ledger control account?

CONFIDENTIALITY

When preparing the final accounts of a sole trader or any other organisation you are likely to have access to much detailed information. This will include details of the business transactions and personal details such as rates of pay or the level of drawings of the owner. It is important, in all areas of finance and accounting, that care should be taken when communicating business matters. You should appreciate the need to consider at all times the confidentiality of the data to which you have access, and the appropriate level of information to which employees or external agents should have access.

For example, if you are responsible for the payroll, you would be expected to keep the data in a safe and secure place, and only make it available to other employees with the appropriate degree of seniority.

CHAPTER OVERVIEW

- start by preparing an initial trial balance from the closing ledger account balances – you may need to set up a suspense account balance if the trial balance does not initially balance

KEY WORD

Drawings cash and goods that the owner of a business takes out of the business for his/her own use

- the suspense account must be cleared by journal entries to correct any errors identified
- make journal entries for the period end adjustments for depreciation, accruals, prepayments, bad and doubtful debts and closing stock
- update the ledger account balances for the adjustments and corrections and prepare a final trial balance
- transfer the balances from the trial balance to the final accounts
- on a final year end adjustment all income and expense balances must be cleared out to the profit and loss ledger account

HOW MUCH HAVE YOU LEARNED?

1 A sole trader had a balance on her capital account of £34,560 on 1 July 2007. During the year ending 30 June 2008 she made a net profit of £48,752 but withdrew £49,860 from the business. What is the capital balance at 30 June 2008?

2 The owner of a business took goods from stock for his own use which had originally cost £1,500 and which had a selling price of £2,100. What are the two alternative double entry accounting treatments for this transaction?

3 The telephone expense and insurance expense accounts of a sole trader have balances of £3,400 and £1,600 respectively at 30 September 2008. However £300 of telephone expense is to be accrued and £200 of insurance has been prepaid. What are the final expense figures that will appear in the profit and loss account for the year?

4 A sole trader has the following balances in her initial trial balance at 31 May 2008:

	£
Fixtures and fittings at cost	12,600
Motor vehicles at cost	38,500
Provision for depreciation at 1 June 2006 – fixtures and fittings	3,400
– motor vehicles	15,500

Fixtures and fittings are depreciated at the rate of 20% per annum on cost and motor vehicles are depreciated on the reducing balance basis at a rate of 30%.

What is the total net book value of the fixed assets that will appear in the balance sheet at 31 May 2008?

5 Given below is the list of initial balances taken from a sole trader's ledger accounts at 30 June 2008.

	£
Sales	308,000
Machinery at cost	67,400
Office equipment at cost	5,600
Carriage inwards	2,300
Carriage outwards	4,100
Sales ledger control	38,400
Telephone	1,800
Purchases ledger control	32,100
Heat and light	3,100
Bank overdraft	3,600
Purchases	196,000
Petty cash	100
Insurance	4,200
Provision for depreciation – machinery	31,200
Provision for depreciation – office equipment	3,300
Stock at 1 July 2006	16,500
Loan	10,000
Miscellaneous expenses	2,200
Wages	86,700
Loan interest	600
Capital	60,000
Drawings	20,000
Provision for doubtful debts	1,000

The following information is also available:

i) After drawing up the initial trial balance the bookkeeper spotted that the heat and light account had been undercast by £200

ii) The value of stock at 30 June 2008 was £18,000

iii) The machinery and office equipment have yet to be depreciated for the year. Machinery is depreciated at 30% on the reducing balance basis and office equipment at 20% of cost

iv) £200 of loan interest has yet to be paid for the year and a telephone bill for £400 for the three months to 30 June 2008 did not arrive until after the trial balance had been drawn up

v) Of the insurance payments £800 is for the year ending 30 September 2008

vi) A bad debt of £1,200 is to be written off and a provision of 3% is required against the remaining debtors

You are required to:

a) draw up an initial trial balance and set up any suspense account required

b) prepare journal entries to clear the suspense account and make all of the year end adjustments required from the information in the question

c) update the ledger accounts for the journal entries

d) prepare a profit and loss account for the year ending 30 June 2008 and balance sheet at that date

chapter 14: THE EXTENDED TRIAL BALANCE

chapter coverage

Unit 5 requires you to be able to present information for preparing final accounts either in the form of a trial balance or an extended trial balance. In this chapter we will work through the preparation of an extended trial balance and then continue with the preparation of the final accounts.

KNOWLEDGE AND UNDERSTANDING AND PERFORMANCE CRITERIA COVERAGE

knowledge and understanding

- the methods of recording information for the organisational accounts of sole traders and partnerships
- the structure of organisational accounts of sole traders and partnerships
- the need to present accounts in the correct form
- the form of final accounts of sole traders and partnerships
- the methods of analysing income and expenditure
- how to draft year end final accounts of sole traders and partnerships
- the function and form of a trial balance and an extended trial balance
- the function and form of a profit and loss account and balance sheet for sole traders and partnerships

Performance criteria – element 5.2

- accurately prepare a trial balance and open a suspense account to record any imbalance
- establish the reasons for any imbalance and clear the suspense account by correcting the errors, or reduce them and refer outstanding items to the appropriate person
- correctly identify, calculate and record appropriate adjustments
- ensure that the organisation's policies, regulations, procedures and timescales relating to preparing final accounts are observed

KNOWLEDGE AND UNDERSTANDING AND PERFORMANCE CRITERIA COVERAGE

Performance criteria – element 5.3

- prepare final accounts of sole traders in proper form, from the trial balance
- observe the organisation's policies, regulations, procedures and timescales in relation to preparing final accounts of sole traders and partnerships
- identify and resolve or refer to the appropriate person discrepancies, unusual features or queries

EXTENDED TRIAL BALANCE

student notes

In this chapter we introduce the EXTENDED TRIAL BALANCE. The extended trial balance (ETB) is a technique that allows the initial trial balance to be adjusted for the necessary year end adjustments, to be corrected for any errors that are found and eventually to form the basis for the preparation of the final accounts.

An extended trial balance will normally have a column for the account name followed by eight further working columns:

student notes

Extended trial balance

Account name	Ledger balance		Adjustments		Profit and loss a/c		Balance sheet	
	DR	CR	DR	CR	DR	CR	DR	CR

student notes

HOW TO PREPARE THE EXTENDED TRIAL BALANCE

We will start with a summary of the procedure for preparing an extended trial balance (ETB) and then work through it on a step by step basis.

Step 1 Enter each ledger account balance as either a debit or a credit in the ledger balance column. This is the initial trial balance and it should balance – however if there is a difference between the debits and the credits a suspense account balance should be added to make the trial balance add up (see Chapter 12). Leave a number of empty lines at the bottom of this trial balance before totalling it as these will be necessary for adjustments and corrections.

Step 2 If there is a suspense account deal with the errors that have caused this by entering the debits and credits to correct the errors in the adjustments column.

Step 3 Enter any year end adjustments as directed in the adjustments column such as the depreciation charge for the year, accruals and prepayments, bad debts written off and adjustments for provision for doubtful debts. When doing this you may need to open up some new account lines in the ETB in the blank lines that you have left at the bottom of the ETB.

Step 4 Enter the closing stock balance in the adjustments column.

Step 5 Total and extend each line of the ETB into the profit and loss account or balance sheet columns as appropriate.

Step 6 Total the profit and loss account columns to find the profit or loss for the year and enter this in the balance sheet columns. Total the balance sheet columns.

student notes

HOW IT WORKS

We will use the same example of John Thompson used in the previous chapter so that you see that the final accounts are the same whichever method is used.

Given below is the list of ledger balances for John Thompson, a wholesaler of small electrical items, at his year end of 31 March 2009.

	£
Building at cost	100,000
Fixtures and fittings at cost	4,800
Motor vehicles at cost	32,700
Computer at cost	2,850
Provisions for depreciation at 1 April 2008	
– building	4,000
– fixtures and fittings	1,920
– motor vehicles	7,850
– computer	950
Stock at 1 April 2008	4,400
Bank (debit balance)	3,960
Petty cash	100
Sales ledger control	15,240
Purchases ledger control	5,010
Capital	130,000
Sales	155,020
Sales returns	2,100
Purchases	80,200
Purchases returns	1,400
Bank charges	200
Discounts allowed	890
Discounts received	1,260
Wages	32,780
Rates	5,500
Telephone	1,140
Electricity	1,480
Insurance	1,500
Motor expenses	1,580
Office expenses	960
Provision for doubtful debts at 1 April 2008	220
VAT (credit balance)	820
Drawings	15,800

Step 1 Enter these balances onto the ETB in the debit and credit columns of the ledger balance columns. Total the trial balance and check your totals carefully. Enter a suspense account balance if necessary.

student notes

Extended trial balance

Account name	Ledger balance		Adjustments		Profit and loss a/c		Balance sheet	
	DR	CR	DR	CR	DR	CR	DR	CR
	£	£	£	£	£	£	£	£
Buildings at cost	100,000							
Fixtures and fittings at cost	4,800							
Motor vehicles at cost	32,700							
Computer at cost	2,850							
Provisions for depreciation at 1 April 2008:								
– buildings		4,000						
– fixtures and fittings		1,920						
– motor vehicles		7,850						
– computer		950						
Stock at 1 April 2008	4,400							
Bank	3,960							
Petty cash	100							
Sales ledger control	15,240							
Purchases ledger control		5,010						
Capital		130,000						
Sales		155,020						
Sales returns	2,100							
Purchases	80,200							
Purchases returns		1,400						
Bank charges	200							

student notes

Account name	Ledger balance		Adjustments		Profit and loss a/c		Balance sheet	
	DR	CR	DR	CR	DR	CR	DR	CR
	£	£	£	£	£	£	£	£
Discounts allowed	890							
Discounts received		1,260						
Wages	32,780							
Rates	5,500							
Telephone	1,140							
Electricity	1,480							
Insurance	1,500							
Motor expenses	1,580							
Office expenses	960							
Provision for doubtful debts at 1 April 2008		220						
VAT		820						
Drawings	15,800							
Suspense account	270							
	308,450	308,450						

student notes

In this case the trial balance does not balance. The total of the debit column is £308,180 and the total of the credit column is £308,450. Therefore a suspense account balance of £270 is entered into the debit column in order to make the trial balance add up.

Take note of some of the entries in the trial balance. The provisions for depreciation and for doubtful debts are as at 1 April 2008. Therefore this means that the depreciation expense for the year has not yet been accounted for nor has there been any adjustment to the provision for doubtful debts for the year.

The stock figure in the trial balance is also at 1 April 2008, it is the opening stock. The stock figure in the trial balance is always the opening stock figure as the closing stock is not entered into the accounts until the year end when the stock is counted and valued (see Chapter 12).

Step 2 Deal with the errors that have caused the balance on the suspense account. The errors that have been found are given below:

- The purchases returns account was overcast by £100
- £200 of office expenses has been charged to the motor expenses account
- Discounts allowed of £170 had been correctly accounted for in the sales ledger control account but omitted from the discounts allowed account

First, work out the double entry that will correct each of these errors and then enter the debits and credits against the correct account totals in the adjustments columns of the ETB.

- The purchases returns account was overcast by £100

As purchases returns are a credit balance if the account has been overstated then the purchases returns account must be debited and the suspense account credited:

Debit	Purchases returns	£100
Credit	Suspense	£100

student notes

- £200 of office expenses has been charged to the motor expenses account

The motor expenses account has been charged with office expenses so the motor expenses account must be credited and the office expenses account debited:

Debit	Office expenses	£200
Credit	Motor expenses	£200

- Discounts allowed of £170 had been correctly accounted for in the sales ledger control account but omitted from the discounts allowed account

The double entry for discounts allowed is to debit the discounts allowed account and credit the sales ledger control account. The credit entry has been made but not the debit entry. Therefore the correcting entry is:

Debit	Discounts allowed	£170
Credit	Suspense	£170

These three double entries will now be entered into the ETB.

student notes

Account name	Ledger balance		Adjustments		Profit and loss a/c		Balance sheet	
	DR	CR	DR	CR	DR	CR	DR	CR
	£	£	£	£	£	£	£	£
Buildings at cost	100,000							
Fixtures and fittings at cost	4,800							
Motor vehicles at cost	32,700							
Computer at cost	2,850							
Provisions for depreciation at 1 April 2008:								
– buildings		4,000						
– fixtures and fittings		1,920						
– motor vehicles		7,850						
– computer		950						
Stock at 1 April 2008	4,400							
Bank	3,960							
Petty cash	100							
Sales ledger control	15,240							
Purchases ledger control		5,010						
Capital		130,000						
Sales		155,020						
Sales returns	2,100							
Purchases	80,200							
Purchases returns		1,400	100					
Bank charges	200							

student notes

Account name	Ledger balance		Adjustments		Profit and loss a/c		Balance sheet	
	DR	CR	DR	CR	DR	CR	DR	CR
	£	£	£	£	£	£	£	£
Discounts allowed	890		170					
Discounts received		1,260						
Wages	32,780							
Rates	5,500							
Telephone	1,140							
Electricity	1,480							
Insurance	1,500							
Motor expenses	1,580			200				
Office expenses	960		200					
Provision for doubtful debts at 1 April 2008		220						
VAT		820						
Drawings	15,800		{	100				
Suspense account	270			170				
	308,450	308,450						

student notes

Step 3 Enter the year end adjustments in the adjustments columns. The adjustments that are to be made are:

a) depreciation is to be provided for the year on the following basis:

   i) Buildings – 2% of cost
   ii) Fixtures and fittings – 20% of cost
   iii) Motor vehicles – 30% on the reducing balance basis
   iv) Computer – 33 1/3% of cost

b) rates of £500 are to be accrued

c) the insurance account includes an amount of £300 prepaid

d) a bad debt of £240 is to be written off

e) a provision for 2% of the remaining debtors is to be made

Firstly calculate the figures required for these adjustments and the double entry for them – you may need to open up new accounts for these adjustments.

a) Depreciation is to be provided for the year on the following basis:

   i) Buildings – 2% of cost

   £100,000 x 2% = £2,000

Debit	Buildings depreciation expense	£2,000
Credit	Buildings provision for depreciation	£2,000

   ii) Fixtures and fittings – 20% of cost

   £4,800 x 20% = £960

Debit	Fixtures depreciation expense	£960
Credit	Fixtures provision for depreciation	£960

   iii) Motor vehicles – 30% on the reducing balance basis

   (£32,700 – 7,850) x 30% = £7,455

Debit	Vehicles depreciation expense	£7,455
Credit	Vehicles provision for depreciation	£7,455

   iv) Computer – 33 1/3% of cost

   £2,850 x 33 1/3% = £950

Debit	Computer depreciation expense	£950
Credit	Computer provision for depreciation	£950

student notes

b) Rates of £500 are to be accrued

Debit	Rates	£500
Credit	Accruals	£500

c) The insurance account includes an amount of £300 prepaid

Debit	Prepayments	£300
Credit	Insurance	£300

d) A bad debt of £240 is to be written off

Debit	Bad debts expense	£240
Credit	Sales ledger control	£240

e) A provision for 2% of the remaining debtors is to be made

Provision required 2% x (£15,240 – 240)	=	£300
Balance on provision account at start of the year	=	£220
Increase in provision required £300 – 220	=	£80

Debit	Bad debts expense	£80
Credit	Provision for doubtful debts	£80

student notes

Account name	Ledger balance		Adjustments		Profit and loss a/c		Balance sheet	
	DR	CR	DR	CR	DR	CR	DR	CR
	£	£	£	£	£	£	£	£
Buildings at cost	100,000							
Fixtures and fittings at cost	4,800							
Motor vehicles at cost	32,700							
Computer at cost	2,850							
Provisions for depreciation at 1 April 2008:								
– buildings		4,000		2,000				
– fixtures and fittings		1,920		960				
– motor vehicles		7,850		7,455				
– computer		950		950				
Stock at 1 April 2008	4,400							
Bank	3,960							
Petty cash	100							
Sales ledger control	15,240			240				
Purchases ledger control		5,010						
Capital		130,000						
Sales		155,020						
Sales returns	2,100							
Purchases	80,200							
Purchases returns		1,400	100					
Bank charges	200							

student notes

Account name	Ledger balance		Adjustments		Profit and loss a/c		Balance sheet	
	DR	CR	DR	CR	DR	CR	DR	CR
	£	£	£	£	£	£	£	£
Discounts allowed	890		170					
Discounts received		1,260						
Wages	32,780							
Rates	5,500		500					
Telephone	1,140							
Electricity	1,480							
Insurance	1,500			300				
Motor expenses	1,580			200				
Office expenses	960		200					
Provision for doubtful debts								
at 1 April 2008		220		80				
VAT		820						
Drawings	15,800			{100				
Suspense account	270			{170				
Buildings depreciation expense			2,000					
Fixtures depreciation expense			960					
Motor vehicles depr'n expense			7,455					
Computer depreciation expense			950					
Accruals				500				
Prepayments			300					
Bad debts expense			240+80					
	308,450	308,450						

Step 4 Enter the closing stock valuation in the ETB in the adjustments column.

student notes

The closing stock at 31 March 2009 has been valued at £5,200.

The entries for this in the ledger accounts (see previous chapter) are:

Debit	Stock account – balance sheet	£5,200
Credit	Stock account – profit and loss account	£5,200

In the adjustment column of the ETB the entries to make are both a debit and a credit entry against the opening stock line with the value of the closing stock.

At this stage you have completed the adjustments. Therefore to check that all of the adjustments have consisted of complete double entry you should total the debit and credit adjustment columns – they should be equal.

student notes

Account name	Ledger balance		Adjustments		Profit and loss a/c		Balance sheet	
	DR	CR	DR	CR	DR	CR	DR	CR
	£	£	£	£	£	£	£	£
Buildings at cost	100,000							
Fixtures and fittings at cost	4,800							
Motor vehicles at cost	32,700							
Computer at cost	2,850							
Provisions for depreciation at 1 April 2008:								
– buildings		4,000		2,000				
– fixtures and fittings		1,920		960				
– motor vehicles		7,850		7,455				
– computer		950		950				
Stock at 1 April 2008	4,400		5,200	5,200				
Bank	3,960							
Petty cash	100							
Sales ledger control	15,240			240				
Purchases ledger control		5,010						
Capital		130,000						
Sales		155,020						
Sales returns	2,100							
Purchases	80,200							
Purchases returns		1,400	100					
Bank charges	200							

student notes

Account name	Ledger balance DR	Ledger balance CR	Adjustments DR	Adjustments CR	Profit and loss a/c DR	Profit and loss a/c CR	Balance sheet DR	Balance sheet CR
	£	£	£	£	£	£	£	£
Discounts allowed	890		170					
Discounts received		1,260						
Wages	32,780							
Rates	5,500		500					
Telephone	1,140							
Electricity	1,480							
Insurance	1,500			300				
Motor expenses	1,580			200				
Office expenses	960		200					
Provision for doubtful debts at 1 April 2008		220		80				
VAT		820						
Drawings	15,800			{ 100				
Suspense account	270			{ 170				
Buildings depreciation expense			2,000					
Fixtures depreciation expense			960					
Motor vehicles depr'n expense			7,455					
Computer depreciation expense			950					
Accruals				500				
Prepayments			300					
Bad debts expense			240+80					
	308,450	308,450	18,155	18,155				

student notes

Step 5 Total and extend each line of the ETB into the profit and loss account or balance sheet columns as appropriate.

The approach here is to take each line in turn and firstly add it across then decide whether this is a profit and loss account balance or a balance sheet balance. As examples:

- the buildings at cost account has a debit balance of £100,000 in the ledger balances column – there are no entries in the adjustment column so the only decision to make is whether this £100,000 is a debit in the profit and loss account or the balance sheet – it is of course a fixed asset that will appear in the debit column in the balance sheet
- the provision for depreciation for buildings has a credit of £4,000 in the ledger balance column and a further credit of £2,000 in the adjustment column – this totals to a credit of £6,000 – this is the provision for depreciation and therefore it is a balance sheet figure – this £6,000 is therefore taken across to the credit column of the balance sheet
- the stock is a complicated one – there are three figures that need to be extended across – opening stock of £4,400, the debit balance in the ledger balance column is taken to the debit of the profit and loss account – the debit in the adjustment column is taken as a debit to the balance sheet, the current asset of stock – the credit in the adjustment column is taken as a credit in the profit and loss account
- the sales ledger control account (debtors account) has a debit balance in the ledger balances column of £15,240 and a credit of £240 in the adjustment column – therefore the credit of £240 is deducted from the debit of £15,240 to give a debit total of £15,000 which is taken to the debit column of the balance sheet
- the suspense account has a debit of £270 in the ledger balances column – there are two credit entries in the adjustment column which total to £270 therefore meaning that there is no balance to be extended across
- the credit entry for accruals and the debit entry for prepayments are both taken across to the balance sheet

Now work carefully through the fully extended ETB ensuring that you are happy with each total and that you understand why the balances appear in the profit and loss account columns or the balance sheet columns.

Remember:

Profit and loss account	–	income
	–	expenses
Balance sheet	–	assets
	–	liabilities

student notes

Account name	Ledger balance		Adjustments		Profit and loss a/c		Balance sheet	
	DR	CR	DR	CR	DR	CR	DR	CR
	£	£	£	£	£	£	£	£
Buildings at cost	100,000						100,000	
Fixtures and fittings at cost	4,800						4,800	
Motor vehicles at cost	32,700						32,700	
Computer at cost	2,850						2,850	
Provisions for depreciation at 1 April 2008:								
– buildings		4,000		2,000				6,000
– fixtures and fittings		1,920		960				2,880
– motor vehicles		7,850		7,455				15,305
– computer		950		950				1,900
Stock at 1 April 2008	4,400		5,200	5,200	4,400	5,200	5,200	
Bank	3,960						3,960	
Petty cash	100						100	
Sales ledger control	15,240			240			15,000	
Purchases ledger control		5,010						5,010
Capital		130,000						130,000
Sales		155,020				155,020		
Sales returns	2,100				2,100			
Purchases	80,200				80,200			
Purchases returns		1,400	100			1,300		
Bank charges	200				200			

student notes

Account name	Ledger balance		Adjustments		Profit and loss a/c		Balance sheet	
	DR	CR	DR	CR	DR	CR	DR	CR
	£	£	£	£	£	£	£	£
Discounts allowed	890		170		1,060			
Discounts received		1,260				1,260		
Wages	32,780				32,780			
Rates	5,500		500		6,000			
Telephone	1,140				1,140			
Electricity	1,480				1,480			
Insurance	1,500			300	1,200			
Motor expenses	1,580			200	1,380			
Office expenses	960		200		1,160			
Provision for doubtful debts at 1 April 2008		220		80				300
VAT		820						820
Drawings	15,800			{100			15,800	
Suspense account	270			{170				
Buildings depreciation expense			2,000		2,000			
Fixtures depreciation expense			960		960			
Motor vehicles depr'n expense			7,455		7,455			
Computer depreciation expense			950		950			
Accruals				500				500
Prepayments			300				300	
Bad debts expense			240+80		320			
	308,450	308,450	18,155	18,155				

Step 6 Total the profit and loss account columns to find the profit or loss for the year and enter this in the balance sheet columns. Total the balance sheet columns.

student notes

If the credits in the profit and loss account exceed the debits then a profit has been made. This is the balancing debit in the ETB which will require a new account line of profit and loss. This same figure is also a credit in the balance sheet columns.

If the debits in the profit and loss account exceed the credits then a loss has been made. This is the balancing credit in the ETB which will again require a new account line of profit and loss. This same figure is entered as a debit in the balance sheet columns.

student notes

Account name	Ledger balance		Adjustments		Profit and loss a/c		Balance sheet	
	DR	CR	DR	CR	DR	CR	DR	CR
	£	£	£	£	£	£	£	£
Buildings at cost	100,000						100,000	
Fixtures and fittings at cost	4,800						4,800	
Motor vehicles at cost	32,700						32,700	
Computer at cost	2,850						2,850	
Provisions for depreciation at 1 April 2008:								
– buildings		4,000		2,000				6,000
– fixtures and fittings		1,920		960				2,880
– motor vehicles		7,850		7,455				15,305
– computer		950		950				1,900
Stock at 1 April 2008	4,400		5,200	5,200	4,400	5,200	5,200	
Bank	3,960						3,960	
Petty cash	100						100	
Sales ledger control	15,240			240			15,000	
Purchases ledger control		5,010						5,010
Capital		130,000						130,000
Sales		155,020				155,020		
Sales returns	2,100				2,100			
Purchases	80,200				80,200			
Purchases returns		1,400	100			1,300		
Bank charges	200				200			

student notes

Account name	Ledger balance DR	Ledger balance CR	Adjustments DR	Adjustments CR	Profit and loss a/c DR	Profit and loss a/c CR	Balance sheet DR	Balance sheet CR
	£	£	£	£	£	£	£	£
Discounts allowed	890		170		1,060			
Discounts received		1,260				1,260		
Wages	32,780				32,780			
Rates	5,500		500		6,000			
Telephone	1,140				1,140			
Electricity	1,480				1,480			
Insurance	1,500			300	1,200			
Motor expenses	1,580			200	1,380			
Office expenses	960		200		1,160			
Provision for doubtful debts								
at 1 April 2008		220		80				300
VAT		820						820
Drawings	15,800			{100			15,800	
Suspense account	270			{170				
Buildings depreciation expense			2,000		2,000			
Fixtures depreciation expense			960		960			
Motor vehicles depr'n expense			7,455		7,455			
Computer depreciation expense			950		950			
Accruals				500				500
Prepayments			300				300	
Bad debts expense			240					
			+ 80		320			
Profit and loss					17,995			17,995
	308,450	308,450	18,155	18,155	162,780	162,780	180,710	180,710

student notes

In this case a profit of £17,995 was made. This is the balancing figure in the profit and loss account columns and is shown as a credit in the balance sheet to be added to the capital for the period.

Once it is entered into the credit column in the balance sheet the balance sheet columns should be totalled and the two column totals should be equal.

Activity 1

List out the procedures that you would follow when preparing an extended trial balance.

Activity 2

If the credit balances exceed the debit balances in the profit and loss columns what does this mean? What other entry is made with this balancing amount?

Final accounts

The final stage is to rearrange the profit and loss columns into the correct profit and loss account format and to rearrange the balance sheet column figures into the correct balance sheet format.

student notes

John Thompson
Profit and loss account for the year ending 31 March 2009

		£	£
Sales			155,020
Less: sales returns			(2,100)
			152,920
Cost of sales			
Opening stock		4,400	
Purchases		80,200	
Less: purchases returns		(1,300)	
		83,300	
Less: closing stock		(5,200)	
			(78,100)
Gross profit			74,820
Discount received			1,260
			76,080
Less: expenses			
Bank charges		200	
Discounts allowed		1,060	
Wages		32,780	
Rates		6,000	
Telephone		1,140	
Electricity		1,480	
Insurance		1,200	
Motor expenses		1,380	
Office expenses		1,160	
Depreciation –	building	2,000	
	fixtures and fittings	960	
	motor vehicles	7,455	
	computer	950	
Bad debts		320	
			58,085
Net profit			17,995

student notes

John Thompson
Balance sheet as at 31 March 2009

	Cost	Provision for depreciation	Net book value
	£	£	£
Fixed assets			
Building	100,000	6,000	94,000
Fixtures and fittings	4,800	2,880	1,920
Motor vehicles	32,700	15,305	17,395
Computer	2,850	1,900	950
	140,350	26,085	114,265
Current assets			
Stock		5,200	
Debtors	15,000		
Less: provision	(300)		
		14,700	
Prepayments		300	
Bank		3,960	
Cash		100	
		24,260	
Current liabilities			
Creditors	5,010		
VAT	820		
Accruals	500		
		(6,330)	
Net current assets			17,930
			132,195
Capital at 1 April 2008			130,000
Net profit for the year			17,995
			147,995
Less: drawings			(15,800)
Capital at 31 March 2009			132,195

CHAPTER OVERVIEW

- once the initial trial balance has been prepared any errors that have caused a suspense account and any year end adjustments must be put through the accounts in order to arrive at the figures for the final accounts – this is all done in the extended trial balance

> **KEY WORD**
>
> **Extended trial balance** an accounting technique of moving from the trial balance, through the year end adjustments to the figures for the final accounts

- the first stage is to enter all of the ledger account balances into the ETB and to check that it then balances – if it does not balance then a suspense account must be entered in order to make the trial balance balance
- the suspense account must then be cleared by entering the correcting entries in the adjustments columns of the ETB
- any year end adjustments must then also be entered in the adjustment columns for depreciation, bad and doubtful debts and accruals and prepayments
- the closing stock figure is then entered as a debit and a credit entry in the adjustment columns
- each line of the ETB is then totalled and extended into either the profit and loss columns or the balance sheet columns as a debit or a credit – in the profit and loss account there are income and expenses – in the balance sheet there are assets and liabilities
- the profit and loss account columns are then totalled and the balancing figure is inserted as a new account line, the profit or loss – this is also inserted in the balance sheet columns – a debit in the profit and loss account column is a credit in the balance sheet column and vice versa
- the final stage is to total the balance sheet columns and these should now agree.
- to prepare the final accounts the profit and loss column figures and balance sheet column figures must be rearranged into the correct format

HOW MUCH HAVE YOU LEARNED?

1 When preparing an extended trial balance what do you do if you discover that the initial trial balance does not balance?

2 What entries are made in the adjustments column for the closing stock?

3 What entries are made in the profit and loss and balance sheet columns for the closing stock?

4 Given below is a list of the balances on the ledger accounts of a small business at its year end 30 April 2009.

	£
Drawings	15,480
Sales	94,300
Stock at 1 May 2008	1,600
Purchases	56,500
Electricity	700
Capital	15,600
Motor vehicle at cost	12,400
Office equipment	5,000
Provision for depreciation at 1 May 2008:	
– motor vehicle	3,720
– office equipment	1,250
Motor expenses	2,100
Bank (debit balance)	1,950
Wages	10,400
Creditors	5,300
Telephone	1,100
VAT (credit balance)	1,100
Debtors	9,950
Provision for doubtful debts at 1 May 2008	100
Rent	1,200
Insurance	1,400
Administration expenses	1,800

You are also given the following information:

i) A number of errors have been discovered:

- The purchases account was overcast by £100
- A total from the sales day book was entered in the debtors account correctly as £2,530 but entered into the sales account as £2,350
- £240 of wages costs have been posted in error to the purchases account
- £70 of electricity cost was correctly entered into the cash payments book but was not entered into the electricity account

ii) Depreciation for the year is to be provided as follows:

- Motor vehicle – 30% reducing balance basis
- Office equipment – 25% on cost

iii) An accrual for £200 of telephone costs is required and the rent account includes £140 that has been prepaid

iv) A debt of £450 is to be written off as bad and a provision of 2% is required against the remaining debtors

v) The stock at 30 April 2009 has been valued at £2,000

You are required to:

a) enter all of these figures onto the extended trial balance and then to total and extend the extended trial balance showing the profit or loss for the year

b) prepare the final accounts for the year ending 30 April 2009

chapter 15: PARTNERSHIPS

chapter coverage 

The standards of competence for Unit 5 require you to be able to prepare final accounts for two types of business entity: sole traders and partnerships. We have looked at sole traders in previous chapters. In this chapter we will consider the records and accounts of partnerships. A partnership is a number of sole traders who are in business together and therefore the financial records and accounts are very similar to those of a sole trader and in this chapter we will highlight the main differences between a sole trader and a partnership. The topics that we shall cover are:

- definition of a partnership
- the partnership agreement
- accounting for capital, profits and drawings in a partnership
- partnership balance sheet
- accounting for partners' salaries and interest on capital
- partnership accounts and the extended trial balance
- final accounts for a partnership
- admission of a new partner
- partnership goodwill
- retirement of a partner
- change in the profit sharing ratio

KNOWLEDGE AND UNDERSTANDING AND PERFORMANCE CRITERIA COVERAGE

Knowledge and understanding

- legal requirements relating to the division of profits between partners
- the methods of recording information for the organisational accounts of sole traders and partnerships
- the structure of the organisational accounts of sole traders and partnerships
- the need to present accounts in the correct form
- the form of final accounts of sole traders and partnerships
- how to use the transfer journal
- the methods of analysing income and expenditure
- how to draft year end final accounts of sole traders and partnerships
- the function and form of a trial balance and an extended trial balance
- the function and form of a profit and loss account and balance sheet for sole traders and partnerships

Performance criteria – element 5.2

- accurately prepare a trial balance and open a suspense account to record any imbalance
- establish the reasons for any imbalance and clear the suspense account by correcting the errors, or reduce them and refer outstanding items to the appropriate person
- correctly identify, calculate and record appropriate adjustments
- make the relevant journal entries to close off the revenue accounts in preparation for the transfer of balances to the final accounts
- ensure that the organisation's policies, regulations, procedures and timescales relating to preparing final accounts are observed

Performance criteria – element 5.3

- prepare final accounts of partnerships in proper form and in compliance with the partnership agreement, from the trial balance
- observe the organisation's policies, regulations, procedures and timescales in relation to preparing final accounts of sole traders and partnerships
- identify and resolve or refer to the appropriate person discrepancies, unusual features or queries

student notes

PARTNERSHIPS

A partnership is a method of trading which arises where a number of sole traders trade together. A partnership is defined in the Partnership Act 1890 as 'the relation which subsists between persons carrying on a business in common with a view of profit'. Most partnerships consist of between two and twenty partners although the large accountancy and legal partnerships have many more partners than this.

Partnership agreement

In a partnership there are a number of people paying capital into the business and sharing the profits of the business. Therefore most partnerships will have a PARTNERSHIP AGREEMENT. This agreement will cover the following common areas:

- The amount of capital that each partner must contribute to the business
- The method of sharing out the profits of the business amongst the partners
- Any restrictions on the taking of drawings out of the business
- Whether any salaries are to be paid to partners as well as their profit share
- Whether any interest is to be paid to partners on their outstanding capital balance

If the partners do not have a partnership agreement then the provisions of the Partnership Act 1890 will apply. However in the exam-based assessment the details of the partnership agreement will always be given so you are not required to know the default provisions of the Partnership Act.

student notes

ACCOUNTING IN A PARTNERSHIP

Most of the accounting in a partnership is exactly the same as for a sole trader. The transactions will initially be recorded in the primary records and then posted to the main ledger and subsidiary ledger accounts. The types of transactions and assets and liabilities in a partnership will also be the same as those for a sole trader.

The difference between a sole trader's accounts and those of a partnership centre around the financing element of the balance sheet, the bottom part of the balance sheet.

For a sole trader all of the capital has been introduced by that sole trader and all of the profits and drawings relate to the sole trader. However in a partnership all of the partners contribute capital, they will each have a share of the profits and they will each make different amounts of drawings. This makes the accounting slightly more complex.

The capital, profits and drawings for each partner are recorded in the partner's CAPITAL ACCOUNT and CURRENT ACCOUNT.

Capital account

The capital account will record the permanent capital that each partner pays into the business:

Debit Bank account
Credit Partner's capital account

This account will only change if there is a permanent increase or decrease in the amount of capital that a partner has in the business.

Current account

The current accounts for each partner will be used to record the partner's share of the profits for the year and the partner's drawings:

Partner's current account

	£		£
Drawings	X	Profit share	X
Balance c/d	X		
	X		X
		Balance b/d	X

In the bottom part of the balance sheet for a partnership the balances on each of the partner's capital accounts and current accounts will be listed.

student notes

HOW IT WORKS

A partnership is set up between Alan, Bill and Chris on 1 January 2009. Each partner contributed the following amounts of capital:

Alan	£30,000
Bill	£28,000
Chris	£25,000

During the year ended 31 December 2008 the profit and loss account shows that the partnership made a net profit of £60,000 which is to be shared equally between all three partners. The drawings made by each partner during the year were:

Alan	£12,000
Bill	£15,000
Chris	£16,000

The assets and liabilities of the business totalled to £100,000 on 31 December 2008.

We will write up the partners' capital and current accounts and show them in the balance sheet at the end of the year.

Capital account – Alan

	£		£
		1 Jan Bank	30,000

Capital account – Bill

	£		£
		1 Jan Bank	28,000

Capital account – Chris

	£		£
		1 Jan Bank	25,000

Capital account – Alan

	£		£
31 Dec Drawings	12,000	31 Dec Profit share	20,000
31 Dec Balance c/d	8,000		
	20,000		20,000
		2009	
		1 Jan Balance b/d	8,000

student notes

Capital account – Bill

	£		£
31 Dec Drawings	15,000	31 Dec Profit share	20,000
31 Dec Balance c/d	5,000		
	20,000		20,000
		2009	
		1 Jan Balance b/d	5,000

Capital account – Chris

	£		£
31 Dec Drawings	16,000	31 Dec Profit share	20,000
31 Dec Balance c/d	4,000		
	20,000		20,000
		2009	
		1 Jan Balance b/d	4,000

The bottom part of the balance sheet will now be shown:

Balance sheet extract:

	£	£
Capital accounts:		
– Alan		30,000
– Bill		28,000
– Chris		25,000
		83,000
Current accounts:		
– Alan	8,000	
– Bill	5,000	
– Chris	4,000	
		17,000
		100,000

This would mean that the balance sheet balances as the top part of the balance sheet, the assets and liabilities, totals £100,000 at the year end.

Activity 1

A partner in a partnership has paid £24,000 of capital into the partnership. His share of the profits for the year is £18,000 and he has taken £13,000 of drawings out of the partnership during the year.

What is the balance on the partner's current account at the end of the year?

student notes

THE APPROPRIATION ACCOUNT

In some partnership agreements the sharing of the profits will be made slightly more complicated by the provision for some partners to be allowed **salaries** to reflect the amount of work they perform within the partnership. The partners may also be allowed **interest** on the capital balance that they have within the partnership.

The important point to remember is that if there are agreements regarding salaries and interest on capital then the salaries and the interest must be shared out to the partners in the APPROPRIATION ACCOUNT **before** the final share of the remaining profit is made.

HOW IT WORKS

Harry, Bob and Gail are in partnership together with the following partnership agreement:

- Profits or losses are to be shared out in the ratio of 3 : 2 : 1
- Bob has a salary of £10,000 per annum and Gail has a salary of £15,000 per annum
- Interest of 5% is allowed to the partners on their capital balance at the start of each accounting year

At 1 January 2008 the balances on the partners' capital and current accounts were as follows:

		£
Capital accounts	Harry	50,000
	Bob	30,000
	Gail	20,000
Current accounts	Harry	2,000 (credit)
	Bob	1,000 (debit)
	Gail	1,500 (credit)

During the year ending 31 December 2008 the partnership made a net profit of £120,000. The balance on each partner's drawings account at 31 December 2008 was as follows:

		£
Drawings account	Harry	40,000
	Bob	36,000
	Gail	28,000

student notes

We will now show how the profit for the year is shared out amongst the partners in the appropriation account. The appropriation account can be shown as a ledger account or more usually in a vertical format. We will start with showing it as a ledger account as this will help with the double entry with the partners' current accounts.

Appropriation account

	£		£
		Balance b/d – net profit	12,000

We start the appropriation account with the net profit as a credit balance. This is the amount due to the partners which is why it is a credit balance – a creditor of the business. If there was a net loss in a partnership this would be a debit balance.

This profit must now be shared out to the partners according to the partnership agreement. All appropriations will be debited to the appropriation account and credited to the partners' current accounts.

So we must now set up the partners' current accounts. In this example the current accounts have opening balances on them. These will normally be credit balances as this is the amount of profit due to each partner which the partner has not yet withdrawn in the form of drawings. However in this case Bob has a debit balance on his current account meaning that last year he withdrew more in drawings that was allocated to him in profits. Watch out for this in an assessment or exam but if you are not told otherwise assume that the current account balances are credit balances.

Current account– Harry

	£		£
		Balance b/d	2,000

Current account– Bob

	£		£
Balance b/d	1,000		

Current account– Gail

	£		£
		Balance b/d	1,500

Now the profit appropriation will begin with the salaries for Bob and Gail and the interest to all three partners on their capital account balances. These will be debited to the appropriation account and credited to each partner's current account.

student notes

Appropriation account

		£		£
Salaries	Bob	10,000	Balance b/d – net profit	120,000
	Gail	15,000		

Current account – Bob

	£		£
Balance b/d	1,000	Salary	10,000

Current account – Gail

	£		£
		Balance b/d	1,500
		Salary	15,000

Next the interest is allowed to each partner:

Harry	£50,000 x 5%	=	£2,500
Bob	£30,000 x 5%	=	£1,500
Gail	£20,000 x 5%	=	£1,000

Appropriation account

		£		£
Salaries	Bob	10,000	Balance b/d – net profit	120,000
	Gail	15,000		
Interest	Harry	2,500		
	Bob	1,500		
	Gail	1,000		

Current account – Harry

	£		£
		Balance b/d	1,000
		Interest on capital	2,500

Current account – Bob

	£		£
balance b/d	1,000	Salary	10,000
		Interest on capital	1,500

Current account – Gail

	£		£
		Balance b/d	1,000
		Salary	15,000
		Interest on capital	2,500

student notes

At this point we are ready to share out the remaining profit in the profit s ratio of 3 : 2 : 1. The appropriation account will normally be balanced at stage in order to determine how much profit remains to be shared out.

Appropriation account

		£		£
Salaries	Bob	10,000	Balance b/d – net profit	120,000
	Gail	15,000		
Interest	Harry	2,500		
	Bob	1,500		
	Gail	1,000		
Balance c/d		90,000		
		120,000		120,000
			Balance b/d	90,000

We therefore have £90,000 to appropriate to the partners in the profit s ratio:

Harry	£90,000 x 3/6	=	£45,000
Bob	£90,000 x 2/6	=	£30,000
Gail	£90,000 x 1/6	=	£15,000

Appropriation account

		£		£
Salaries	Bob	10,000	Balance b/d – net profit	120,000
	Gail	15,000		
Interest	Harry	2,500		
	Bob	1,500		
	Gail	1,000		
Balance c/d		90,000		
		120,000		120,000
			Balance b/d	90,000
Profit share	Harry	45,000		
	Bob	30,000		
	Gail	15,000		
		90,000		90,000

Current account – Harry

	£		£
		Balance b/d	1,000
		Salary	2,500
		Profit share	45,000

student notes

Current account – Bob

	£		£
Balance b/d	1,000	Salary	10,000
		Interest on capital	1,500
		Profit share	30,000

Current account – Gail

	£		£
		Balance b/d	1,500
		Salary	15,000
		Interest on capital	1,000
		Profit share	15,000

Finally the balances from the partners' drawings accounts are transferred to the debit of their current accounts and the current accounts can then be balanced for inclusion in the balance sheet.

Current account – Harry

	£		£
Drawings	40,000	Balance b/d	1,000
		Interest on capital	2,500
Balance c/d	8,500	Profit share	45,000
	48,500		48,500
		Balance b/d	8,500

Current account – Bob

	£		£
Balance b/d	1,000	Salary	10,000
Drawings	36,000	Interest on capital	1,500
Balance c/d	4,500	Profit share	30,000
	41,500		41,500
		Balance b/d	4,500

Current account – Gail

	£		£
Drawings	28,000	Balance b/d	1,500
		Salary	15,000
Balance c/d	4,500	Interest on capital	15,000
	32,500		32,500
		Balance b/d	4,500

student notes

The capital and current account balances will then be shown in the bottom part of the balance sheet as:

		£	£
Capital accounts	Harry		50,000
	Bob		30,000
	Gail		20,000
			100,000
Current accounts	Harry	8,500	
	Bob	4,500	
	Gail	4,500	
			17,500
			117,500

Activity 2

Petra and Ginger are in partnership together with the agreement that Ginger receives a salary of £8,000 per annum and that 6% interest is paid on capital balances at the start of the year. Petra has introduced £40,000 of capital to the business and Ginger £24,000 of capital. At the start of the year Petra had a debit balance of £1,800 on her current account and Ginger had a credit balance on his current account of £500. All profits and losses are to be shared in the ratio of 2 : 1.

Petra took drawings of £38,000 during the year and Ginger withdrew £25,000 from the business. The partnership made a net profit of £71,840 during the year.

Write up the appropriation account and the partners' current accounts at the year end.

Appropriation account in vertical format

Often the appropriation account will be shown in a vertical format rather than in the form of a ledger account. Remember, though, that it is a ledger account and does form part of the double entry.

student notes

For Harry, Bob and Gail, the appropriation account in vertical format would appear as follows:

		£	£
Net profit for the year			120,000
Salaries	Bob	10,000	
	Gail	15,000	
			(25,000)
Interest on capital	Harry	2,500	
	Bob	1,500	
	Gail	1,000	
			(5,000)
Profit available for distribution			90,000
Profit share	Harry	45,000	
	Bob	30,000	
	Gail	15,000	
			90,000

Activity 3

Show the appropriation account from Activity 2 in vertical format.

Partnership losses

If a partnership makes a loss then this must be split amongst the partners in the profit share ratio. However if the partnership agreement includes salaries and provisions for interest on capital these appropriations must be accounted for first (therefore making the loss larger) before the final loss is split in the profit share ratio.

HOW IT WORKS

Suppose that in the following year the partnership of Harry, Bob and Gail made a net loss of £15,000 and no partners made any drawings during the year.

student notes

The appropriation account and current accounts would appear as follows:

Appropriation account

		£		£
Net loss		15,000		
Salaries	Bob	10,000		
	Gail	15,00		
Interest	Harry	2,500		
	Bob	1,500		
		1,000	Balance c/d	45,000
		45,000		45,000
Balance b/d		45,000	Loss share	
			Harry (45,000 × 3/6)	22,500
			Bob (45,000 × 2/6)	15,000
			Gail (45,000 × 1/6)	7,500
		45,000		90,000

Current account – Harry

	£		£
Drawings	22,500	Balance b/d	8,500
		Interest on capital	2,500
		Balance c/d	11,500
	22,500		22,500
Balance b/d	11,500		

Current account – Bob

	£		£
Share of loss	15,000	Balance b/d	4,500
		Salary	1,000
Balance c/d	1,000	Interest on capital	1,500
	16,000		16,000
		Balance b/d	1,000

Current account – Gail

	£		£
Share of loss	7,500	Balance b/d	4,500
		Salary	15,000
Balance c/d	13,000	Interest on capital	1,000
	20,500		20,500
		Balance b/d	13,000

Having dealt with the basic accounting for partnerships we will now move on to consider the preparation of final accounts for a partnership from an extended trial balance and from a trial balance.

student notes

Partnership accounts and the extended trial balance

n just the same way as with a sole trader, a partnership's final accounts can
be brought together using an extended trial balance.

HOW IT WORKS

Jamie and Freya are in partnership together sharing any profits or losses equally. The list of ledger balances at their year end 31 March 2009 are given below:

	£
Capital accounts:	
Jamie	16,000
Freya	15,000
Stock at 1 April 2008	6,300
Purchases	94,200
Sales	145,000
Motor vehicles at cost	38,000
Office equipment at cost	16,000
Expenses	19,000
Current accounts:	
Jamie	1,000
Freya	200
Bank	4,200
Creditors	9,000
Debtors	14,600
VAT	1,000
Drawings:	
Jamie	10,400
Freya	10,500
Provision for depreciation at 1 April 2008:	
motor vehicles	18,000
office equipment	8,000

You are also provided with the following information:

a) The stock at 31 March 2009 has been valued at £6,800

b) Depreciation is to be charged for the year on the following basis:

   i) Motor vehicles – 30% reducing balance basis
   ii) Office equipment – 25% straight line basis

c) Expenses of £300 are to be accrued

student notes

We will record these balances and adjustments on the extended trial balance.

Step 1 List the ledger balances in the ledger balance column and total the debits and credits to ensure that the trial balance balances. Remember that unless told otherwise the current account balances are credit balances.

Step 2 As the trial balance balances the next stage is to put through the year end adjustments for stock, depreciation and accruals:

Depreciation charges:

Motor vehicles (£38,000 – 18,000) x 30%	=	£6,000
Office equipment £16,000 x 25%	=	£4,000

Once the adjustments have been entered in the adjustments column then the debit and credit adjustments columns can be totalled to ensure that they are equal.

Step 3 Total and extend the trial balance into the profit and loss account and balance sheet columns.

Step 4 Total the profit and loss account columns, find the profit as the balancing figure and then divide the profit equally between the two partners. Transfer the profit to the balance sheet and then total the balance sheet columns.

student notes

Account name	Ledger balance		Adjustments		Profit and loss a/c		Balance sheet	
	DR	CR	DR	CR	DR	CR	DR	CR
Capital – Jamie		16,000						16,000
Capital – Freya		15,000						15,000
Stock at 1 April 2008	6,300		6,800	6,800	6,300	6,800	6,800	
Purchases	94,200				94,200			
Sales		145,000				145,000		
Motor vehicles at cost	38,000						38,000	
Office equipment at cost	16,000						16,000	
Expenses	19,000		300		19,300			
Current – Jamie		1,000						1,000
Current – Freya		200						200
Bank	4,200						4,200	
Creditors		9,000						9,000
Debtors	14,600						14,600	
VAT		1,000						1,000
Drawings – Jamie	10,400						10,400	
Drawings – Freya	10,500						10,500	
Provision for depreciation:								
motor vehicles		18,000		6,000				24,000
office equipment		8,000		4,000				12,000
Accruals				300				300
Depreciation expense:								
motor vehicles			6,000		6,000			
office equipment			4,000		4,000			
Profit – Jamie					11,000			11,000
Profit – Freya					11,000			11,000
	213,200	213,200	17,100	17,100	151,800	151,800	100,500	100,500

student notes

Final accounts

The final accounts can now be prepared in just the same way as with a sole trader by rearranging the figures in the profit and loss columns and balance sheet columns into the format of a profit and loss account and balance sheet.

Profit and loss account for the year ended 31 March 2009

	£	£
Sales		145,000
Cost of sales		
Opening stock	6,300	
Purchases	94,200	
	100,500	
Less: closing stock	(6,800)	
		93,700
Gross profit		51,300
Less: expenses		
Expenses	19,300	
Depreciation – motor vehicles	6,000	
Depreciation – office equipment	4,000	
		29,300
Net profit		22,000

Balance sheet as at 31 March 2009

student notes

	Cost	Accumulated depreciation	Net book value
	£	£	£
Fixed assets			
Motor vehicles	38,000	24,000	14,000
Office equipment	16,000	12,000	4,000
	54,000	36,000	18,000
Current assets			
Stock		6,800	
Debtors		14,600	
Bank		4,200	
		25,600	
Current liabilities			
Creditors	9,000		
VAT	1,000		
Accruals	300		
		(10,300)	
Net current assets			15,300
			33,300
Capital accounts Jamie			16,000
Freya			15,000
			31,000
Current accounts Jamie			
(1,000 + 11,000 – 10,400)		1,600	
Freya			
(200 + 11,000 – 10,500)		700	
			2,300
			33,300

In order to determine the current account balances we need to start with the opening balance on the current accounts, add the profit share for each partner and subtract each partner's drawings.

FROM TRIAL BALANCE TO FINAL ACCOUNTS

The final accounts of a partnership can also be prepared directly from the trial balance in just the same way as we saw for a sole trader earlier in this book. Journal entries would be required for all of the adjustments and corrections of errors as with a sole trader; however there are additional journal entries required for the APPROPRIATION of the profit between the partners and for the partners' drawings.

student notes

Remember that the sharing of the profit or appropriation of the profit is done in the profit and loss appropriation account. This starts when the net profit has been calculated for a partnership in the profit and loss account. This is a credit balance on the profit and loss account which is carried down into the appropriation account. This credit balance is cleared to the partners' current accounts according to the partnership agreement.

Each partner's drawings will have been debited to a drawings account and this must also be transferred to the partners' current accounts in order to find a balance for each current account to appear in the balance sheet.

HOW IT WORKS

Tina, Gavin and Fred are in partnership together. For the year ending 30 September 2008 the profit and loss account has been prepared and the net profit for the partnership is £120,000. Profits are shared between the three partners in the ratio of 3 : 2 : 1. During the year the partners' drawings have been recorded in individual drawings accounts and the balances at 30 September 2007 were:

Tina	£40,000
Gavin	£20,000
Fred	£10,000

We need to prepare the final journal entries required to complete the final accounts of the partnership.

Journal entries

Profit share

	Debit	*Credit*
Profit and loss appropriation account	£120,000	
Tina – current account (£120,000 x 3/6)		£60,000
Gavin – current account (£120,000 x 2/6)		£40,000
Fred – current account (£120,000 x 1/6)		£20,000

Drawings

		Debit	*Credit*
Current accounts	Tina	£40,000	
	Gavin	£20,000	
	Fred	£10,000	
Drawings accounts	Tina		£40,000
	Gavin		£20,000
	Fred		£10,000

student notes

Activity 4

Jane, Mike and Simon are in partnership sharing profits in the ratio of 4 : 3 : 2. During the year ending 30 June 2008 the partnership made a net profit of £180,000. What is the journal entry required to record the appropriation of profit to the partners?

Salaries and interest on capital

We have seen earlier that the appropriation of profit becomes slightly more complicated when the partnership agreement includes provisions regarding salaries for partners and interest on partners' capital. When preparing the final accounts in order to find the total transfer from the appropriation account to each partner's current account you will need to prepare the appropriation account to find the correct figures.

HOW IT WORKS

Jenny and Clare are in partnership sharing profits in the ratio of 2 to 1. Clare is allowed a salary of £10,000 per annum and both partners are allowed interest at 4% per annum on their capital balances. During the year ending 30 September 2008 the partnership made a net profit of £72,000. An extract from the trial balance at 30 September 2008 shows the following balances:

		£
Capital	Jenny	30,000
	Clare	20,000
Current account balance at 1 October 2007		
	Jenny	2,000
	Clare	3,500
Drawings	Jenny	39,000
	Clare	31,000

As the partnership profit and loss account has already been prepared we know the net profit for the period. Now we need to determine how this profit is to be appropriated to the partners in order to determine the journal entries that are required.

student notes

Appropriation account

		£		£
			Net profit	72,000
Salary	Clare	10,000		
Interest	Jenny (4% ×30,000)	1,200		
	Clare (4% ×20,000)	800		
Balance c/d		60,000		
		72,000		72,000
			Balance b/d	60,000
Profit share				
	Jenny (60,000 ×2/3)	40,000		
	Clare (60,000 ×1/3)	20,000		
		60,000		60,000

From the appropriation account we can determine the total amounts to be appropriated to each partner:

		£
Jenny	interest	1,200
	profit share	40,000
		41,200
Clare	salary	10,000
	interest	800
	profit share	20,000
		30,800

Now the journal entries can be prepared:

	Debit	*Credit*
	£	£
Appropriation account	72,000	
Current account – Jenny		41,200
Current account – Clare		30,800

Being profit share for the year.

Remember the drawings also have to be transferred to the current accounts.

	Debit	*Credit*
	£	£
Current account – Jenny	39,000	
Current account – Clare	31,000	
Drawings account – Jenny		39,000
Drawings account – Clare		31,000

student notes

Finally the current accounts for the partners can be drawn up after the journal entries to give the balances which will appear in the balance sheet. Don't forget the opening balances on each current account which will be credit balances unless you are told otherwise.

Current account – Jenny

	£		£
Drawings	39,000	Balance b/d	2,000
Balance c/d	4,200	Profit share	41,200
	43,200		43,200
		Balance c/d	4,200

Current account – Clare

	£		£
Drawings	31,000	Balance b/d	3,500
Balance c/d	3,300	Profit share	30,800
	34,300		34,300
		Balance b/d	3,300

The figures that will appear as the bottom part of the balance sheet are:

		£	£
Capital accounts	Jenny		30,000
	Clare		20,000
			50,000
Current accounts –	Jenny	4,200	
	Clare	3,300	
			7,500
			57,500

Extended trial balance

If you were preparing an extended trial balance and the partnership agreement included salaries and interest on capital the method to use to find the balance sheet credit entry for each partner would be the method used above. Use an appropriation account to determine the total profit share to each partner, including salaries and interest, and enter these figures in the balance sheet credit column for each partner, so, in the case of Jenny and Clare, the entries would be £41,200 and £30,800 respectively.

student notes

Activity 5

Frank and Butch are in partnership and the profit and loss account for the year ending 31 March 2009 shows that they have a net profit of £75,000. The partnership agreement is that Frank should receive a salary of £5,000 per annum and that interest is paid on capital balances at 5% per annum. Profits and losses are to be shared equally.

Extracts from the trial balance are given below:

		£
Capital	–Frank	30,000
	Butch	30,000
Current	–Frank	1,000
	Butch	1,000 (debit balance)
Drawings	– Frank	34,000
	Butch	30,000

Prepare the journal entries required to produce the final balance on the current accounts.

ADMISSION OF A NEW PARTNER

If a partnership requires more capital, for example if it is trying to expand its business, or it needs more expertise in the form of another partner, then a further individual to join the partnership will be sought. When the new partner has been found and the terms of the partnership have been agreed then he will be required to pay a certain amount of cash into the partnership bank account as his capital. The double entry for this is:

Debit	Bank account
Credit	New partner's capital account

There will also then be agreement between the original partners and the new partner regarding his profit share in the business.

HOW IT WORKS

Kylie and Jake have been in partnership together for a number of years sharing profits in the ratio of 2 to 1. However as the business requires urgent investment in new equipment for an envisaged expansion they have decided to admit a new partner to the business, Craig. It has been agreed that Craig will join the partnership on 1 March 2008 and will pay £60,000 into the business bank account for his share of the partnership assets. The profit share ratio for the three partners will then be 2 : 2 : 1.

student notes

During the year to 31 December 2008 the partnership made a profit of £120,000.

We will start with the double entry for the capital paid into the partnership by Craig. This is debited to the bank account and credited to a newly opened capital account for Craig.

Capital account – Craig

	£		£
		Bank	60,000

At the end of the year to 31 December 2008 the profits must be shared between the partners. This will be done in a two stage calculation:

Step 1 First the profit for the period up until the admission of Craig will be split between Kylie and Jake in their old profit sharing ratio of 2 : 1.

Profit from 1 January to 1 March 2008	=	£120,000 x 2/12
	=	£20,000
Kylie profit share	=	£20,000 x 2/3
	=	£13,333
Jake profit share	=	£20,000 x 1/3
	=	£6,667

Step 2 The profits for the period from 1 March to 31 December 2008 must then be split between all three partners in the new profit sharing ratio of 2 : 2 : 1.

Profit from 1 March to 31 December 2008	=	£120,000 x 10/12
	=	£100,000
Kylie profit share	=	£100,000 x 2/5
	=	£40,000
Jake profit share	=	£100,000 x 2/5
	=	£40,000
Craig profit share	=	£100,000 x 1/5
	=	£20,000

Therefore the total profit for each partner to be credited to their current accounts would be:

	Kylie	*Jake*	*Craig*
	£	£	£
1 Jan to 1 Mar	13,333	6,667	–
1 Mar to 31 Dec	40,000	40,000	20,000
	53,333	46,667	20,000

student notes

An alternative presentation of the appropriation of profit over a year in which there has been a change in the partnership is the use of a three-column proforma. Steps 1 and 2 above would therefore be combined as follows.

Kylie, Jake and Craig – Appropriation account for the year ended 31 December 2008

	1/1/08–28/2/08	*1/3/08–31/12/08*	*Total*
	£	£	£
Profit available for distribution	20,000	100,000	120,000
Profit share			
Kylie	(13,333)	(40,000)	(53,333)
Jake	(6,667)	(40,000)	(46,667)
Craig		(20,000)	(20,000)
	0	0	0

Activity 6

A new partner, Howard, is admitted to a partnership and agrees to pay in £25,000 of capital. What is the double entry for the admission of this partner?

GOODWILL

We have already seen in an earlier chapter that a business can have not only tangible fixed assets, such as buildings and machinery, but also an intangible fixed asset called goodwill. Most businesses will have goodwill, due to factors such as good reputation, good location, quality service etc. However in normal circumstances goodwill is not recognised in the balance sheet due to uncertainty regarding its valuation.

However when there is any form of change in a partnership, the true value of the partnership will need to be recognised. This is done by initially setting up the goodwill as an asset in order to correctly value the partnership. However as the goodwill cannot remain in the balance sheet it must then be removed again, once the change in the partnership has been accounted for.

HOW IT WORKS

Jane and Pete are in partnership sharing profits in the ratio of 2 : 1. The value of their net assets in the balance sheet at 30 June 2008 was £120,000. It was also estimated that the business had goodwill valued at £24,000. Liam was to be admitted to the partnership on 30 June and the profit sharing ratio was to be 3 : 2 : 1.

student notes

As such, Liam is buying into one sixth of the partnership by paying £24,000 of capital into the partnership. This is made up of one sixth of the balance sheet net assets of £20,000 (£120,000/6) and also one sixth of the unrecorded asset of goodwill for £4,000 (£24,000/6).

The capital account balances of Jane and Pete at 30 June 2008 were as follows:

Capital accounts

	Jane	Pete		Jane	Pete
	£	£		£	£
31/03			30/6 bal b/d	40,000	30,000

Step 1 The first stage in accounting for the admission of Liam is to initially set up the goodwill as an asset:

Debit Goodwill account
Credit Capital accounts in the **old** profit sharing ratio

Goodwill account

	£		£
Capital accounts	24,000		

Capital accounts

	Jane	*Pete*		*Jane*	*Pete*
	£	£		£	£
			30/6 bal b/d	40,000	30,000
			30/6 Goodwill	16,000	8,000

This is giving Jane and Pete their share of the goodwill that has been built up to date.

Step 2 Introduce Liam and his capital payment of £24,000.

Capital accounts

Jane	*Pete*	*Liam*		*Liam*	*Jane*	*Pete*
£	£	£		£	£	£
			30/6 bal b/d	40,000	30,000	
			30/6 Goodwill	16,000	8,000	
			30/6 Bank			24,000

Having credited Jane and Pete with their share of the goodwill that they built up in the business the goodwill must then be removed from the accounting records:

Debit Capital accounts in the **new** profit sharing ratio
Credit Goodwill account

student notes

Goodwill account

	£		£
Capital account	24,00	Capital accounts	24,000

This has now removed the goodwill from the accounting records.

Capital accounts

	Jane	*Pete*	*Liam*		*Liam*	*Jane*	*Pete*
	£	£	£		£	£	£
30/6 Goodwill	12,000	8,000	4,000	30/6 bal b/d	40,000	30,000	
				30/6 Goodwill	16,000	8,000	
				30/6 Bank			24,000

Step 3 Finally the capital accounts can be balanced.

Capital accounts

	Jane	*Pete*	*Liam*		*Liam*	*Jane*	*Pete*
	£	£	£		£	£	£
30/6 Goodwill	12,000	8,000	4,000	30/6 bal b/d	40,000	30,000	
				30/6 Goodwill	16,000	8,000	
30/6 Bal c/d	44,000	30,000	20,000	30/6 Bank			24,000
	56,000	38,000	24,000		56,000	38,000	24,000
				1/7 Bal b/d	44,000	30,000	20,000

RETIREMENT OF A PARTNER

A further scenario that you may have to deal with is that of the retirement of a partner. The accounting processes are similar to that for admission of a partner, as prior to the retirement each partner's capital account must be credited with their share of the goodwill earned in the business (so that the retiring partner can take his share) but then the goodwill must be removed from the accounting records.

HOW IT WORKS

Jo, Luke and Pat have been in partnership for a number of years sharing profits equally. Jo is about to retire from the partnership and any balances due to her are to be paid off in cash.

At the date of the retirement the capital and current account balances of the partners were as follows:

student notes

		£
Capital accounts	Jo	40,000
	Luke	35,000
	Pat	35,000
Current accounts	Jo	2,000
	Luke	5,000
	Pat	3,000

The goodwill of the partnership was estimated at £30,000, and after Jo's retirement profits are to be shared between Luke and Pat in the ratio of 2 : 1.

Step 1 Set up the partners' capital accounts and current accounts.

Capital accounts

	Jo	*Luke*	*Pat*		*Jo*	*Luke*	*Pat*
	£	£	£		£	£	£
				Bal b/d	40,000	35,000	35,000

Current accounts

	Jo	*Luke*	*Pat*		*Jo*	*Luke*	*Pat*
	£	£	£		£	£	£
				Bal b/d	2,000	5,000	3,000

Step 2 Transfer the balance on Jo's current account to her capital account so that all amounts due to Jo are recorded in her capital account.

Capital accounts

	Jo	*Luke*	*Pat*		*Jo*	*Luke*	*Pat*
	£	£	£		£	£	£
				Bal b/d	40,000	35,000	35,000
				Current a/c	2,000		

Current accounts

	Jo	*Luke*	*Pat*		*Jo*	*Luke*	*Pat*
	£	£	£		£	£	£
Capital a/c	2,000			Bal b/d	2,000	5,000	3,000

Step 3 Recognise the goodwill that has been earned by each of the partners by setting up a goodwill account and crediting each partner with their share of that goodwill in the old profit sharing ratio.

Debit Goodwill account
Credit Partners' capital accounts in old profit sharing ratio

Goodwill

	£		£
Capital accounts	30,000		

student notes

Capital accounts

	Jo	Luke	Pat		Jo	Luke	Pat
	£	£	£		£	£	£
				Bal b/d	40,000	35,000	35,000
				Current a/c	2,000		
				Goodwill	10,000	10,000	10,000

Step 4 Remove the goodwill from the accounting records.

Debit Partners' capital accounts in the new profit sharing ratio

Credit Goodwill account

Goodwill

	£		£
Capital accounts	30,000	Capital accounts	30,000

Capital accounts

	Jo	Luke	Pat		Jo	Luke	Pat
	£	£	£		£	£	£
				Bal b/d	40,000	35,000	35,000
				Current a/c	2,000		
Goodwill		20,000	10,000	Goodwill	10,000	10,000	10,000

Step 5 Pay Jo the amount that is due to her from the bank account – £52,000 (£40,000 + 2,000 + 10,000)

Bank

	£		£
		Capital a/c – Jo	52,000

Capital accounts

	Jo	Luke	Pat		Jo	Luke	Pat
	£	£	£		£	£	£
				Bal b/d	40,000	35,000	35,000
				Current a/c	2,000		
Goodwill		20,000	10,000	Goodwill	10,000	10,000	10,000
Bank	52,000						

Step 6 Finally balance the capital accounts to find the opening capital balances for the two remaining partners.

student notes

Capital accounts

	Jo	Luke	Pat		Jo	Luke	Pat
	£	£	£		£	£	£
				Bal b/d	40,000	35,000	35,000
				Current a/c	2,000		
Goodwill		20,000	10,000	Goodwill	10,000	10,000	10,000
Bank	52,000						
Balance c/d		25,000	35,000				
	52,000	45,000	45,000		52,000	45,000	45,000
				Bal b/d		25,000	35,000

Paying off the retiring partner

When a partner retires it is likely that he will be owed a significant amount by the partnership, being the capital that he has paid into the partnership, the balance on his current account and his share of any goodwill. Therefore in many instances the partnership may not have enough money in the bank account to pay off the amount due to the retiring partner. In such circumstances the retiring partner might agree to leave all or part of the amounts due to him within the partnership as a loan.

HOW IT WORKS

Let's return to Jo, Luke and Pat. When Jo retires we have seen that she is owed £52,000 in total by the partnership. Suppose that the partners discuss the retirement and agree to pay Jo £12,000 in cash but for the remainder to remain as a loan to the partnership from Jo until such time as the partnership has enough cash to pay off the full amount.

In this case the final stages of the accounting for the retirement would be slightly different. Having dealt with the goodwill adjustment there will be two remaining accounting entries.

Step 1 Pay Jo the agreed £12,000

Debit Jo's capital account
Credit Bank account

Capital accounts

	Jo	Luke	Pat		Jo	Luke	Pat
	£	£	£		£	£	£
				Bal b/d	40,000	35,000	35,000
				Current a/c	2,000		
Goodwill		20,000	10,000	Goodwill	10,000	10,000	10,000
Bank	12,000						

student notes

Step 2 Set up the loan from Jo to the partnership

There is a further £40,000 due to Jo which is to remain within the partnership as a loan from Jo. This is therefore transferred from Jo's capital account to a loan account.

Debit Jo's capital account
Credit Loan account – Jo

Capital accounts

	Jo	*Luke*	*Pat*		*Jo*	*Luke*	*Pat*
	£	£	£		£	£	£
				Bal b/d	40,000	35,000	35,000
				Current a/c	2,000		
Goodwill		20,000	10,000	Goodwill	10,000	10,000	10,000
Bank	12,000						
Loan	40,000						

Loan account – Jo

	£		£
		Capital account	40,000

Step 3 Finally the capital accounts can be balanced as before.

Capital accounts

	Jo	*Luke*	*Pat*		*Jo*	*Luke*	*Pat*
	£	£	£		£	£	£
				Bal b/d	40,000	35,000	35,000
				Current a/c	2,000		
Goodwill		20,000	10,000	Goodwill	10,000	10,000	10,000
Bank	12,000						
Loan	40,000						
Balance c/d		25,000	35,000				
	52,000	45,000	45,000		52,000	45,000	45,000
				Bal b/d		25,000	35,000

student notes

Activity 7

Nick, Sue and Trish have been in partnership for a number of years sharing profits equally. However at the year end of 31 March 2009 Sue has decided to retire. The partnership between Nick and Trish will continue and profits will be shared in the ratio of 2: 1.

The capital and current account balances for the partners at the year end of 31 March 2009 were as follows:

		£
Capital accounts	Nick	50,000
	Sue	40,000
	Trish	30,000
Current accounts	Nick	3,000
	Sue	2,000
	Trish	1,000

The value of the partnership goodwill is estimated to be £15,000. On retirement it has been agreed that Sue will receive £10,000 in cash and the remainder of what is due to her will be in the form of a loan to the partnership.

Write up the partners' capital accounts to reflect the retirement of Sue.

CHANGE IN PROFIT SHARING RATIO

A further change that might take place within a partnership is that during an accounting period the partners might decide to change the profit sharing ratio. This will mean that there will be two separate profit appropriation calculations – one for the period up to the date of change and one for the period after the date of change. Therefore the total profit made in the year must be split into each of these periods.

HOW IT WORKS

During the year ended 31 December 2008 the partnership of Phil and Bob made a total profit of £60,000. At the start of the year the profit sharing ratio was 2 : 1 but on 31 March 2008 the partners decided to change the ratio to equal shares of profit and for Phil to receive a salary of £12,000 per annum. The profit has accrued evenly over the year.

student notes

Step 1 In order to appropriate the profit correctly we need to firstly appropriate the profit up to 31 March in accordance with the old profit sharing ratio of 2 : 1.

	£
Profit to 31 March (£60,000 x 3/12)	15,000
Appropriation:	
Phil (£15,000 x 2/3)	10,000
Bob (£15,000 x 1/3)	5,000
	15,000

Step 2 Next the profit for the remainder of the year is appropriated according to the new profit sharing agreement.

		£
Profit from 1 April to 31 December (£60,000 x 9/12)		45,000
Appropriation:		
Salary	Phil (£12,000 x 9/12)	9,000
Profit share	Phil (36,000 x 1/2)	18,000
	Bob (36,000 x 1/2)	18,000
		45,000

Step 3 Finally the partners' current accounts can be written up. Phil had an opening debit balance of £2,000 while Bob had an opening credit balance of £1,000. Phil had made drawings of £33,000 during the year and Bob had made drawings of £20,000.

Capital accounts

	Phil	*Bob*		*Phil*	*Bob*
	£	£		£	£
Bal b/d	2,000		Bal b/d		1,000
Drawings	33,000	20,000	Profit to 31 March	10,000	5,000
			Salary	9,000	
Bal c/d	2,000	4,000	Profit to 31 Dec	18,000	18,000
	37,000	24,000		37,000	24,000
			Bal b/d	2,000	4,000

Activity 8

Pat and Ray have been in partnership for a number of years sharing profits in the ratio of 2 : 1. On 31 May 2008 it was decided to change the profit sharing ratio so that each partner received an equal share of profits. The partnership profit for the year to 31 December 2008 was £48,000 and this accrued evenly over the year.

The current account balances of the two partners at 1 January 2008 were a credit balance of £7,400 for Pat and a debit balance of £1,200 for Ray. The partners' drawings for the year were £32,000 for Pat and £19,000 for Ray.

Using a three column format, calculate the profit appropriation for the year and write up the partners' current accounts for the year.

student notes

CHAPTER OVERVIEW

- the financing section of the balance sheet for a sole trader shows the opening capital, plus profit for the year less drawings in the year
- drawings are always a debit entry in the drawings account – if the drawings are in cash the credit is to the bank account, if the drawings are in goods then the cost price of the goods is normally used and the credit entry is to purchases – if the selling price of the goods taken is used then the credit entry should be to the sales account
- a partnership is a number of people in business together trying to make a profit – most partnerships will have a partnership agreement covering the sharing of profits and other financial details
- most of the accounting for a partnership is the same as that for a sole trader – the difference lies in the accounting for capital, profits and drawings
- the partners' capital accounts are used to record the permanent capital that a partner pays into the partnership
- the partners' current accounts are used to record each partner's share of the profits for the year and each partner's drawings during the year
- the appropriation account is used to split the net profit for the period between the parties. Net profit can be appropriated by salary and interest on capital, then the remaining net profit is appropriated in the profit sharing ratio
- the extended trial balance can be used to prepare final accounts for a partnership in just the same way as for a sole trader
- the final accounts can also be prepared from the draft trial balance and journal entries – additional journal entries are required to complete the current accounts with profit share and drawings
- if a new partner is admitted to the partnership he or she will pay cash for their share of the partnership assets
- if the partnership has goodwill then this should be adjusted for when the new partner is admitted by crediting the partners' capital accounts in the old profit sharing ratio and debiting the capital accounts in the new profit sharing ratio

KEY WORDS

Drawings the amounts that the owner of the business withdraws from the business either as cash or goods

Partnership agreement agreement between the partners concerning the sharing out of the profits of the partnership and other financial details

Capital account the partners' account that records the permanent capital that each partner pays into the business

Current account the partners' account that records the partners' profit share for the year and the partners' drawings for the year

Appropriation sharing of profit between partners

Appropriation account ledger account used to split the profit according to the partnership agreement

CHAPTER OVERVIEW cont.

- if a partner retires there should also be an adjustment for goodwill by crediting the partners' capital accounts in the old profit sharing ratio and debiting with the new profit sharing ratio. The retiring partner's current account balance is also transferred to the capital account and the retiring partner is either paid what is due in cash or all or part of what is owed remains as a loan to the partnership
- if the partners change the profit sharing ratio during the accounting period then the appropriation of profit should take place in two separate calculations. The profit for the period should be split into the profit before the change which is appropriated using the old profit sharing ratio and the profit after the change which is appropriated using the new profit sharing ratio

HOW MUCH HAVE YOU LEARNED?

1 What areas are likely to be considered when a partnership is drawing up its partnership agreement?

2 A partnership was set up on 1 May 2008 by Fred and George. Fred paid in £32,000 of capital and George £27,000 of capital. During the year ended 30 April 2009 the business made a net profit of £50,000 which is to be split between Fred and George with Fred getting 60%. Fred's drawings during the year were £20,000 and George's were £16,000.

Write up the capital and current accounts for the two partners for the year and show the balances on these accounts that would appear in the balance sheet at 30 April 2009.

3 Kristin and Gary are in partnership with profits being shared equally. Their ledger balances at 31 March 2009, their year end, are as follows:

		£
Expenses		24,980
Machinery at cost		100,000
Motor vehicles at cost		60,000
Sales		210,000
Stock at 1 April 2008		10,200
Bank		6,400
Creditors		13,000
Drawings –	Kristin	22,000
	Gary	25,000
VAT		2,400
Purchases		134,000

Provision for depreciation at 1 April 2008:

		£
Machinery		30,000
Motor vehicles		30,600
Current accounts –	Kristin	1,500
	Gary	2,680
Capital accounts –	Kristin	60,000
	Gary	53,000
Debtors		20,600

The following information is also available:

i) The closing stock has been valued at £12,000

ii) The depreciation charges for the year are at the rate of:

Machinery	15% on cost
Motor vehicles	30% reducing balance

iii) The expenses figure includes £1,000 of prepaid amounts

You are required to:

a) enter these balances and adjustments in an extended trial balance and total and extend the trial balance

b) prepare the final accounts for the partnership

4 Jake and Lyle were in partnership with the following partnership agreement:

- Jake would receive a salary of £10,000 per annum and Lyle would receive a salary of £20,000 per annum
- Interest on capital was allowed at 4% per annum
- Profits and losses were to be shared in the ratio of 3 : 2

An extract from the trial balance at 30 September 2008 shows the following:

		£
Capital accounts	Jake	100,000
	Lyle	60,000
Current accounts	Jake	5,000
	Lyle	8,000
Drawings	Jake	31,000
	Lyle	34,000

The partnership made a net profit of £66,400 for the year ending 30 September 2008.

Prepare the appropriation account and the partners' current accounts clearly and show the figures that would in appear in the balance sheet for the partners' capital and current accounts.

5 Anna, Bill and Cheryl are in partnership sharing profits in the ratio of 2 : 1 : 1. Bill has a salary of £10,000 and Cheryl a salary of £5,000 per annum. All partners are allowed interest at 4% on their capital balance.

Their draft trial balance at 30 June 2008 has the following balances.

		£
Stock at 1 July 2007		45,000
Debtors		54,000
Sales		465,000
Fixed assets at cost		80,000
Provision for depreciation at 1 July 2007		42,000
Provision for doubtful debts at 1 July 2007		1,500
Expenses		68,000
Drawings	Anna	38,000
	Bill	15,000
	Cheryl	18,000
Creditors		40,000
Bank		2,000 (debit)
Current accounts at 1 July 2007	Anna	2,500 (credit)
	Bill	5,000 (credit)
	Cheryl	3,000 (credit)
Purchases		302,000
Capital accounts	Anna	30,000
	Bill	23,000
	Cheryl	10,000

You are also given the following information:

i) Stock at 30 June 2008 has been valued at £50,000

ii) Depreciation for the year has yet to be provided at 20% on cost

iii) A bad debt of £4,000 is to be written off and the provision for doubtful debts is to be 2% of the remaining debtors

iv) Expenses of £5,000 are to be accrued

You are required to:

a) draft an initial trial balance
b) draft journal entries for all of the adjustments required
c) complete the ledger accounts for which journals have been drafted
d) prepare the profit and loss account of the partnership
e) draft journal entries for the appropriation of profits and drawings
f) draw up the partners' current accounts
g) prepare the balance sheet as at 30 June 2008

6 Kate, Hal and Mary have been in partnership for a number of years sharing profits equally, but on 31 December 2008 Kate has decided to retire. During the year ended 31 December 2007 the partnership made a profit of £75,000.

The partners' capital and current account balances at 1 January 2008 and their drawings for the year were:

		£
Capital account	Kate	48,000
	Hal	38,000
	Mary	27,000
Current account (credit)	Kate	1,200
	Hal	800
(debit)		
	Mary	2,500
(credit)		
Drawings	Kate	20,000
	Hal	23,500
	Mary	24,400

At 31 December 2008 the goodwill of the partnership was estimated to be £27,000. After Kate's retirement it has been decided that Hal should receive a salary of £15,000 per annum and that profits should be shared equally between the two remaining partners.

It has been agreed that the partnership will pay Kate £15,000 of the amount due to her in cash and that the remainder should remain as a loan to the partnership.

Write up the capital and current accounts for the partners for the year ending 31 December 2008.

7 Paul and Gill have been in partnership for a number of years sharing profits in the ratio of 3:2. On 1 July 2008 they have decided to change the partnership agreement to Gill receiving a salary of £10,000 per annum and for profits to be split in the ratio of 2 : 1. During the year ending 30 September 2008 the partnership profits totalled £45,000.

At 1 October 2007 both partners had credit balances of £2,000 on their current accounts. Paul made drawings of £26,400 during the year to 30 September 2008 and Gill's drawings for the period totalled £18,700.

Write up the partners' current accounts for the year ending 30 September 2008.

chapter 16: INCOMPLETE RECORDS

chapter coverage 

In this penultimate chapter of the Course Companion we are dealing with small businesses that do not keep the type of accounting records considered so far, such as primary records, ledger accounts, fixed asset registers etc. However such businesses will keep some records – incomplete records – and from these it is necessary to find the missing information and reconstruct the figures needed for the final accounts. The topics we shall cover are:

- what is meant by incomplete records
- using the accounting equation
- reconstructing the cash and bank accounts
- reconstructing the debtors and creditors accounts
- using mark ups and profit margins
- the approach to follow for incomplete records examples
- finding a missing stock value

KNOWLEDGE AND UNDERSTANDING AND PERFORMANCE CRITERIA COVERAGE

knowledge and understanding

- the methods of restructuring accounts from incomplete evidence
- the principles of double entry accounting

student notes

WHAT ARE INCOMPLETE RECORDS?

Many small businesses do not keep full accounting records made up of primary records, ledger accounts, monthly reconciliations and trial balances. Instead they will keep the basic records necessary to keep track of the transactions of the business. A typical small business may well have the following information from which details of the transactions can be determined:

- Bank statements, paying in slips, cheque counterfoils
- Copies of sales invoices sent out to customers
- Purchase invoices received from suppliers
- Lists of customers who have not yet paid – debtors
- Lists of suppliers who have not yet been paid – creditors

This type of information is what we mean by INCOMPLETE RECORDS.

However limited the information, the owner of the business is likely to want to know how much profit or loss has been made in the year and what assets and liabilities he has at the end of the year. This is where an accountant is required in order to be able to piece together the information that is required to prepare a statement showing the profit or loss and a statement listing the assets and liabilities at the end of the period.

There are a variety of techniques that are available to the accountant in order to be able to reconstruct the figures that are needed. Each of these will be considered in turn:

- The accounting equation – assets minus liabilities equals capital
- Reconstruction of the cash/bank account
- Use of debtors and creditors accounts
- Use of mark ups and margins

In assessments and exams you may be required to prepare a profit and loss account and a balance sheet from incomplete records.

THE ACCOUNTING EQUATION

student notes

We came across the accounting equation in an early chapter of this Course Companion so just a brief reminder here. The accounting equation is:

ASSETS – LIABILITIES = CAPITAL

Opening capital

If we are to prepare the final accounts of a business with incomplete records then we may need to determine the opening capital balance. This can be done by finding the total of the assets minus the liabilities at the start of the year.

HOW IT WORKS

Stan Kelly runs a small business. He does not keep any primary records or ledger accounts but he can provide you with information about the assets and liabilities of his business. He has only a small number of fixed assets – a car and a computer – and he can fairly easily determine the value of his stock at any time. He keeps copies of all of his sales invoices and marks each one as paid when the customer sends a cheque therefore he knows exactly what the debtors position is – the unmarked invoices. Similarly he keeps all of his suppliers' invoices and marks them as paid when he sends out a cheque to the supplier therefore his creditors are any unmarked invoices.

Stan has an accounting year that runs to 31 March each year and he has provided you with the following information on his assets and liabilities:

	31 March 2008	*31 March 2009*
	£	£
Car – valuation	7,000	6,000
Computer – valuation	3,000	2,500
Stock	7,300	8,900
Debtors	10,500	11,200
Creditors for purchases	6,400	5,200
Creditors for expenses	400	200
Bank	1,200	1,800
Cash in till	100	100

These are all of the assets and liabilities that Stan has and therefore from this his opening capital balance can be determined by finding the total of assets minus liabilities at 31 March 2008.

student notes

Statement of assets and liabilities at 31 March 2008

	£
Car – valuation	7,000
Computer – valuation	3,000
Stock	7,300
Debtors	10,500
Creditors for purchases	(6,400)
Creditors for expenses	(400)
Bank	1,200
Cash in till	100
Opening capital	22,300

Alternative use of the accounting equation

The accounting equation can also be viewed in a different manner. The assets minus the liabilities are known as the NET ASSETS of the business. If the net assets of the business increase then for the accounting equation to balance the capital balance must also increase.

The capital balance is made up of:

OPENING CAPITAL + CAPITAL INTRODUCED + PROFIT – DRAWINGS

If the net assets of the business have increased then the closing capital balance must also be larger than the opening capital balance – therefore this must have been caused by capital being introduced or more profit being made than drawings.

Therefore the accounting equation can also be said to be:

INCREASE IN NET ASSETS =
CAPITAL INTRODUCED + PROFIT – DRAWINGS

student notes

HOW IT WORKS

We know Stan Kelly's opening capital balance is £22,300. We also have the list of his assets and liabilities at 31 March 2009 – therefore we can calculate the increase in net assets over the year.

	31 March 2009
	£
Car – valuation	6,000
Computer – valuation	2,500
Stock	8,900
Debtors	11,200
Creditors for purchases	(5,200)
Creditors for expenses	(200)
Bank	1,800
Cash in till	100
Net assets at 31 March 2007	25,100

	£
Net assets at 31 March 2008	22,300
Net assets at 31 March 2009	25,100
Increase in net assets	2,800

Stan has told you that he has not paid in any additional capital to the business during the year and from his bank statements and cheque counterfoils you have determined that his drawings were £15,700 during the year. We can now use the accounting equation in order to find the missing figure – profit for the year.

Increase in net assets	= capital introduced	+ profit	– drawings
£2,800	= £0	+ profit	– £15,700
Profit	= £18,500		

Activity 1

A small business has opening net assets of £31,400 and closing net assets of £40,600. The owner tells you that he has paid an additional £5,000 of capital into the business during the year and has withdrawn £10,200 of drawings for living expenses.

What profit did the business make during the year?

student notes

CASH AND BANK ACCOUNT

The use of the accounting equation allows you to calculate the total profit made in a year by a business but gives no details of how this profit is made up. This information can only be found by a more detailed consideration of the actual transactions of the business. The place to start here when trying to reconstruct the transactions is the cash and bank account movements.

HOW IT WORKS

Maria Donald runs a small business selling computer accessories largely on credit but with some cash sales. You have had access to her bank statements, paying-in slips, cheque stubs and till rolls for the year to 31 December 2008 and have been able to summarise the transactions that have taken place as follows:

Till summary

Money paid into the till – per till rolls	£4,200

Bank account summary

Receipts

Cash paid into the bank account from the till	£3,600
Cheques paid into the bank from debtors	£48,700

Payments

Cheques written to pay creditors	£37,600
Cheques written to pay expenses	£4,100

Maria tells you that she always keeps a float of £100 in the till and you discover from the bank statements that the bank balance on 1 January 2008 was £650 and on 31 December 2008 was £720. The figures that Maria cannot however tell you are how much cash she took out of the till and the bank account as drawings during the year.

By reconstructing a cash account (effectively the till account) and the bank account we will be able to determine the figures for drawings.

student notes

Cash account

	£		£
Opening balance	100	Cash paid into the bank	3,600
Money paid into the till	4,200		?
		Closing balance	100

You can see immediately that the account does not add up – there is a missing figure on the credit side. This will be the amount of cash Maria took out of the till as drawings. If we balance the account then we can find this missing figure.

Cash account

	£		£
Opening balance	100	Cash paid into the bank	3,600
Money paid into the till	4,200	Drawings	600
		Closing balance	100
	4,300		4,300

We will do the same with the bank account:

Bank account

	£		£
Opening balance	650	Cheques to creditors	37,600
Cash paid into the bank	3,600	Cheques for expenses	4,100
Cheques paid into the bank	48,700		?
		Closing balance	720

Again the account does not add up as there is a missing credit entry – the drawings from the bank account. Balance the account to find this missing figure:

Bank account

	£		£
Opening balance	650	Cheques to creditors	37,600
Cash paid into the bank	3,600	Cheques for expenses	4,100
Cheques paid into the bank	48,700	Drawings	10,530
		Closing balance	720
	52,950		52,950

student notes

Therefore Maria's total drawings for the year are:

	£
Cash drawings	600
Bank drawings	10,530
	11,130

It is often the case that the cash and bank accounts are drawn up together in a single two-column ledger account:

Cash and bank account

	Cash £	Bank £		Cash £	Bank £
Opening balance	100	650	Cash paid into bank	3,600	
Money paid in	4,200		Creditors		37,600
Cash paid in		3,600	Expenses		4,100
Cheques paid in		48,700	Drawings	600	10,530
			Closing balance	100	720
	4,300	52,950		4,300	52,950

The important point to note here is the double entry between the cash and the bank columns. The cash paid into the bank must have come out of the till therefore the bank account is debited and the cash account credited with the £3,600 of bankings.

DEBTORS AND CREDITORS ACCOUNTS

We have seen how to reconstruct the cash and bank accounts from information that we can find in the business and how to use these accounts to find a missing figure, such as drawings. Now we will reconstruct the debtors and creditors accounts in order to find the missing figures for sales and purchases.

HOW IT WORKS

Maria Donald has now provided you with information about her debtors and creditors at 31 December 2007 and 31 December 2008.

	31 Dec 2007 £	*31 Dec 2008* £
Debtors	4,500	4,800
Creditors for purchases	3,900	3,100
Creditors for expenses	400	700

student notes

From the bank account we know that £48,700 was received from debtors during the year and £37,600 was paid to creditors for purchases. Take care that you do not confuse these receipts and payments with the sales and purchases for the year. As there are opening and closing debtors and creditors these cash movements are not the sales and purchases – the cash figures must be adjusted for the opening and closing balances. This is done most easily by reconstructing a debtors and creditors account.

Debtors account

	£		£
Opening balance	4,500	Receipts from debtors	48,700
	?	Closing balance	4,800

Clearly the account has a large missing figure – this will be the sales made on credit – the double entry being a debit in the debtors account and a credit to the sales account. If we balance the account we can find the missing figure for sales on credit.

Debtors account

	£		£
Opening balance	4,500	Receipts from debtors	48,700
Sales on credit	49,000	Closing balance	4,800
	53,500		53,500

We now know that sales on credit totalled £49,000. Remember however that Maria also has a till and the cash account shows that the receipts into the till were £4,200. These must be sales for cash – therefore the total sales for the year are:

	£
Credit sales	49,000
Cash sales	4,200
	53,200

In this example the only entries in the debtors account were the opening and closing balances and the cash receipts from debtors – if there were discounts allowed to customers and/or bad debts written off they must also be entered onto the credit side of the account before finding the balance.

Now we will do the same for credit purchases using the creditors account:

Creditors account

	£		£
Payments to creditors	37,600	Opening balance	3,900
Closing balance	3,100		?

student notes

Again there is a large missing figure – the credit purchases – this can be found by balancing the account and finding the purchases as the balancing figure.

Creditors account

	£		£
Payments to creditors	37,600	Opening balance	3,900
Closing balance	3,100	Credit purchases	36,800
	40,700		40,700

The credit purchases are £36,800 – the full double entry would be a debit in the purchases account and this credit in the creditors account.

Finally we can do the same for the expenses – the payment out of the bank account was £4,100 but as there are opening and closing creditors for expenses this is not the expenses total – we need to set up an expenses account to adjust the cash payment.

Expenses account

	£		£
Payment from bank	4,100	Opening balance	400
Closing balance	700		?

The missing figure will be the expenses incurred for the period.

Expenses account

	£		£
Payment from bank	4,100	Opening balance	400
Closing balance	700	Expenses	4,400
	4,800		4,800

Activity 2

A business has opening debtors of £3,300, closing debtors of £2,800 and had receipts from debtors of £38,700 during the year. At the end of the year it was decided that one debt of £300 was to be written off.

What are the credit sales for the year?

student notes

Using these ledger accounts

As you can see each of these ledger accounts has four main entries (there may be others such as discounts but these are the main ones):

- Opening balance
- Closing balance
- Cash paid/received
- Sales/purchases/expenses

Provided that you know three of these four figures you can always determine the final one by finding the balance on the account. In these examples we had to find sales and purchases. However it is also possible that the missing figure could be the closing balance on the account or the cash movement. As long as you know the other three figures then this is possible.

Activity 3

A business has opening creditors of £4,100 and closing creditors of £3,600. The owner of the business knows that the credit purchases for the year totalled £40,000.

How much was paid to the creditors during the year?

Preparing the profit and loss account

Having reconstructed the debtors and creditors accounts we now have the key profit and loss account figures – sales and purchases as well as the expenses. The only figures now required are the opening and closing stocks and then the profit and loss account can be completed.

HOW IT WORKS

Maria now informs you that her stocks were as follows:

	31 Dec 2007	*31 Dec 2008*
	£	£
Stock	3,000	4,000

student notes

We will now prepare the profit and loss account for the year to 31 December 2008:

	£	£
Sales		53,200
Less: cost of sales		
opening stock	3,000	
purchases	36,800	
	39,800	
Less: closing stock	(4,000)	
		(35,800)
Gross profit		17,400
Less: expenses		(4,400)
Net profit		13,000

Preparing the balance sheet

The top part of the balance sheet is simply a list of the assets and liabilities of the business at the end of the year. These can be found by searching through the information and listing each of these assets and liabilities.

The bottom part of the balance sheet is made up of:

	£
Opening capital	X
Add: profit	X
	X
Less: drawings	(X)
	X

The opening capital can be found using the accounting equation (assets less liabilities = capital); if the assets and liabilities at the start of the year are totalled then this is the opening capital.

The profit figure is the net profit from the profit and loss account. The drawings may be given in the information or you may have to determine them by reconstructing the cash/bank account.

HOW IT WORKS

student notes

If we look back at the information that Maria has given us we can first list the assets and liabilities at the start of the year to give the opening capital balance.

	31 Dec 2007
	£
Cash	100
Bank	650
Debtors	4,500
Creditors for purchases	(3,900)
Creditors for expenses	(400)
Stock	3,000
Opening capital	3,950

We have the profit figure from the profit and loss account and the drawings were calculated from the cash and bank accounts. Now we can list the assets and liabilities at the end of the year and prepare the balance sheet.

Balance sheet at 31 December 2008

	£	£
Current assets:		
Stock		4,000
Debtors		4,800
Bank		720
Cash		100
		9,620
Current liabilities:		
Creditors for purchases	3,100	
Creditors for expenses	700	
		(3,800)
		5,820
Opening capital		3,950
Add: profit		13,000
		16,950
Less: drawings		11,130
		5,820

The accounts for Maria have now been completed by piecing together the information that we do have and using the three techniques learned so far:

- Using the accounting equation
- Reconstructing the bank and cash accounts
- Reconstructing debtors and creditors accounts

student notes

USE OF MARK UPS AND MARGINS

In a retail organisation the owner is likely to know how he prices his goods. He will normally take the cost of the goods and add some percentage of profit margin in order to reach the selling price of the goods. The percentage that he uses can be useful in an incomplete records situation in finding either the sales figure or the cost of sales.

Profit mark up

A PROFIT MARK UP is a percentage of the cost of the goods that is added to the cost in order to reach the sales price.

HOW IT WORKS

A retailer uses a 20% mark up on cost. The cost of the goods he is selling is £150. What is their selling price?

This can be determined using percentages first which is known as the COST STRUCTURE:

	%
Sales	
Cost	
Gross profit	

As this is a mark up on cost the cost figure is put in as 100% – the mark up is 20% therefore the sales percentage is 120%.

	%
Sales	120
Cost	100
Gross profit	20

Now we add in the figure that we know for cost:

	%	£
Sales	120	
Cost	100	150
Gross profit	20	

If this £150 is equivalent to 100% then the sales of 120% must be:

$$£150 \times \frac{120}{100} = £180$$

student notes

We can now complete the figures for sales and gross profit:

	%	£
Sales	120	180
Cost	100	150
Gross profit	20	30

Alternatively you could have been told that the sales were £180 and required to find the cost of these sales. Using the cost structure the sales figure of £180 is equivalent to 120% therefore the cost can be calculated as:

$$£180 \times \frac{100}{120} = £150$$

Activity 4

A business operates with a mark up on cost of 30%. The sales for a period were £1,950.

What was the cost of those sales?

Profit margin

A PROFIT MARGIN (or SALES MARGIN) is the percentage of gross profit made expressed as a percentage of the sales figure.

HOW IT WORKS

A retailer operates with a gross profit margin (or sales margin) of 30%. His sales for the period are £1,200. What is the cost of those sales?

Set up the cost structure – this time as a profit margin is a percentage of sales value then the sales figure will be 100%:

	%
Sales	100
Cost	70
Gross profit	30

If the gross profit is to be 30% of sales then the cost of the sales must be 70%.

student notes

Now put in the figure that you know:

	%	£
Sales	100	1,200
Cost	70	
Gross profit	30	

Use the cost structure to determine the missing figures. If sales are £1,200 then the cost must be:

$$£1{,}200 \times \frac{70}{100} = £840$$

	%	£
Sales	100	1,200
Cost	70	840
Gross profit	30	360

Alternatively you might have been told that the cost of sales was £840 and asked to find the sales figure:

$$£840 \times \frac{100}{70} = £1{,}200$$

Activity 5

A business operates with a gross profit margin of 40%. The cost of the goods sold in a period was £2,000.

What were the sales for the period?

APPROACH TO AN EXAMPLE

Incomplete records problems can at first appear to be very daunting, however with practice you will become used to the approach that you must have and the techniques to use.

Remember that you have a variety of techniques to choose from:

- accounting equation
- cash/bank account
- debtors/creditors accounts
- mark up/margin

In an assessment or exam if you are given information about the mark up or profit margin then you will need to use it – therefore if you think you can find

student notes

the sales or cost of sales figures without the cost structure you have gone wrong somewhere!

You need a clear and logical approach to these questions and the following steps may be useful:

Step 1 Read through the example to get a feel for the information that you have been given.

Step 2 Decide whether or not you need to reconstruct the cash and/or bank account – in many assessment or exam examples you are given a neat summary of the bank transactions and therefore there is no need to include this in your answer.

Step 3 Set up the debtors and creditors accounts and put in the opening and closing balances.

Step 4 Set up the cost structure in percentages if you are given a mark up or a margin.

Step 5 Head up one sheet of paper for your profit and loss account and another for your balance sheet.

Step 6 Work carefully through the example entering each figure either in the working ledger accounts or onto the profit and loss account or balance sheet as appropriate. Take special care with the cash and bank transactions – this is only one side of the double entry and the other side of the transaction must also be entered – for example a payment of the electricity bill in the bank account must be entered as an expense in the profit and loss account, and the receipt of money from debtors must be entered as a credit in the debtors account.

Step 7 When you have entered as many figures as you can take a look at what you have in the working ledger accounts, cost structure and profit and loss account and balance sheet in order to determine how you can find the figures that are missing.

student notes

HOW IT WORKS

Jack Eagle runs a small business selling his goods on credit at a gross profit margin of 25%. He does not keep proper accounting records but has produced a summary of his bank statements for the year to 31 March 2009.

Bank statement summary

	£
Opening balance – 1 April 2008	380
Receipt from loan	5,000
Receipts from debtors	61,200
	66,580
Payments for expenses	(2,100)
Other payments	(54,900)
Closing balance – 31 March 2009	9,580

The figure for other payments is for both payments to credit suppliers and drawings but Jack does not know how much his drawings were in the year.

The loan was taken out on 1 January 2009 at an interest rate of 6% and is repayable in 2012.

Jack has also provided you with figures for his assets and liabilities at the start and end of the year:

	1 April 2008	*31 Mar 2009*
	£	£
Fixed asset cost	10,000	10,000
Stock	4,100	3,800
Debtors	5,200	4,000
Creditors	2,100	2,900
Prepayment of expenses	100	200

The fixed asset originally cost £10,000 on 1 April 2007 and is being depreciated on the straight line basis over a ten year life.

You now need to prepare the profit and loss account for the year ended 31 March 2009 and a balance sheet at that date.

Set up the debtors and creditors control accounts and the cost structure

student notes

Debtors account

	£		£

Creditors account

	£		£

Expenses account

	£		£

Cost structure:

	%
Sales	
Cost of sales	
Gross profit	

Work through the example entering figures as you come across them

The cost structure is a gross profit margin of 25% therefore the sales must be 100%

Cost structure:

	%
Sales	100
Cost of sales	75
Gross profit	25

Debtors account

	£		£
Opening balance	5,200	Bank – receipts	61,200
		Closing balance	4,000

Expenses account

	£		£
Opening balance	100		
Bank – payments	2,100	Closing balance	200

student notes

Creditors account

	£		£
		Opening balance	2,100
Closing balance	2,900		

Profit and loss account for the year ended 31 March 2009

	£	£
Sales		
Less: cost of sales		
Opening stock	4,100	
Purchases		
Less: closing stock	(3,800)	

Now look at the information you have:

- The debtors account has three entries therefore the missing figure of sales can be determined:

Debtors account

	£		£
Opening balance	5,200	Bank – receipts	61,200
Sales	60,000	Closing balance	4,000
	65,200		65,200

- The creditors account has only two entries therefore no balance can be found – however as you know the sales figure this can be entered into the cost structure to find the cost of sales

Cost structure:

	%	£	
Sales	100	60,000	As sales are £60,000
Cost of sales	75	45,000	cost must be
Gross profit	25	15,000	£60,000 x 75/100
			= £45,000

Take care with this cost of sales figure – it is cost of sales not purchases. However, if you now go to the profit and loss account and apply the opening and closing stock figures to the cost of sales the balancing figure is the purchases for the year.

student notes

Profit and loss account for the year ended 31 March 2009

	£	£
Sales		60,000
Less: cost of sales		
Opening stock	4,100	
Purchases (balancing figure)	44,700	
	48,800	
Less: closing stock	(3,800)	
		45,000
Gross profit		15,000

- The purchases figure of £44,700 has now been found and must be entered as a credit in the creditors account:

Creditors account

	£		£
		Opening balance	2,100
Closing balance	2,900	Purchases	44,700

- The creditors account now has three figures so the remaining balance – the payments to creditors can be found:

Creditors account

	£		£
Payment to creditors	43,900	Opening balance	2,100
Closing balance	2,900	Purchases	44,700
	46,800		46,800

- Remember from the bank summary that the total for other payments of £54,900 is made up of the payments to creditors and the drawings – as we now know the payments to creditors the drawings can be determined:

	£
Total payment	54,900
Less: payment to creditors	43,900
Drawings	11,000

- The expenses account has three entries and therefore the expenses figure for the profit and loss account can be found as the balancing figure:

Expenses account

	£		£
Opening balance	100	Profit and loss a/c	2,000
Bank – payments	2,100	Closing balance	200
	2,200		2,200

student notes

It is not always necessary to open a ledger account for expenses – instead the working for the figure could be shown on the face of the profit and loss account as follows:

Expenses (2,100 + 100 – 200)	2,000

The opening prepayment must be added in to the bank payment figure as this is part of this year's expense but the closing prepayment must be deducted as this is part of next year's expense.

The profit and loss account can now be completed:

- Do not forget to include the depreciation of the fixed asset as part of the expenses for the year
- We also need to accrue loan interest for the three months from 1 January

Profit and loss account for the year ended 31 March 2009

	£	£
Sales		60,000
Less: cost of sales		
Opening stock	4,100	
Purchases (balancing figure)	44,700	
	48,800	
Less: closing stock	(3,800)	
		45,000
Gross profit		15,000
Less: expenses		
Expenses	2,000	
Loan interest (£5,000 × 6% × 3/12)	75	
Depreciation (£10,000 × 10%)	1,000	
		3,075
Net profit		11,925

Finally the balance sheet should be prepared:

- For this we will need the opening capital therefore using the accounting equation a list of all the opening assets and liabilities is made:

	£
Bank	380
Fixed asset (10,000 – 1,000)	9,000
Stock	4,100
Debtors	5,200
Creditors	(2,100)
Prepayment	100
Opening capital	16,680

student notes

Balance sheet as at 31 March 2009

	£	£	£
Fixed asset (10,000 – 2,000)			8,000
Current assets:			
Stock		3,800	
Debtors		4,000	
Prepayment		200	
Bank		9,580	
		17,580	
Current liabilities:			
Creditors	2,900		
Accrual – loan interest	75		
		(2,975)	
			14,605
			22,605
Non–current liability			
Loan			(5,000)
			17,605
Opening capital			16,680
Add: profit			11,925
			28,605
Less: drawings			(11,000)
			17,605

Activity 6

A business has made sales for a period of £49,000 but the purchases figure is unknown. The sales have been made at a mark up of 40% and opening and closing stocks were £3,000 and £5,000 respectively.

What were the purchases for the period?

MISSING STOCK FIGURE

A final situation that you may come across in assessments or exams is a missing figure for closing stock – for example there may have been a fire or flood that destroyed the stock at the year end before it was counted and valued or indeed it may have been stolen.

In order to find the missing stock figure it must be found as the balancing figure in the profit and loss account – therefore opening stock, sales and purchases must be known and the cost structure used to find the cost of sales – the only figure missing will be the closing stock.

student notes

HOW IT WORKS

Janis Harvey runs a small retail business with a mark up on cost of 30%. Unfortunately her entire stock at her year end has been stolen before it could be counted and valued. However you have already been able to determine the following figures:

Sales for the year	£52,000
Purchases for the year	£37,000
Opening stock	£5,000

What was the value of her closing stock?

We can use the cost structure to determine the total for cost of sales:

	%	£
Sales	130	52,000
Cost of sales	100	40,000
Gross profit	30	12,000

Cost of sales $= £52{,}000 \times \frac{100}{130}$
$= £40{,}000$

The profit and loss account can then be set up:

	£	£
Sales		52,000
Less: cost of sales		
Opening stock	5,000	
Purchases	37,000	
	42,000	
Less: closing stock	?	
		40,000
Gross profit		12,000

In order to reach a cost of sales figure of £40,000 the closing stock must have been valued at £2,000.

Type of organisation

In this chapter we have used sole traders in all of the examples for incomplete records. However in an assessment or exam an incomplete records problem could be set in the context of a partnership. However the principles and the techniques are exactly the same and should simply be applied to the details you are given in the assessment or exam.

Activity 7

A partnership sells their goods at a mark up of 50%. Sales in the year were £10,500 and the purchases were £7,300. The opening stocks were £1,300 but the entire closing stock has been stolen.

What was the value of the stock stolen?

CHAPTER OVERVIEW

- many sole traders and other small businesses do not keep full accounting records – this is what is known as incomplete records
- there are a variety of techniques that can be used to piece together the information required for a profit and loss account and balance sheet even if the accounting records are incomplete
- the opening capital balance can be found by applying the accounting equation: assets – liabilities = capital
- a further use of the accounting equation is in the fact that the increase in net assets = capital introduced + profit – drawings; this can be used to find a missing figure such as profit or drawings
- in some cases the first task will be to reconstruct the cash account and bank account – these are often shown together in a two column ledger account
- the cash account and bank account can be balanced to find a missing figure such as drawings for the period
- debtors and creditors accounts can also be reconstructed to find missing figures – there are four main entries in these accounts – opening balance, closing balance, cash movement, sales/purchases – if three of the figures are known then the fourth can be found by balancing the account
- mark ups or profit margins in a retail business can be used by setting up the cost structure – this can then be used to find sales if cost of sales is known or to find cost of sales if sales are known
- all of the techniques covered may need to be used in an assessment or exam – a clear, logical approach is required together with plenty of practice of incomplete records problems
- the cost structure and the profit and loss account can also be used to find the value of any missing stock at the end of the accounting period

KEY WORDS

Incomplete records accounting records which are not a full set of primary records and ledger accounts

Net assets total of the assets of a business minus the liabilities

Profit mark up the percentage added to cost of goods to arrive at their selling price

Cost structure the relationship in percentage terms between sales, cost of sales and gross profit

Profit margin the percentage of gross profit expressed as a percentage of sales. Also called sales margin

HOW MUCH HAVE YOU LEARNED?

1 A business has made a profit for the year of £17,800. The opening net assets were £58,900 and the closing net assets were £71,400. The owner had paid in an additional £10,000 of capital during the year.

What were the drawings during the year?

2 A business had creditors on 30 April 2009 of £4,700 and on 1 May 2008 of £3,800. During the year payments were made to creditors of £56,900 and settlement discounts were received of £1,300.

What were the purchases for the year?

3 At 1 April 2008 a business's bank balance showed a balance of £1,020. During the year takings of £48,700 were paid into the bank account and payments for purchases were made of £24,600 and for expenses of £12,500. The closing bank balance was £890.

What were the owners drawings out of the bank account for the year ending 31 March 2009?

4 A business sells its goods at a mark up of 45% on cost. The sales for the year were £184,150.

What was the cost of sales for the year?

5 A business operates with an average profit margin of 35%. The cost of sales during the year was £130,000.

What were the sales for the year?

6 A small business has asked you to help in the preparation of a profit and loss account and balance sheet for the year ended 31 March 2009. A summary of the bank statements for the year is given below:

	£
Receipts from debtors	108,500
Payments to creditors for purchases	74,400
Payments for expenses	12,600

You are also given the opening and closing figures for the assets and liabilities, however the owner does not know what the closing debtors figure is.

	1 April 2008	*31 March 2009*
	£	£
Bank	430	7,200
Stock	7,600	6,100
Debtors	10,400	not known
Creditors	6,200	8,300
Accruals of expenses	800	600

The business also has fixed assets with a net book value of £12,600 at 1 April 2008. It has been decided that £1,600 of depreciation should be charged for the year to 31 March 2009.

The sales are made at a mark up of 40%.

Prepare the profit and loss account and balance sheet for the business for the year ended 31 March 2009.

7 A business has had all of its closing stock destroyed by a flood at the end of the year and needs a valuation in order to put in an insurance claim. Thc information that is known about the business's transactions for the year are:

Sales	£240,000
Purchases	£162,000
Opening stock	£12,000
Profit margin	30%

What is the value of the closing stock that was destroyed?

chapter 17: INTERNATIONAL ACCOUNTING STANDARDS

chapter coverage

Since June 2006, Unit 11 Drafting Financial Statements has been examined on the basis of International Accounting Standards. However, Unit 5 will continue to be assessed on UK Accounting Standards. Therefore you may find this chapter useful as a bridge between Units 5 and 11.

The topics we shall cover are:

- what is meant by International Accounting Standards
- the differences between UK and international terminology
- how UK and International Accounting Standards relevant to Unit 5 compare

student notes

WHAT ARE INTERNATIONAL ACCOUNTING STANDARDS?

International Accounting Standards (IASs) are set by the International Accounting Standards Board. IASs have been adopted by the European Union and affected companies in all the member states will have to submit consolidated accounts under IAS.

As a result the UK Accounting Standards Board has been issuing revised accounting standards that comply with IAS and use international terminology. However there are still a significant number of differences between UK and International Accounting Standards.

GLOSSARY OF UK/INTERNATIONAL ACCOUNTING TERMINOLOGY

UK	International
Sales ledger	Accounts receivable/ Receivables ledger
Purchase ledger/bought ledger	Accounts payable/ Payables ledger
Balance sheet *Balance sheet items*	Statement of financial position
Fixed assets	Non-current assets
Tangible fixed assets	Property, plant and equipment
Intangible fixed assets	Intangible non-current assets
Stock	Inventory
Debtors	Receivables
Creditors	Payables
Long term liabilities	Non-current liabilities
Debenture	Loan stock
Capital and reserves	Equity
Profit and loss account (in the balance sheet)/ Accumulated profits	Retained earnings
Profit and loss account items	
Profit and loss account	Statement of comprehensive income
Turnover/sales	Revenue
Taxation	Tax expense
Other items	
Statement of total recognised gains and losses	Statement of recognised income and expense

student notes

COMPARISON OF UK AND INTERNATIONAL ACCOUNTING STANDARDS COVERED IN UNIT 5

UK standard	**International Accounting Standard**
SSAP 5 – VAT	No equivalent
SSAP 9 – Stock valuation: Valuation: ■ Cost of purchase ■ Costs of Conversion FIFO or weighted average preferred LIFO not normally allowed	IAS 2 *Inventories* Valuation: ■ Costs of purchase ■ Costs of conversion ■ Other costs FIFO or weighted average allowed LIFO not permitted
FRS 15 – Depreciation provisions only	IAS 16 *Property, plant and equipment* – no significant differences regarding depreciation
FRS 18 – Accounting policies Key concepts ■ Going concern ■ Accruals	IAS 1 *Presentation of financial statements* Important assumptions ■ Going concern ■ Accrual basis of accounting ■ Consistency of presentation ■ Materiality and aggregation (small items can be aggregated) ■ Offsetting (not allowed) ■ Prudence ■ Substance over form

ANSWERS TO CHAPTER ACTIVITIES

CHAPTER 1 Revision of how accounting systems work

A debtor

A credit note

Purchases day book

Subsidiary ledger – the purchases ledger

CHAPTER 2 Revision of double entry bookkeeping

the bank balance decreases
the creditor also decreases

a)

Debtors account

Date	Details	£	Date	Details	£
4 Mar	Sales	240			

Sales account

Date	Details	£	Date	Details	£
			4 Mar	Debtors	2,400

b)

Purchase account

Date	Details	£	Date	Details	£
4 Mar	Creditors	1,800			

Creditors account

Date	Details	£	Date	Details	£
			4 Mar	Purchases	1,800

c), d)

Telephone account

Date	Details	£	Date	Details	£
4 Mar	Creditors	1,800			

Bank account

Date	Details	£	Date	Details	£
4 Mar	Bank	500			

Drawings account

Date	Details	£	Date	Details	£
			4 Mar	Telephone	140
			4 Mar	Drawings	500

3

Purchases account

Date	Details	£	Date	Details	£
1 Feb	Bank	680			
8 Feb	Creditor	1,000	28 Feb	Balance c/d	1,680
		1,680			1,680
1 Mar	Balance b/d	1,680			

Sales account

Date	Details	£	Date	Details	£
			12 Feb	Bank	1,380
			17 Feb	Debtors	900
28 Feb	Balance c/d	3,840	26 Feb	Bank	1,560
		3,840			3,840
			1 Mar	Balance b/d	3,840

Creditors account

Date	Details	£	Date	Details	£
22 Feb	Bank	600	8 Feb	Purchases	1,000
28 Feb	Balance c/d	400			
		1,000			1,000
			1 Mar	Balance b/d	400

Debtors account

Date	Details	£	Date	Details	£
17 Feb	Sales	900	25 Feb	Bank	700
			28 Feb	Balance c/d	200
		900			900
1 Mar	Balance b/d	200			

4 Debit Discounts allowed account
Credit Sales ledger control account

5
- To serve as a check on the correctness of the double entry
- As a basis for preparing the financial statements

CHAPTER 3 Introduction to financial statements

1

	Debits £	*Credits* £	*Description*
Rent	480		Expense
Motor van	7,400		Asset
Creditors		1,900	Liability
Gas	210		Expense
Discounts received		50	Income
Carriage outwards	310		Expense
Sales		40,800	Income
Opening stock	2,100		Expense
Loan		2,000	Liability
Electricity	330		Expense
Capital		7,980	Liability
Telephone	640		Expense
Discount allowed	60		Expense
Purchases	22,600		Expense
Debtors	3,400		Asset
Wages	9,700		Expense
Drawings	4,000		Reduction of liability
Carriage inwards	220		Expense
Motor expenses	660		Expense
Bank	620		Asset
	52,730	52,730	

2

	£	£
Sales		136,700
Less: cost of sales		
Opening stock	11,300	
Purchases	97,500	
	108,800	
Less: closing stock	(10,600)	
		98,200
Gross profit		38,500

	Debits	*Credits*	*Profit and loss a/c*
	£	£	*or balance sheet?*
Rent	480		P&L
Motor van	7,400		Balance sheet
Creditors		1,900	Balance sheet
Gas	210		P&L
Discounts received		50	P&L
Carriage outwards	310		P&L
Sales		40,800	P&L
Opening stock	2,100		P&L
Loan		2,000	Balance sheet
Electricity	330		P&L
Capital		7,980	Balance sheet
Telephone	640		P&L
Discount allowed	60		P&L
Purchases	22,600		P&L
Debtors	3,400		Balance sheet
Wages	9,700		P&L
Drawings	4,000		Balance sheet
Carriage inwards	220		P&L
Motor expenses	660		P&L
Bank	620		Balance sheet
	52,730	52,730	

A debtor owes your business £10,000 at the year end but is rumoured to be in financial difficulties. At the year end **relevant** information is that the business has a debt of £10,000 but the **reliability** of this information will only be known some time after the year end as and when the debtor pays.

CHAPTER 4 Value Added Tax

Output VAT is VAT charged on sales
Input VAT is VAT on purchases and expenses

VAT account

	£		£
Input VAT	10,500	Output VAT	14,700

Debit	Purchases account	£14,800
Debit	VAT account	£2,590
Credit	Creditors account	£17,390

The input VAT incurred on the goods and services purchased cannot be reclaimed from HM Revenue & Customs and therefore must be included as part of the cost of the goods and services.

CHAPTER 5 Capital expenditure

1 The £15,000 of expenditure on Machine A is capital expenditure as it is a major improvement of the asset. The £4,000 repair costs of Machine B would be treated as revenue expenditure as this is just the running costs of the machine.

2

Plant and machinery account

	£		£
Creditors	17,000		
Wages	1,400		

Creditors account

	£		£
		Plant and machinery	17,000

Wages account

	£		£
		Plant and machinery	1,400

3

Date	*Account*	*Ref*	*Debit*	*Credit*
			£	£
	Motor vehicles		78,800	
	Motor expenses		800	
	Bank account			79,600
			79,600	79,600

Being purchase of four cars for the sales force

CHAPTER 6 Depreciation of fixed assets

1 NBV = Cost – depreciation to date
NBV = £8,000 – 3,000 = £5,000

2 Depreciation charge $= \dfrac{£22,000 - 9,000}{4}$

= £3,250 per annum

NBV = £22,000 – (2 x 3,250)
= £15,500

3

	£
Original cost	22,000
Year 1 depreciation 22,000 x 20%	4,400
NBV at end of year 1	17,600
Year 2 depreciation 17,600 x 20%	3,520
NBV at end of year 2	14,080
Year 3 depreciation 14,080 x 20%	2,816
NBV at end of year 3	11,264
Year 4 depreciation 11,264 x 20%	2,253
NBV	9,011

4

Depreciation expenser

	£		£
Provision for depreciation	24,000		

Provision for depreciation

	£		£
		Depreciation expense	24,000

Profit and loss account

Expenses:	£
Depreciation expense	24,000

Balance sheet

Fixed assets:	*Cost*	*Accumulated depreciation*	*NBV*
	£	£	£
Machinery	120,000	24,000	96,000

CHAPTER 7 Disposal of fixed assets

1 a)

	£
Original cost	11,200
2007 depreciation 11,200 x 30%	3,360
NBV 31 Dec 2007	7,840
2008 depreciation 7,840 x 30%	2,352
NBV 31 Dec 2008	5,488

b)

NBV at 31 December 2008	5,488
Disposal proceeds	5,000
Loss on disposal	488

c)

Motor car cost account

	£		£
1 Jan 2007 Bank	11,200	31 Dec 2008 Disposal	11,200

Motor car provision for depreciation account

	£		£
31 Dec 2007 Balance c/d	3,360	31 Dec 2007 Depreciation	3,360
31 Dec 2008 Disposal	5,712	1 Jan 2008 Balance b/d	3,360
		31 Dec 2008 Depreciation	2,352
	5,712		5,712

Disposal account

	£		£
31 Dec 2008 Motor car at cost	11,200	31 Dec 2008 Motor car depreciation	5,712
		31 Dec 2008 Proceeds	5,000
		31 Dec 2008 P&L – loss	488
	11,200		11,200

2

Motor car account

	£		£
1 Mar 2006 Bank	10,000	31 May 2008 Disposal	10,000
31 May 2008 Bank	6,200		
31 May 2008 Disposal	4,800	31 May 2008 Balance c/d	11,000
	21,000		21,000
1 June 2008 Balance b/d	11,000		

Disposal account

	£		£
31 May 2008 Disposal	5,500	31 May 2008 Balance b/d	5,500

Disposal account

	£		£
31 May 2008 Cost	10,000	31 May 2008 Depreciation	5,500
31 May 2008 P&L – profit on disposal	300	31 May 2008 Part exchange allowance	4,800
	10,300		10,300

3

FIXED ASSET REGISTER

Fixed asset number	24116									
Description	Fork lift truck XC355									
Location	Warehouse									
Supplier	Leyland Machinery									
Date	*Cost*	*Expected life (years)*	*Estimated scrap value*	*Depreciation method*	*Depreciation rate*	*Depreciation charge for the year*	*Provision at end of the year*	*Net book value at end of year*	*Disposal proceeds*	*Profit or loss on disposal*
	£		£			£	£	£	£	£
2005										
1 May	34,000	4	6,250	Reducing balance	30%					
31 Dec						10,200	10,200	23,800		
2006										
31 Dec						7,140	17,340	16,660		
2007										
31 Dec						4,998	22,338	11,662		
2008										
20 Mar									10,500	(1,162)

CHAPTER 8 Accruals and prepayments

1
- the expense in the profit and loss account should be increased to £1,370
- the balance sheet should show a current liability, an accrual for £260

2

Telephone account

	£		£
31 Dec Balance b/d	2,600		
31 Dec Accruals	480	31 Dec Profit and loss a/c	3,080
	3,080		3,080

Accruals account

	£		£
		31 Dec Telephone	480

3

Rent account

	£		£
31 Dec Balance b/d	3,200	31 Dec Profit and loss a/c	2,900
		31 Dec Profit and loss a/c	300
	3,200		3,200
1 Jan Prepayment b/d	300		

4
- The rental income in the profit and loss account must be reduced to £2,600
- The balance sheet will show a current liability, rental received in advance, of £800

CHAPTER 9 Bad and doubtful debts

1	Debit	Bad debts expense account	£976
	Credit	Debtors account	£976
2	Debit	Bank account	£1,000
	Credit	Debtors account	£1,000
	Debit	Debtors account	£1,000
	Credit	Bad debts expense account	£1,000

3

Bad debts expense account

	£		£
Debtors	680		
Provision for doubtful debts	630	Profit and loss account	1,310
	1,310		1,310

Debtors account

	£		£
Balance b/d	21,680	Bad debts expense	680
		Balance c/d	21,000
	21,860		21,680
Balance b/d	21,000		

Provision for doubtful debts account

	£		£
		Bad debts expense	630

4

Debtors account

	£		£
31 Dec 2008 Balance b/d	60,000	31 Dec 2008 Bad debts	2,400
		31 Dec 2008 Balance c/d	57,600
	60,000		60,000
31 Dec 2008 Balance b/d	57,600		

Bad debts expense account

	£		£
31 Dec 2008 Debtors	680		
31 Dec 2008 Provision for doubtful debts	630	31 Dec 2008 Profit and loss a/c	1,310
	1,310		1,310

Provision for doubtful debts account

	£		£
31 Dec 2008 Balance c/d	1,728	31 Dec 2008 balance b/d	1,500
		31 Dec 2008 Bad debts	228
	1,728		1,728
		31 Dec 2008 Balance b/d	1,728

CHAPTER 10 Control account reconciliations

1 DR Sales ledger control account with the gross amount
CR VAT account with the VAT
CR Sales account with the net amount

2 DR Purchases account with the net amount
DR VAT account with the VAT
CR Purchases ledger control account with the gross amount

3 DR Bad debts expense account
CR Debtors account (or sales ledger control account)

4 DR Purchases ledger control account £500
CR Sales ledger control account £500

5 The sales ledger control account but not the individual balances in the subsidiary ledger.

6 CR Sales ledger control account £120

The other side of the entry would be a debit to the discounts allowed account.

7 If the invoice was entered on the wrong side of the account then it was debited to the account. To correct this the creditor's account must be credited with twice the amount of the invoice in order to remove the debit and put in place the credit. Therefore the list of creditors balances would increase by £700. No adjustment would be made to the purchase ledger control account.

CHAPTER 11 Errors and the suspense account

1 A transposition error

2 Error of commission

3 £1,809 – credit balance

4

Debit	Telephone account	£330
Credit	Electricity account	£330
Debit	Suspense account	£800
Credit	Discounts received (in the trial balance)	£800

5

Journal number: 01276

Date: 7 January 2009

Authorised by:

Account	*Reference*	*Debit* £	*Credit* £
Telephone		330	
Electricity			330

Being correction of the misposting of the telephone payment

Journal number: 01277

Date: 7 January 2009

Authorised by:

Account	*Reference*	*Debit* £	*Credit* £
Suspense		800	
Discounts received			800

Being correction in the trial balance of discounts received listing

6

Journal number: 1245

Date: 31 January 2009

Authorised by:

Account	*Reference*	*Debit* £	*Credit* £
Depreciation expense		2,450	
Provision for depreciation			2,450

Being annual charge for machinery depreciation

CHAPTER 12 Stock

1 Cost = £13.80
Net realisable value = £14.00 – 0.50
= £13.50

Each unit should be valued at £13.50, the lower of cost and net realisable value

2 12 May – sale – 70 units @ £3.50

30 May – sale – 80 units 30 units @ £3.50
50 units @ £4.00

Closing stock – 50 units @ £4.00 = £200.00

3 As a current asset.

CHAPTER 13 From trial balance to final accounts – sole trader

1

	£
Opening capital	23,400
Add: profit for the year	14,500
Less: drawings for the year	(12,200)
Closing capital	25,700

2 Debit Drawings £400
Credit Purchases £400

3 Drawings are a reduction of the amount owed by the business to the owner. Therefore they are deducted from capital in the balance sheet rather than being shown as an expense in the profit and loss account.

4 a) Debit Purchases returns
Credit Profit and loss account

b) Debit Profit and loss account
Credit Insurance

c) No adjustment required as this is a balance sheet item.

CHAPTER 14 The extended trial balance

1
- List all of the ledger balances as debits and credits in the first two columns of the extended trial balance
- Total the trial balance, check your totals and insert a suspense account balance if you are sure that the trial balance does not balance
- Clear the suspense account balance by putting through the correcting double entries in the adjustments column
- Enter the double entries for any year end adjustments such as depreciation charges, bad and doubtful debts and accruals and prepayments in the adjustment columns
- Enter the closing stock figure in the adjustment columns and then total the adjustment columns to ensure that the debits equal the credits
- Total each account line and extend it into the correct debit or credit column in the profit and loss account or balance sheet
- Total the profit and loss account columns – put the balancing figure into the debit or credit column as appropriate – if the figure is in the debit column then this must be put in the credit column of the balance sheet and vice versa
- Total the balance sheet columns which should now balance

2 This means that a profit has been made and the other entry is a credit to the balance sheet column.

CHAPTER 15 Partnerships

	£
Profit share	18,000
Less: drawings	(13,000)
Current account balance (credit balance)	5,000

Appropriation account

	£		£
Salary – Ginger	8,000	Net profit	71,840
Interest on capital			
Petra (40,000 × 6%)	2,400		
Ginger (24,000 × 6%)	1,440		
Balance shared 2:1	60,000		
Balance b/d	71,840		71,840

Current account – Petra

	£		£
Balance b/d	1,800	Interest	2,400
Drawings	38,000	Profit share	40,000
Balance c/d	2,600		
	42,400		42,400
		Balance b/d	2,600

Current account – Ginger

	£		£
Drawings	25,000	Balance b/d	500
		Salary	8,000
		Interest	1,440
Balance c/d	4,950	Profit share	20,000
	29,940		29,940
		Balance b/d	4,940

3 Appropriation account

		£	£
Net profit			71,840
Salary	Ginger		(8,000)
Interest on capital	Petra	2,400	
	Ginger	1,440	
			(3,840)
Balance to share in profit sharing ratio			60,000
Profit share	Petra (2/3)		40,000
	Ginger (1/3)		20,000
			60,000

4

		Debit	Credit
		£	£
Profit and loss account		180,000	
Current accounts	Jane (£180,000 x 4/9)		80,000
	Mike (£180,000 x 3/9)		60,000
	Simon (£180,000 x 2/9)		40,000

5 Journal entries

		Debit	Credit
		£	£
Appropriation account		75,000	
Current account	Frank (5,000 + 1,500 + 33,500)(W)		40,000
	Butch (1,500 + 33,500)(W)		35,000

Being profit share for the year

	Debit	Credit
Current account – Frank	34,000	
Current account – Butch	30,000	
Drawings account – Frank		34,000
Drawings account – Butch		30,000

Being drawings for the year

Working

Appropriation account

		£	£
Net profit			75,000
Salary – Frank			(5,000)
Interest on capital –	Frank (30,000 x 5%)	1,500	
	Butch (30,000 x 5%)	1,500	
			(3,000)
			67,000
Profit share	Frank		33,500
	Butch		33,500
			67,000

6

Debit	Bank account	£25,000
Credit	Howard's capital account	£25,000

7

Capital accounts

	Nick	Sue	Trish		Nick	Sue	Trish
	£	£	£		£	£	£
				Ba b/d	50,000	40,000	30,000
				Current a/c		2,000	
Goodwill	10,000		5,000	Goodwill	5,000	5,000	5,000
Bank		10,000					
Loan		37,000					
Bal c/d	45,000		30,000				
	55,000	47,000	35,000		55,000	47,000	35,000
				Bal b/d	45,000		30,000

8 **Pat and Ray – Appropriation account for the year ended 31 December 2008**

	1/1/08 – 31/5/08	*1/6/08 – 31/12/08*	*Total*
	£	£	£
Profit available for distribution			
£48,000 × 5/12	20,000		
£48,000 × 7/12		28,000	48,000
Profit share			
Pat 2/3 / 1/2	(13,333)	(14,000)	(17,333)
Ray 1/3 / 1/2	(6,667)	(14,000)	(20,667)
	0	0	0

Current accounts

	Pat	Ray		Sue	Trish
	£	£		£	£
Bal b/d		1,200	Ba b/d	7,400	
			Profit	13,333	6,667
Drawings	32,000	19,000	Profit	14,000	14,000
Bal c/d	2,733	467			
	34,733	20,667		34,733	20,667
			Bal b/d	2,733	467

CHAPTER 16 Incomplete records

1

	£
Opening net assets	31,400
Closing net assets	40,600
Increase in net assets	9,200

Increase in net assets	=	capital introduced + profit – drawings
9,200	=	5,000 + profit – 10,200
Profit	=	£14,400

2

Debtors account

	£		£
Opening balance	3,300	Receipts	38,700
		Bad debt written off	300
Credit sales (bal fig)	38,500	Closing balance	2,800
	41,800		41,800

Credit sales = £38,500

3

Creditors account

	£		£
Payments (bal fig)	40,500	Opening balance	4,100
Clsoing balance	3,600	Purchases	40,000
	44,100		44,100

4

	%	£
Sales	130	1,950
Cost	100	1,500
Gross profit	30	450

5

	%	£
Sales	100	3,333
Cost	60	2,000
Gross profit	40	1,333

	%	£
Sales	140	49,000
Cost of sales	100	35,000
Gross profit	40	14,000

	£	£x
Sales		49,000
Less: cost of sales		
Opening stock	3,000	
Purchases (bal fig)	37,000	
	40,000	
Less: closing stock	(5,000)	
		35,000
Gross profit		14,000

	%	£
Sales	150	10,500
Cost of sales	100	7,000
Gross profit	50	3,500

	£	£
Sales		10,500
Less: Cost of sales		
Opening stock	1,300	
Purchases	7,300	
	8,600	
Less: closing stock	?	7,000
Gross profit		3,500

The closing stock must have been valued at £1,600.

HOW MUCH HAVE YOU LEARNED? – ANSWERS

CHAPTER 1 Revision of how accounting systems work

1 There are three main aims of an effective accounting system. First it is necessary that all of the transactions of a business are recorded in the system. Second there must be checks to ensure that the transactions are recorded correctly and finally the accounting system must be able to produce financial statements for the business whenever required.

2 Bank giro credit

3 a) Sales invoice
b) Credit note received
c) The cheque itself or a remittance list
d) The cheque counterfoil
e) The petty cash voucher

4 a) Cash receipts book
b) Purchases returns day book or purchases day book (as a negative amount)
c) Sales day book
d) Cash payments book
e) Cash payments book

5 The sales ledger holds records of the transactions with each individual credit customer showing the amount due from that customer. The purchases ledger holds records of the transactions with each individual credit supplier showing the amount owing to that supplier.

CHAPTER 2 Revision of double entry bookkeeping

1 a) Debit Debtors
Credit Sales

b) Debit Purchases
Credit Bank

c) Debit Fixed assets
Credit Bank

d) Debit Bank
Credit Debtors

e) Debit Wages
Credit Bank

f) Debit Drawings
Credit Bank

2

Bank account

Date	Details	£	Date	Details	£
1 Mar	Capital	14,000	3 Mar	Purchases	3,500
10 Mar	Sales	4,000	8 Mar	Delivery van	7,400
28 Mar	Sales	6,200	15 Mar	Purchases	15,100
31 Mar	Balance c/d	2,000	20 Mar	Telephone	200
		26,200			26,200
			1 Apr	Balance b/d	2,000

3

Bank account

Date	Details	£	Date	Details	£
1 Mar	Capita	20,000	1 Mar	Fixed asset	3,200
10 Mar	Sales	1,800	4 Mar	Purchases	4,400
24 Mar	Debtors	3,500	6Mar	Rent	600
			28 Mar	Drawings	200
			30 Mar	Creditors	1,800
			31 Mar	Wages	900
			31 Mar	balance c/d	13,400
		25,300			25,300
1 Apr	Balance b/d	13,400			

Debtors account

Date	Details	£	Date	Details	£
			1 Mar	Bank	20,000

Fixed asset account – fixtures and fittings

Date	Details	£	Date	Details	£
1 Mar	Bank	3,200			

Purchases account

Date	Details	£	Date	Details	£
4 Mar	Bank	4,400			
20 Mar	Creditors	2,700	31 Mar	Balance c/d	7,100
		7,100			7,100
1 Apr	Balance b/d	7,100			

Rent account

Date	Details	£	Date	Details	£
6 Mar	Bank	600			

Sales account

Date	Details	£	Date	Details	£
			10 Mar	Bank	1,800
			15 Mar	Debtors	4,900
31 Mar	Balance c/d	8,300	29 Mar	Debtors	1,600
		8,300			8,300
			1 Apr	Balance b/d	8,300

Debtors account

Date	Details	£	Date	Details	£
15 Mar	Sales	4,900	24 Mar	Bank	3,500
29 Mar	Sales	1,600	31 Mar	Balance c/d	3,000
		6,500			6,500
1 Apr	Balance b/d	3,000			

Creditors account

Date	Details	£	Date	Details	£
30 Mar	Bank	1,800	20Mar	Purchases	2,700
30 Mar	Bank	900	15 Mar	Debtors	4,900
		2,700			2,700
			1 Apr	Balance b/d	900

Bank account

Date	Details	£	Date	Details	£
28 Mar	Bank	1,000			

Drawings account

Date	Details	£	Date	Details	£
31 Mar	Bank	900			

Trial balance as at 31 March

	Debits £	*Credits* £
Bank	13,400	
Capital		20,000
Fixtures and fittings	3,200	
Purchases	7,100	
Rent	600	
Sales		8,300
Debtors	3,000	
Creditors		900
Drawings	1,000	
Wages	900	
	29,200	29,200

4 Main ledger

Creditors account

Date	Details	£	Date	Details	£
31 Mar	SDB	1,390	31 Mar	SRDB	60
			31 Mar	CRB	720
			31 Mar	CRB - discounts	10
			31 Mar	Balance c/d	600
		1,390			1,390
1 Apr	Balance b/d	600			

Sales account

Date	Details	£	Date	Details	£
			31 Mar	SDB	1,390
31 Mar	Balance c/d	3,060	31 Mar	CRB	1,670
		3,060			3,060
			1 Apr	Balance b/d	3,060

Sales returns account

Date	Details	£	Date	Details	£
31 Mar	SRBD	60			

Creditors account

Date	Details	£	Date	Details	£
31 Mar	PDB	1,400			
31 Mar	CPB	2,250	31 Mar	Balance c/d	3,650
		3,650			3,650
1 Apr	Balance b/d	3,650			

Purchase ledger control account

Date	Details	£	Date	Details	£
31 Mar	PRDB	80	31 Mar	PDB	1,400
31 Mar	CPB	870			
31 Mar	CPB - discounts	40			
31 Mar	Balance c/d	410			
		1,400			1,400
			1 Apr	Balance b/d	410

Purchases returns account

Date	Details	£	Date	Details	£
			31 Mar	PRDB	80

Capital account

Date	Details	£	Date	Details	£
			31 Mar	CRB	15,000

Discounts allowed account

Date	Details	£	Date	Details	£
31 Mar	CRB	10			

Wages account

Date	Details	£	Date	Details	£
31 Mar	CPB	2,200			

Fixed asset – shop fittings account

Date	Details	£	Date	Details	£
31 Mar	CPB	1,100			

Discounts received account

Date	Details	£	Date	Details	£
			31 Mar	CPB	40

Subsidiary ledger – sales ledger

J Simpson

Date	Details	£	Date	Details	£
4 Mar	SDB 0001	420	20 Mar	CRB	420

F Barnet

Date	Details	£	Date	Details	£
12 Mar	SDB 0002	350	19Mar	SRDB CN0001	40
			31 Mar	CRB	300
			31 Mar	CRB – discount	10
		350			350

H Jerry

Date	Details	£	Date	Details	£
18 Mar	SDB 0003	180	25 Mar	SRDB CN002	20
			31 Mar	Balance c/d	160
		180			180
1 Apr	Balance b/d	160			

D Dawson

Date	Details	£	Date	Details	£
28 Mar	SDB 0004	440			

Subsidiary ledger – purchases ledger

L LIlley

Date	Details	£	Date	Details	£
12 Mar	CPB 0003	560	1 Mar	PDB	590
12 Mar	CPD – discounts	30			
		590			590

Purchases account

Date	Details	£	Date	Details	£
10 Mar	PRDB C357	80	7 Mar	PDB	400
20 Mar	CPB	310			
20 Mar	CPB – discounts	10			
		400			400

Purchases account

Date	Details	£	Date	Details	£
			24 Mar	PDB	410

Bank

	£
Total cash receipts	17,390
Total cash payments	(6,420)
	10,970

Trial balance as at 31 March

	Debits £	*Credits* £
Bank (see working above)	10,970	
Sales ledger control	600	
Sales		3,060
Sales returns	60	
Purchases	3,650	
Purchases ledger control		410
Purchases returns		80
Capital		15,000
Discounts allowed	10	
Wages	2,200	
Shop fittings	1,100	
Discounts received		40
	18,590	18,590

5 **Bank reconciliation statement at 30 June**

	£
Balance per bank statement	67.82 o/d
Less: unpresented cheques	141.35
	209.17 o/d
Add: outstanding lodgements	393.67
Cash book balance	184.50

CHAPTER 3 Introduction to financial statements

1

	Debit £	*Credit* £	*Type of balance*	*P&L or balance sheet*
Sales		41,200	Income	P&L
Loan		1,500	Liability	Balance sheet
Wages	7,000		Expense	P&L
Fixed assets	7,100		Asset	Balance sheet
Opening stock	1,800		Expense	P&L
Debtors	3,400		Asset	Balance sheet
Discounts received		40	Income	P&L
Postage	100		Expense	P&L
Bank	300		Asset	Balance sheet
Capital		9,530	Liability	Balance sheet
Rent	500		Expense	P&L
Purchases	30,100		Expense	P&L
Creditors		2,500	Liability	Balance sheet
Discounts allowed	70		Expense	P&L
Drawings	3,000		Reduction of liability	Balance sheet
Electricity	800		Expense	P&L
Telephone	600		Expense	P&L
	54,770	54,770		

2 a) The gross profit of a business is the profit from the trading activities.
b) Carriage inwards is dealt with in the profit and loss account in the trading account.
c) The total of the current assets minus the current liabilities is known as net current assets.
d) Current liabilities are amounts that are payable within one year.
e) Long-term liabilities are amounts payable after more than one year.

3 a) accruals concept
b) historical cost concept, also going concern concept
c) materiality concept

4 The four objectives stated by FRS 18 that should be considered when selecting appropriate accounting policies are relevance, reliability, comparability and understandability.

Financial information is relevant if it has the ability to influence the economic decisions of users of that information and is provided in time to influence those decisions.

Reliable information is a wider concept. In order for information to be reliable it must represent the substance of the transaction or event, it must be free from bias and material error and if there is uncertainty about the information then a degree of caution or prudence must have been applied in making any judgements.

The information in financial statements should be comparable over time and as far as possible between different organisations. Therefore the accounting policies chosen should be applied consistently.

Finally accounting policies should be chosen to ensure ease of understanding by users of the final accounts. Users can be assumed to have a reasonable knowledge of business and economic activities and accounting and a willingness to study the information diligently.

CHAPTER 4 Value Added Tax

1

Sales ledger control account

	£		£
Sales (168,000 × 1.178)	197,400		

Sales account

	£		£
		Sales ledger control	168,000

VAT account

	£		£
Purchase ledger control	22,050	Sales ledger control	29,400

Purchase ledger control account

	£		£
		Purchases (126,000 × 1.178)	148,050

Purchase account

	£		£
Purchase ledger control	126,000		

2 Main ledger

Sales ledger control account

Date	Details	£	Date	Details	£
31 May	SDB	900.05	31 May	SRDB	37.60
			31 May	CRB	411.25

Sales account

Date	Details	£	Date	Details	£
			31 May	SDB	766.00
			31 May	CRB	592.00

Sales return account

Date	Details	£	Date	Details	£
31 May	SRBD	32.00			

VAT account

Date	Details	£	Date	Details	£
31 May	SRDB	5.60	31 May	SDB	134.05
31 May	PDB	120.05	31 May	CRB	103.60
31 May	CPB	71.75			

Purchase ledger control account

Date	Details	£	Date	Details	£
31 May	CPB	514.65	31 May	PDB	806.05

Purchase account

Date	Details	£	Date	Details	£
31 May	PDB	686.00			
31 May	CPD	410.00			

Subsidiary ledger – sales ledger

F Leonard

Date	Details	£	Date	Details	£
3 May	SDB	185.65	12 May	CRB	185.65

K Olsen

Date	Details	£	Date	Details	£
12 May	SDB	263.20	16 May	SRDB	37.60
			28 May	CRB	225.60

Claire & Sons

Date	Details	£	Date	Details	£
28 May	SDB	451.20			

Subsidiary ledger – purchases ledger

David & Co

Date	Details	£	Date	Details	£
15 May	CPB	178.60	2 May	PDB	178.60

Norman Bros

Date	Details	£	Date	Details	£
21 May	CPB	336.05	7 May	PDB	336.05

Field & Sons

Date	Details	£	Date	Details	£
			22 May	PDB	291.40

3 a) Input VAT is VAT on **purchases** and output VAT is VAT on **sales**.

b) If a business is not registered for VAT then the input VAT that it incurs must be **included in the costs** in the accounting records.

c) Postage costs are an example of **an exempt** supply for VAT purposes.

d) Irrecoverable VAT is **included in the cost of the items** in the accounting records.

CHAPTER 5 Capital expenditure

1 a) Capital expenditure – £15,700
Revenue expenditure – £100

b) Capital expenditure – £61,100

c) Capital expenditure – £68,600
Revenue expenditure – £800

2

Account	*Ref*	*Debit*	*Credit*
		£	£
Fixtures and fittings		4,200	
Bank			4,200
		4,200	4,200
Being purchase of desks and chairs for head office			
Computers		2,300	
Computer expenses		100	
Creditors			2,400
		2,400	2,400
Being purchase of computer and rewritable CDs			
Plant and machinery		10,600	
Purchases			200
Wages			800
Bank			9,600
		10,600	10,600
Being purchase and installation of machine			

3 On the date of payment of the deposit

4
- A description of the asset and possibly a fixed asset number
- Its physical location within the business
- The supplier and the date of purchase
- The cost of the asset
- The estimated life of the asset
- The estimated scrap value of the asset at the end of its life
- The method of depreciation to be applied
- The depreciation percentage
- The amount of depreciation charged each year
- The provision for depreciation at the end of each year
- The net book value of the asset at the end of each year
- Eventually the details of the disposal of the asset including any sale proceeds and the profit or loss on disposal

CHAPTER 6 Depreciation of fixed assets

1 The main purpose of depreciation is to ensure that the amount of the cost of the fixed assets that have been used up in the accounting period is charged to the profit and loss account as an expense. This accords with the accounting concept of accruals or matching which requires the expenses incurred in the earning of income to be matched with that income in the profit and loss account. The fixed assets have been used to earn the income and therefore a portion of the cost of the fixed assets must be charged as an expense in the form of depreciation.

2 Depreciation charge $= \dfrac{£11{,}500 - 2{,}500}{5 \text{ years}} = £1{,}800$ per annum

NBV at 31 December 2008 = £11,500 – (2 x £1,800) = £7,900

3

	£
Original cost	16,400
Depreciation to 31 Dec 2007 (16,400 x 35%)	5,740
NBV at 31 Dec 2007	10,660
Depreciation to 31 Dec 2008 (10,660 x 35%)	3,731
NBV at 31 Dec 2008	6,929

4 The reducing balance method of depreciation gives a higher amount of depreciation in the early years of an asset's life and lower amounts in the later years. Depreciation is a method of attempting to estimate the amount of the cost of the fixed asset that has been used or consumed during the year. If an asset is one that typically loses more value, ie. more cost is consumed, in the early years of its life, such as motor vehicles, then although a more complicated method of depreciation than the straight-line method it does give a fairer representation of the cost of the asset used in the period.

5 Depreciation charge = (£240,000 – £135,000) x 30%

= £31,500

6 Depreciation charge = £24,000 x 20% x 7/12

= £2,800

7 a)

Depreciation expense account

Date	Details	£	Date	Details	£
31 Dec 2006	Provision	18,000	31 Dec 2006	P&L a/c	18,000
31 Dec 2007	Provision	18,000	31 Dec 2007	P&L a/c	18,000
31 Dec 2008	Provision	18,000	31 Dec 2008	P&L a/c	18,000

Provision for depreciation account

Date	Details	£	Date	Details	£
31 Dec 2006	Balance c/d	18,000	31 Dec 2006	Expense	18,000
				Balance b/d	18,000
31 Dec 2007	Balance c/d	36,000	31 Dec 2007	Expense	18,000
		36,000			36,000
				Balance b/d	36,000
31 Dec 2008	Balance c/d	54,000	31 Dec 2008	Expense	18,000
		54,000			54,000
				Balance b/d	54,000

b) **Balance sheet extracts:**

Fixed assets:

	Cost	*Accumulated depreciation*	*NBV*
	£	£	£
31 Dec 2006	120,000	18,000	102,000
31 Dec 2007	120,000	36,000	84,000
31 Dec 2008	120,000	54,000	66,000

CHAPTER 7 Disposal of fixed assets

1 a)

	£
Original cost	2,200
2005 depreciation 2,200 x 40%	880
2005 NBV	1,320
2006 depreciation 1,320 x 40%	528
2006 NBV	792
2007 depreciation 792 x 40%	317
2007 NBV	475
Disposal proceeds	200
Loss on disposal	275

b)

Computer at cost

Date	Details	£	Date	Details	£
1 April 2005	Bank	2,200	14 May 2008	Disposal	2,200

Computer depreciation expense account

Date	Details	£	Date	Details	£
31 Dec 2005	Provision	880	31 Dec 2005	P&L a/c	880
31 Dec 2006	Provision	528	31 Dec 2006	P&L a/c	528
31 Dec 2007	Provision	317	31 Dec 2007	P&L a/c	317

Computer provision for depreciation account

Date	Details	£	Date	Details	£
31 Dec 2005	Balance c/d	880	31 Dec 2005	Expense	880
			1 Jan 2006	Balance b/d	880
31 Dec 2006	Balance c/d	1,408	31 Dec 2006	Expense	528
		1,408			1,408
			1 Jan 2007	Balance b/d	1,408
31 Dec 2007	Balance c/d	1,725	31 Dec 2007	Expense	317
		1,725			1,725
14 May 2008	Disposal	1,725	1 Jan 2008	Balance b/d	1,725

Disposal account

Date	Details	£	Date	Details	£
14 May 2008	Cost	2,200	14 May 2008	Depreciation	1,725
			14 May 2008	Proceeds	200
			14 May 2008	P&L a/c – loss	275
		2,220			2,200

2 a)

	£
Original cost	7,200
2006 depreciation 7,200 x 25% x 2/12	(300)
2007 depreciation 7,200 x 25%	(1,800)
2008 depreciation 7,200 x 25% x 8/12	(1,200)
Net book value 31 July 2008	3,900
Proceeds	3,800
Loss on disposal	100

b)

Machine at cost account

Date	Details	£	Date	Details	£
1 Oct 2006	Bank	7,200	31 July 2008	Disposal	7,200

Machine – depreciation expense account

Date	Details	£	Date	Details	£
30 Nov 2006	Provision	300	30 Nov 2006	P&L a/c	300
30 Nov 2007	Provision	1,800	30 Nov 2007	P&L a/c	1,800
31 July 2008	Provision	1,200	30 Nov 2008	P&L a/c	1,200

Machine – provision for depreciation account

Date	Details	£	Date	Details	£
30 Nov 2006	Balance c/d	300	30 Nov 2006	Expense	300
			1 Dec 2006	Balance b/d	300
30 Nov 2007	Balance c/d	2,100			
		2,100			
			1 Dec 2007	Balance b/d	2,100
30 July 2008	Disposal	3,300	31 July 2008	Expense	1,200
		1,200			1,200

Machine – disposal account

Date	Details	£	Date	Details	£
31 July 2008	Cost	7,200	31 July 2008	Depreciation	3,300
			31 July 2008	Proceeds	3,800
			31 July 2008	P&L a/c – loss	100
		2,220			7,200

3 a) A loss on disposal can also be described as under depreciation.

b) A profit on disposal can also be described as over depreciation.

4

Van at cost account

Date	Details	£	Date	Details	£
1 July 2005	Bank	13,600	30 Apr 2008	Disposal	13,600
30 Apr 2008	Bank	12,200			
30 Apr 2008	Disposal				
	(16,700 12,200)	4,500	30 Apr 2008	Balance c/d	16,700
		30,300			30,300

Van – provision for depreciation account

Date	Details	£	Date	Details	£
30 Apr 2008	Disposal	9,000	30 Apr 2008	Balance b/d	9,000

Disposal account

Date	Details	£	Date	Details	£
30 Apr 2008	Cost	13,600	30 Apr 2008	Depreciation	9,000
			30 Apr 2008	Cost	4,500
			30 Apr 2008	P&L a/c – loss	100
		13,600			13,600

5

Fixed asset number	10435									
Description	Computer 1036525									
Location	Sales department									
Supplier	Timing Computers Ltd									
Date	*Cost* £	*Expected life (years)*	*Estimated scrap value* £	*Depreciation method*	*Depreciation rate*	*Depreciation charge for the year* £	*Provision at end of year* £	*Net book value at end of year* £	*Disposal proceeds* £	*Profit or loss on disposal* £
2006										
1 Mar	4,800	4	600	Reducing balance	40%					
31 Jul						1,920	1,920	2,880		
2007										
31 Jul						1,152	3,072	1,728		
2008										
27 Jun									700	(1,028)

CHAPTER 8 Accruals and prepayments

1 a) Rent paid in advance for the following accounting period would appear as **a prepayment** in the balance sheet.

b) Motor expenses owing to the local garage would appear as **an accrual** in the balance sheet.

2 a) In the profit and loss account the expense would appear as £870 and there would be an accrual in the balance sheet for £200.

b) The rental income in the profit and loss account would be reduced to £340 and the balance sheet would show a creditor, rental income received in advance of £40.

c) The insurance expense would appear as £1,100 in the profit and loss account and there would be a prepayment shown in the balance sheet of £300.

d) In the profit and loss account commissions income would be £200 and the balance sheet would show a debtor, commissions receivable, of £20.

3

Motor expenses account

Date	Details	£	Date	Details	£
30 June	Balance b/d	845	30 June	Prepayments	
				(150 × 6/12)	75
			30 June	Profit and loss	770
		845			845

Prepayments account

Date	Details	£	Date	Details	£
30 June	Motor expenses	75			

4 a)

Electricity account

Date	Details	£	Date	Details	£
31 Mar	Balance b/d	470	31 Mar	Profit and loss a/c	650
31 Mar	Accruals c/d	180			
		650			650
			14 Apr	Accrual b/d	180

b)

Electricity account

Date	Details	£	Date	Details	£
25 Apr	Bank	180	1 Apr	Accrual b/d	180

CHAPTER 9 Bad and doubtful debts

1 Main ledger

Sales ledger control account

	£		£
Balance b/d	25,673	Bad debts expense (157 + 2880	445
		Balance c/d	25,228
	25,673		25,673
Balance b/d	25,228		

Bad debts expense account

	£		£
Sales ledger control	445	Profit and loss account	445

Sales ledger

H Taylor

	£		£
Balance b/d	157	Bad debts expense	157

C Phelps

	£		£
Balance b/d	288	Bad debts expense	288

2

Bank account

	£		£
Sales ledger control	250		

Sales ledger control account

	£		£
Bad debts expense	250	Bank account	250

Bad debts expense account

	£		£
		Sales ledger control	250

3 a)

	£
Total debtors	11,650
Bad debt	(350)
	11,300
Specific provision	(200)
Remaining debtors	11,100
General provision 2% x 11,100	222
Specific provision	200
Total provision for doubtful debts	422

b)

Bad debts expense account

	£		£
Debtors	350		
Provision for doubtful debts	422	Profit and loss account	772
	772		772

Debtors account

	£		£
Balance b/d	11,650	Bad debts expense	350
		Balance c/d	11,300
	11,650		11,650
Balance b/d	11,300		

Provision for doubtful debts account

	£		£
		Bad debts expense	422

4

Purchases account

		£			£
2007			2007		
31 Dec	Debtors	370			
31 Dec	Provision for doubtful debts	228	31 Dec	Profit and loss a/c	598
		598	28 Feb	Balance c/d	598
2008			2008		
31 Dec	Debtors	400	31 Dec	Provision for doubtful debts	168
			31 Dec	Profit and loss a/c	232
		400			400

Provision for doubtful debts account

		£			£
2007			2007		
			1 Jan	Balance b/d	1,460
31 Dec	Balance c/d	1,688	31 Dec	Bad debts expense	228
		1,688			1,688
2008			2008		
31 Dec	Bad debts expense	168	1 Jan	Balance b/d	1,688
31 Dec	Balance c/d	1,520			
		1,688			1,688
			2009		
			1 Jan	Balance b/d	1,520

CHAPTER 10 Control account reconciliations

1 Main ledger

Sales ledger control account

	£		£
Opening balance	1,216.26	CRB	1,078.97
SDB	1,602.32	CRB – discounts	8.73
		Balance c/d	1,730.88
	2,818.58		2,818.58
Balance b/d	1,730.88		

Subsidiary ledger

Virgo Partners

	£		£
Opening balance	227.58	CRB	117.38
SDB	94.70		
SDB	210.00	Balance c/d	414.90
	532.28		532.28
Balance b/d	414.90		

McGowan & Sons

	£		£
Opening balance	552.73	CRB	552.73
SDB	582.69	Balance c/d	582.69
	1,135.42		1,135.42
Balance b/d	582.69		

JJ Westrope

	£		£
Opening balance	317.59	CRB	308.86
SDB	163.90	CRB – discount	435.47
SDB	271.57	Balance c/d	435.47
	753.06		753.06
Balance b/d	435.47		

Jacks Ltd

	£		£
Opening balance	118.36	CRB	100.00
SDB	105.47		
SDB	173.99	Balance c/d	297.82
	397.82		397.82
Balance b/d	297.82		

Reconciliation of month-end balances

	£
Virgo Partners	414.90
McGowan & Sons	582.69
J J Westrope	435.47
Jacks Ltd	297.82
Sales ledger control account balance	1,730.88

2 Main ledger

Purchases ledger control account

	£		£
CPB	959.39	Opening balance	839.46
CPB – discounts	30.07	PDB	1,573.72
Balance c/d	1,423.72		
	2,413.18		2,413.18
		Balance b/d	1,423.72

Subsidiary ledger

Jenkins Supplies

	£		£
CPB	423.89	CRB	441.56
CPB – discount	17.67	PDB	215.47
Balance c/d	657.37	PDB	441.90
	1,098.93		1,098.93

Kilnfarm Paper

	£		£
CPB	150.00	Opening balance	150.00
CPB – discount	150.00	PDB	150.00
Balance c/d	150.00	PDB	150.00
	450.00		450.00
		Balance b/d	150.00

Barnfield Ltd

	£		£
CPB	235.50	Opening balance	247.90
CPB – discount	12.40	PDB	310.58
Balance c/d	616.35	PDB	305.77
	864.25		864.25
		Balance b/d	616.35

Reconciliation of month-end balances

	£
Jenkins Supplies	657.37
Kilnfarm Paper	150.00
Barnfield Ltd	616.35
Purchases ledger control account balance	1,423.72

3

Sales ledger control account

	£		£
Opening balance	16,339	Sales returns	3,446
Credit sales	50,923	Cash received	47,612
Returned cheque	366	Settlement discounts	1,658
		Bad debt written off	500
		Balance c/d	14,415
	67,631		67,631

4

Purchases ledger control account

	£		£
Purchases returns	2,568	Opening balance	12,587
Cheques paid	38,227	Credit purchases	40,827
Settlement discounts	998		
	11,621		
	53,414		53,414

5

Sales ledger control account

	£		£
Original balance	41,774	Sales returns	450
SDB undercast	100	Bad debt written off	210
		Balance c/d	41,214
	41,874		41,874
Balance b/d	41,214		

	£
Original total of list of balances	41,586
Less: invoice misposted (769 – 679)	(90)
Less: discount (2 x 16)	(32)
Less: credit balance included as a debit balance (2 x 125)	(250)
Amended control account balance	41,214

6

Purchases ledger control account

	£		£
Settlement	267	Original balance	38,694
		Purchases returns – overcast	300
Balance c/d	38,997	CPB error – (3,415 – 3,145)	270
	39,264		39,264
		Balance b/d	38,997

	£
Original total of list of balances	39,741
Less: settlement discount omitted	(267)
Less: credit note adjustment (210 – 120)	(90)
Less: debit balance omitted	(187)
Less: credit balance misstated	(200)
Amended control account balance	38,997

CHAPTER 11 Errors and the suspense account

1
- The discounts received have been entered on the wrong side of the account
- The closing balance has been incorrectly calculated

2 Transposition error

3 This is not correct.
Error of reversal – the debit and credit entries have been reversed

4 Error of commission

5 a) The difference between the two figures is exactly divisible by 9 therefore the error may be a transposition error in one of the balances in the trial balance

b) £270 debit balance

6

Suspense account

	£		£
Balance	290	Sales returns	170
Rental income	180	Balance c/d	300
	470		470

7 a) Debit Electricity account £400
Credit Suspense account £400

b) Debit Sales account in the TB £1,000
Credit Suspense account £1,000

c) Debit Suspense account £280
Credit Commission income account £280

d) Debit Cleaning costs account £100
Credit Wages account £100

e) Debit Discount allowed in the TB £680
Credit Suspense account £680

Suspense account

	£		£
Balance	1,800	Electricity	400
Commission incomes		Sales	1,000
		Discount allowed	680
	2,080		2,080

CHAPTER 12 Stock

1 a) Cost = £25.80 + 1.00 = £26.80
NRV = £28.00 – 1.10 = £26.90

b) 120 x £26.80 = £3,216.00

2

Stock line	*Cost*	*NRV*	*Value*	*Units*	*Total*
	£	£	£		£
A	12.90	20.00	12.90	80	1,032.00
B	14.60	14.20	14.20	65	923.00
C	19.80	29.30	19.80	90	1,782.00
D	17.50	17.20	17.20	30	516.00
					4,253.00

3 a) **FIFO**

9 Apr Sale	50 units @ 5.20			
15 Apr Sale	50 units –	30 units @ 5.20		
		20 units @ 5.50		
17 Apr Sale	60 units @ 5.50			
28 Apr Sale	70 units –	20 units @ 5.50		
		50 units @ 5.80		
Closing stock		50 units @ 5.80	=	£290

b) **LIFO**

9 Apr Sale	50 units @ 5.20			
15 Apr Sale	50 units @ 5.50			
17 Apr Sale	60 units –	50 units @ 5.50		
		10 units @ 5.20		
28 Apr Sale	70 units @ 5.80			
Closing stock	50 units –	20 units @ 5.20	=	£104
		30 units @ 5.80	=	£174
				£278

c) **AVCO**

		Unit cost	Units	Total
				£
3 Apr	Purchase	5.20	80	416.00
9 Apr	Sale	5.20	(50)	(260.00)
		5.20	30	156.00
10 Apr	Purchase	5.50	100	550.00
		5.43	130	706.00
15 Apr	Sale	5.43	(50)	(271.50)
17 Apr	Sale	5.43	(60)	(325.80)
		5.43	20	108.70
20 Apr	Purchase	5.80	100	580.00
		5.74	120	688.70
28 Apr	Sale	5.74	(70)	(401.80)
Closing stock		5.74	50	286.90

CHAPTER 13 From trial balance to final accounts – sole trader

1

	£
Opening capital	34,560
Net profit	48,752
	83,312
Less: drawings	(49,860)
Closing capital	33,452

2

	£	£
Debit Drawings	1,500	
Credit Purchases		1,500
OR		
Debit Drawings	2,100	
Credit Sales		2,100

3

Telephone	= £3,400 + 300	=	£3,700
Insurance	= £1,600 – 200	=	£1,400

4 Depreciation charge:

Fixtures and fittings	(12,600 x 20%)	=	£2,520
Motor vehicles	(38,500 – 15,500) x 30%	=	£6,900

Accumulated depreciation:

Fixtures and fittings	3,400 + 2,520	=	£5,920
Motor vehicles	15,500 + 6,900	=	£22,400

Fixed assets	*Cost*	*Accumulated depreciation*	*Net book value*
	£	£	£
Fixtures and fittings	12,600	5,920	6,680
Motor vehicles	38,500	22,400	16,100
			22,780

5 a) **Initial trial balance**

	Debit	*Credit*
	£	£
Sales		308,000
Machinery at cost	67,400	
Office equipment at cost	5,600	
Carriage inwards	2,300	
Carriage outwards	4,100	
Sales ledger control	38,400	
Telephone	1,800	
Purchases ledger control		32,100
Heat and light	3,100	
Bank overdraft		3,600
Purchases	196,000	
Petty cash	100	
Insurance	4,200	
Provision for depreciation – machinery		31,200
Provision for depreciation – office equipment		3,300
Stock at 1 July 2006	16,500	
Loan		10,000
Miscellaneous expenses	2,200	
Wages	86,700	
Loan interest	600	
Capital		60,000
Drawings	20,000	
Provision for doubtful debts		1,000
Suspense	200	
	449,200	449,200

b) **Journal entries**

		Debit	Credit
		£	£
i)	Heat and light	200	
	Suspense		200
ii)	Stock – balance sheet	18,000	
	Stock – profit and loss		18,000
iii)	Depreciation expense – machinery		
	((67,400 – 31,200) x 30%)	10,860	
	Provision for depreciation – machinery		10,860
	Depreciation expense – office equipment		
	(5,600 x 20%)	1,120	
	Provision for depreciation – office equipment		1,120
iv)	Loan interest	200	
	Telephone	400	
	Accruals		600
v)	Prepayments (800 x 3/12)	200	
	Insurance		200
vi)	Bad debts expense	1,200	
	Sales ledger control		1,200
	Bad debts expense		
	((38,400 – 1,200) x 3%) – 1,000)	116	
	Provision for doubtful debts		116

Ledger accounts

c) i)

Heat and light

		£			£
30 June	Balance b/d	3,100			
30 June	Journal	200	30 June	Balance c/d	3,300
		3,300			3,300
30 June	Balance b/d	3,300			

Suspense account

		£			£
30 June	Balance b/d	200	30 June	Journal	200

ii)

Stock – balance sheet

		£			£
30 June	Journal	18,000			

Stock – profit and loss account

		£			£
			30 June	Journal	18,000

iii)

Depreciation expense – machinery

		£			£
30 June	Journal	10,860			

Provision for depreciation – machinery

		£			£
			30 June	Balance b/d	31,200
30 June	Balance c/d	42,060	30 June	Journal	10,860
		42,060			42,060
			30 June	Balance b/d	42,060

Depreciation expense – office equipment

		£			£
30 June	Journal	1,120			

Provision for depreciation – office equipment

		£			£
			30 June	Balance b/d	3,300
30 June	Balance c/d	4,420	30 June	Journal	1,120
		4,420			4,200
			30 June	Balance b/d	4,420

iv)

Loan interest

		£			£
30 June	Balance b/d	600			
30 June	Journal	200	30 June	Balance c/d	800
		800			2,200
30 June	Balance b/d	800			

Telephone

		£			£
30 June	Balance b/d	1,800			
30 June	Journal	400	30 June	Balance c/d	2,200
		2,200			2,200
30 June	Balance b/d	2,200			

Accruals

		£			£
			30 June	Journal	600

v)

Prepayments

		£			£
30 June	Balance b/d	200			

Insurance

		£			£
30 June	Balance b/d	4,200	30 June	Journal	200
			30 June	Balance c/d	4,000
		4,200			4,200
30 June	Balance b/d	4,000			

vi)

Bad debts expense

		£			£
30 June	Journal	1,200			
30 June	Journal	116	30 June	Balance c/d	1,316
		1,316			1,316
30 June	Balance b/d	1,316			

Sales ledger control

		£			£
30 June	Balance c/d	38,400	30 June	Journal	1,200
			30 June	Balance c/d	37,200
		38,400			38,400
30 June	Balance b/d	37,200			

Provision for doubtful debts

		£			£
			30 June	balance b/d	1,000
30 June	balance c/d	1,116	30 June	Balance c/d	116
		1,116			1,116
			30 June	Balance b/d	1,116

d) **Profit and loss account for the year ending 30 June 2008**

	£	£
Sales		308,000
Cost of sales		
Opening stock	16,500	
Purchases	196,000	
Carriage inwards	2,300	
	214,800	
Less: closing stock	18,000	
		196,800
Gross profit		111,200
Less: expenses		
Carriage outwards	4,100	
Tele phone	2,200	
Heat and light	3,300	
Insurance	4,000	
Miscellaneous expenses	2,200	
Wages	86,700	
Loan interest	800	
Depreciation – machinery	10,860	
Depreciation – office equipment	1,120	
Bad debts	1,316	
		116,596
Net loss		(5,396)

Balance sheet as at 30 June 2008

	Cost	Provision for depreciation	Net book value
	£	£	£
Fixed assets			
Machinery	67,400	42,060	25,340
Office equipment	5,600	4,420	1,180
	73,000	46,480	26,520
Current assets			
Stock		18,000	
Debtors	37,200		
Less: provision	(1,116)		
		36,084	
Prepayments		200	
Petty cash		100	
		54,384	
Current liabilities			
Creditors	32,100		
Bank overdraft	3,600		
Accruals	600		
		36,300	
Net current assets			18,084
			44,604
Long term loan			(10,000)
			34,604
Capital			60,000
Net loss			(5,396)
			54,604
Less: drawings			20,000
			34,604

CHAPTER 14 The extended trial balance

1 Find the difference and set up a suspense account to record this difference.

2 Both a debit and a credit entry for the value of the closing stock.

3 Profit and loss columns: Debit with opening stock
Credit with closing stock

Balance sheet columns: Debit with closing stock

4 a) **Extended trial balance**

Account name	Ledger balance DR £	Ledger balance CR £	Adjustments DR £	Adjustments CR £	Profit and loss a/c DR £	Profit and loss a/c CR £	Balance sheet DR £	Balance sheet CR £
Drawings	15,480						15,480	
Sales		94,300		180		94,480		
Stock at 1 May 2008	1,600		2,000	2,000	1,600	2,000	2,000	
Purchases	56,500			100	56,160			
				240				
Electricity	700		70		770			
Capital		15,600						15,600
Motor vehicle at cost	12,400						12,400	
Office equipment at cost	5,000						5,000	
Provision for depreciation at 1 May 2008								
– motor vehicle		3,720		2,604				6,324
– office equipment		1,250		1,250				2,500
Motor expenses	2,100				2,100			
Bank	1,950						1,950	
Wages	10,400		240		10,640			
Creditors		5,300						5,300
Telephone	1,100		200		1,300			
VAT		1,100						1,100
Debtors	9,950			450			9,500	
Provision for doubtful debts at 1 May 2008		100		90				190

Account name	Ledger balance		Adjustments		Profit and loss a/c		Balance sheet	
	DR	CR	DR	CR	DR	CR	DR	CR
	£	£	£	£	£	£	£	£
Rent	1,200			140	1,060			
Insurance	1,400				1,400			
Administration expenses	1,800				1,800			
Suspense account		210	100	70				
			180					
Depreciation expense:								
– motor vehicle			2,604		2,604			
– office equipment			1,250		1,250			
Accrual				200				200
Prepayment			140				140	
Bad debts expense			450					
			90		540			
Profit and loss account					15,256			15,256
	121,580	121,580	7,324	7,324	96,480	96,480	46,470	46,470

b) **Profit and loss account for the year ending 30 April 2009**

	£	£
Sales		94,480
Cost of sales		
Opening stock	1,600	
Purchases	56,160	
	57,760	
Less: closing stock	(2,000)	
		55,760
Gross profit		38,720
Less: expenses		
Electricity	770	
Motor expenses	2,100	
Wages	10,640	
Telephone	1,300	
Rent	1,060	
Insurance	1,400	
Administration expenses	1,800	
Depreciation		
– motor vehicles	2,604	
– office equipment	1,250	
Bad debts	540	
		23,464
Net profit		15,256

Balance sheet as at 30 April 2009

	Cost	*Provision for depreciation*	*Net book value*
	£	£	£
Fixed assets			
Motor vehicles	12,400	6,324	6,076
Office equipment	5,000	2,500	2,500
	17,400	8,824	8,576
Current assets			
Stock		2,000	
Debtors	9,500		
Less: provision	(190)		
		9,310	
Prepayments		140	
Bank		1,950	
		13,400	
Current liabilities			
Creditors	5,300		
VAT	1,100		
Accruals	200		
		(6,600)	
Net current assets			6,800
			15,376
Capital at 1 May 2008			15,600
Net profit for the year			15,256
			30,856
Less: drawings			15,480
			15,376

Workings for adjustments

i) **Errors:**

Purchases account is overcast by £100 therefore the purchases account must be credited and suspense account debited.

Debit Suspense £100
Credit Purchases
£100

Sales account has been credited with £180 too little therefore credit sales and debit the suspense account:

Debit Suspense £180
Credit Sales
£180

Wages account must be debited with £240 and purchases credited:

Debit	Wages	£240	
Credit	Purchases		£240

Electricity account must be debited with £70 and suspense account credited:

Debit	Electricity	£70	
Credit	Suspense		£70

ii) **Depreciation**:

Motor vehicles (£12,400 – 3,720) x 30% = £2,604

Debit	Depreciation expense – motor vehicles	£2,604	
Credit	Provision for depreciation – motor vehicles		£2,604

Office equipment £5,000 x 25% = £1,250

Debit	Depreciation expense – office equipment	£1,250	
Credit	Provision for depreciation – office equipment		£1,250

iii) **Accrual**:

Debit	Telephone	£200	
Credit	Accruals		£200

Prepayment:

Debit	Prepayment	£140	
Credit	Rent		£140

iv) **Bad debt**:

Debit	Bad debts expense	£450	
Credit	Debtors		£450

Provision for doubtful debts:

Provision required (£9,950 – 450) x 2% =	£190
Provision at the start of the year =	£100
Expense £90	

Debit	Bad debts expense	£90	
Credit	Provision for doubtful debts		£90

CHAPTER 15 Partnerships

1
- The amount of capital that each partner should introduce
- Whether interest on capital should be charged
- Whether partners should be paid any salaries
- Restrictions regarding drawings
- How the profit should be shared between the partners

2

Capital account – Fred

Date	Details	£	Date	Details	£
			1 May 2008	Bank	32,000

Capital account – George

Date	Details	£	Date	Details	£
			1 May 2008	Bank	27,000

Capital account – Fred

Date	Details	£	Date	Details	£
30 Apr 2009	Drawings	20,000	30 Apr 2009	Profit share	30,000
30 Apr 2009	Balance c/d	10,000			
		30,000			30,000
			1 May 2009	Balance b/d	10,000

Capital account – Geroge

Date	Details	£	Date	Details	£
30 Apr 2009	Drawings	16,000	30 Apr 2009	Profit share	20,000
30 Apr 2009	Balance c/d	4,000			
					20,000
			1 May 2009	Balance b/d	4,000

Balance sheet extract

	£	£
Capital accounts:		
Fred		32,000
George		27,000
		59,000
Current accounts:		
Fred	10,000	
George	4,000	
		14,000
		73,000

3 a)

Account name	Ledger balance DR £	Ledger balance CR £	Adjustments DR £	Adjustments CR £	Profit and loss a/c DR £	Profit and loss a/c CR £	Balance sheet DR £	Balance sheet CR £
Expenses	24,980			1,000	23,980			
Machinery at cost	100,000						100,000	
Motor vehicles at cost	60,000						60,000	
Sales		210,000				210,000		
Stock at 1 April 2008	10,200		12,000	12,000	10,200	12,000	12,000	
Bank	6,400						6,400	
Creditors		13,000						13,000
Drawings – Kristin	22,000						22,000	
– Gary	25,000						25,000	
VAT		2,400						2,400
Purchases	134,000				134,000			
Provision for depreciation:								
Machinery		30,000		15,000				45,000
Motor vehicles		30,600		8,820				39,420
Current accounts – Kristin		1,500						1,500
– Gary		2,680						2,680
Capital accounts – Kristin		60,000						60,000
– Gary		53,000						53,000
Debtors	20,600						20,600	
Prepayments			1,000				1,000	
Machinery – depreciation			15,000		15,000			
Motor vehicles – depreciation			8,820		8,820			
Profit share – Kristin					15,000			15,000
Profit share – Gary					15,000			15,000
	403,180	403,180	36,820	36,820	222,000	222,000	247,000	247,000

b) **Profit and loss account for the year ending 31 March 2009**

	£	£
Sales		
210,000		
Less: cost of sales		
Opening stock	10,200	
Purchases	134,000	
	144,200	
Less: closing stock	(12,000)	
		132,200
Gross profit		77,800
Expenses	23,980	
Depreciation – machinery	15,000	
Depreciation – motor vehicles	8,820	
		47,800
Net profit		30,000

Balance sheet as at 31 March 2009

	Cost	Accumulated depreciation	Net book value
	£	£	£
Fixed assets			
Machinery	100,000	45,000	55,000
Motor vehicles	60,000	39,420	20,580
	160,000	84,420	75,580
Current assets			
Stock		12,000	
Debtors		20,600	
Prepayments		1,000	
Bank		6,400	
		40,000	
Current liabilities			
Creditors	13,000		
VAT	2,400		
		15,400	
Net current assets			24,600
			100,180

Balance sheet extract

Capital accounts	Kristin	60,000
	Gary	53,000
		113,000
Current accounts –		
Kristin (1,500 + 15,000 – 22,000)		(5,500)
Gary (2,680 + 15,000 – 25,000)		(7,320)
		100,180

4

Appropriation

	£		£
Salaries Jake	10,000	Net profit	66,400
Lyle	20,000		
Interest			
Jake (100,000 × 4%)	4,000		
Lyle (60,000 × 4%)	2,400		
Balance c/d	30,000		
	66,400		66,400
		Balance b/d	30,000
Profit share			
Jake (30,000 × 3/5)	18,000		
Lyle (30,000 × 2/5)	12,000		
	30,000		30,000

Current account – Jake

	£		£
Drawings	31,000	Balance b/d	5,000
		Salary	10,000
		Interest	4,000
Balance c/d	6,000	Profit share	18,000
	37,700		37,000
		Balance b/d	6,000

Current account – Lyle

	£		£
Drawings	34,000	Balance b/d	8,000
		Salary	20,000
		Interest	2,400
Balance c/d	8,400	Profit share	12,000
	42,400		42,400
		Balance b/d	8,400

Balance sheet extract

		£	£
Capital accounts	Jake		100,000
	Lyle		60,000
			160,000
Current accounts	Jake	6,000	
	Lyle	8,400	
			14,400
			174,400

5 a) **Trial balance as at 30 June 2008**

		£	£
Stock at 1 July 2007		45,000	
Debtors		54,000	
Sales			465,000
Fixed assets at cost		80,000	
Provision for depreciation at 1 July 2007			42,000
Provision for doubtful debts at 1 July 2007			1,500
Expenses		68,000	
Drawings	Anna	38,000	
	Bill	15,000	
	Cheryl	18,000	
Creditors			40,000
Bank		2,000	
Current accounts at 1 July 2007	Anna		2,500
	Bill		5,000
	Cheryl		3,000
Purchases		302,000	
Capital accounts	Anna		30,000
	Bill		23,000
	Cheryl		10,000
		622,000	622,000

b) **Journal entries**

		Debit	Credit
		£	£
i)	Stock – balance sheet	50,000	
	Stock – profit and loss account		50,000
ii)	Depreciation expense (£80,000 x 20%)	16,000	
	Provision for depreciation		16,000
iii)	Bad debts expense	4,000	
	Debtors		4,000
	Provision for doubtful debts	500	
	Bad debts expense		500
	(2% x £50,000 = £1,000 less existing provision of £1,500 = £500 decrease)		
iv)	Expenses	5,000	
	Accruals		5,000

c) **Ledger accounts**

Stock – balance sheet

	£		£
Journal	50,000		

Stock – profit and loss account

	£		£
		Journal	50,000

Depreciation expense

	£		£
Journal	16,000		

Provision for depreciation

	£		£
		Per trial balance	42,000
Balance c/d	58,000	Journal	16,000
	58,000		58,000
		Balance b/d	58,000

Bad debts expense

	£		£
Journal	4,000	Journal	500
		Balance c/d	3,500
	4,000		4,000
Balance b/d	3,500		

Debtors

	£		£
Per trial balance	54,000	Journal	4,000
		Balance c/d	50,000
	54,000		54,000
Balance b/d	50,000		

Provision for doubtful debts

	£		£
Journal	500	Per trial balance	1,500
Balance c/d	1,000		
	1,500		1,500
		Balance b/d	1,000

Expenses

	£		£
Per trial balance	68,000		
	5,000	Balance c/d	73,000
	73,000		73,000
Balance b/d	73,000		

Accruals

	£		£
		Journal	5,000

d) **Profit and loss account for the year ending 30 June 2008**

		£	£
Sales			
465,000			
Less:	cost of sales		
	opening stock	45,000	
	purchases	302,000	
		347,000	
	Less: closing stock	(50,000)	
			297,000
Gross profit			168,000
Less:	expenses	73,000	
	depreciation	16,000	
	bad debts	3,500	
			92,500
Net profit			75,500

e) **Appropriation of profit**

			£	£
Net profit				75,500
Salaries	Bill		10,000	
	Cheryl		5,000	
			(15,000)	
Interest on capital	Anna	30,000 x 4%	1,200	
	Bill	23,000 x 4%	920	
	Cheryl	10,000 x 4%	400	
				(2,520)
				57,980
Profit share	Anna	57,980 x 2/4	28,990	
	Bill	57,980 x 1/4	14,495	
	Cheryl	57,980 x 1/4	14,495	
				57,980

Journal entries

		Debit £	*Credit* £
Profit and loss appropriation account		75,500	
Current account			
Anna (1,200 + 28,990)			30,190
Bill (10,000 + 920 + 14,495)			25,415
Cheryl (5,000 + 400 + 14,495)			19,895
Current account	Anna	38,000	
	Bill	15,000	
	Cheryl	18,000	
Drawings account	Anna		38,000
	Bill		15,000
	Cheryl		18,000

f) **Current accounts**

Current account – Anna

	£		£
Drawings	38,000	Opening balance	2,500
		Profit share	30,190
		Balance c/d	5,310
	38,000		38,000
Balance b/d	5,310		

Current account – Bill

	£		£
Drawings	15,000	Opening balance	5,000
Balance c/d	15,415	Profit share	25,415
	30,415		30,415
		Balance b/d	15,415

Current account – Cheryl

	£		£
Drawings	18,000	Opening balance	3,000
Balance c/d	4,895	Profit share	19,895
	22,895		22,895
		Balance b/d	4,895

g) **Balance sheet as at 30 June 2008**

		Cost	Accumulated depreciation	Net book value
		£	£	£
Fixed assets		80,000	58,000	22,000
Current assets				
Stock			50,000	
Debtors		50,000		
Less: provision		(1,000)		
			49,000	
Bank			2,000	
			101,000	
Current liabilities				
Creditors		40,000		
Accrual		5,000		
			(45,000)	
Net current assets				56,000
				78,000
Capital accounts	Anna			30,000
	Bill			23,000
	Cheryl			10,000
				63,000
Current accounts	Anna		(5,310)	
	Bill		15,415	
	Cheryl		4,895	
				15,000
				78,000

6

Capital accounts

	Kate	Hal	Mary		Kate	Hal	Mary
	£	£	£		£	£	£
				Bal b/d	48,000	38,000	27,000
				Current a/c	6,200		
Goodwill		13,500	13,500	Goodwill	9,000	9,000	9,000
Bank	15,000						
Loan	48,200						
Bal c/d		33,500	22,500				
	63,200	47,000	36,000		63,200	47,000	36,000

Current accounts

	Kate	Hal	Mary		Kate	Hal	Mary
	£	£	£		£	£	£
Bal b/d		800		Bal b/d	1,200		2,500
Drawings	20,000	23,500	24,400	Profit	25,000	25,000	25,000
Capital a/c	6,200						
Bal c/d		700	3,100				
	26,200	25,000	27,500		26,200	25,000	27,500

7

Current accounts

	Paul	Gill		Paul	Gill
	£	£		£	£
Drawings	26,400	18,700	Bal b/d	2,000	2,000
			Profit	20,250	13,500
			Salary		2,500
Bal c/d	1,683	2,217	Profit	5,833	2,917
	28,083	20,917		28,083	20,917

Appropriation of profit

	£
1 Oct to 30 June (£45,000 x 9/12)	33,750
Paul (£33,750 x 3/5)	20,250
Gill (£33,750 x 2/5)	13,500
	33,750
1 July to 30 Sept (£45,000 x 3/12)	11,250
Paul ((£11,250 – 2,500) x 2/3)	5,833
Gill salary	2,500
profit ((£11,250 – 2,500) x 1/3)	2,917
	11,250

OR

	1/10 – 30/6	1/7/ – 30/9	Total
	£	£	£
Profit for distribution	33,750	11,250	45,000
Paul: salary	(20,250)	(5,833)	(26,083)
Gill: profit share	(13,500)	(2,917)	(18,917)
	0	0	0

CHAPTER 16 Incomplete records

1

	£
Opening net assets	58,900
Closing net assets	71,400
Increase in net assets	12,500

Increase in net assets	=	capital introduced + profit – drawings
£12,500	=	£10,000 + 17,800 – drawings
Drawings	=	£15,300

2

Creditors account

	£		£
Payments	56,900	Opening balance	3,800
Discounts	1,300		
Closing balance	4,700	Purchases (bal fig)	59,100
	62,900		62,900

Purchases = £59,100

3

Bank account

	£		£
Opening balance	1,020	Purchases	24,600
Receipts	48,700	Expenses	12,500
		Drawings (bal fig)	11,730
		Closing balance	890
	49,720		49,720

Drawings = £11,730

4

	%	£
Sales	145	184,150
Cost of sales	100	127,000
Gross profit	45	57,150

Cost of sales = £127,000

5

	%	£
Sales	100	200,000
Cost of sales	65	130,000
Gross profit	35	70,000

Sales = £200,000

6

Debtors account

	£		£
Opening balance	10,400	Receipts	108,500

Creditors account

	£		£
Payments	74,400	Opening balance	6,200
Closing balance	8,300	Purchases (bal fig)	76,500
	82,700		82,700

Cost structure:

	%
Sales	140
Cost of sales	100
Gross profit	40

If purchases are £76,500 then the cost of sales is:

	£
Opening stock	7,600
Purchases	76,500
	84,100
Less: closing stock	(6,100)
	78,000

Using the cost structure the sales figure can be determined:

Cost structure:

	%	£
Sales	140	109,200
Cost of sales	100	78,000
Gross profit	40	31,200

The sales figure can then be entered into the debtors account and the closing balance found.

Debtors account

	£		£
Opening balance	10,400	Receipts	108,500
Sales	109,200	Closing balance	11,100
	119,600		119,600

The profit and loss account can now be prepared:

Profit and loss account for the year ended 31 March 2009

	£	£
Sales		109,200
Less: cost of sales		
Opening stock	7,600	
Purchases	76,500	
	84,100	
Less: closing stock	(6,100)	
		78,000
Gross profit		31,200
Less: expenses		
Expenses (12,600 – 800 + 600)	12,400	
Depreciation	1,600	
		14,000
Net profit		17,200

In order to draw up the balance sheet we need the opening capital and the drawings figures.

Net assets at 1 April 2008

	£
Bank	430
Stock	7,600
Debtors	10,400
Creditors	(6,200)
Accrual	(800)
Fixed assets	12,600
Opening capital	24,030

The drawings can be found as the balancing figure in the bank account:

Bank account

	£		£
Opening balance	430	Creditors	74,400
Receipts from debtors	108,500	Expenses	12,600
		Drawings (bal fig)	14,730
		Closing balance	7,200
	108,930		108,930

Balance sheet as at 31 March 2009

	£	£	£
Fixed assets (12,600 – 1,600)			11,000
Current assets:			
Stock		6,100	
Debtors		11,100	
Bank		7,200	
		24,400	
Current Liabilities:			
Creditors	8,300		
Accruals	600		
		(8,900)	
			15,500
			26,500
Opening capital			24,030
Add: profit for the year			17,200
			41,230
Less: drawings			(14,730)
			26,500

7 Cost structure:

	%	£
Sales	100	240,000
Cost of sales	70	168,000
Gross profit	30	72,000

	£	£
Sales		240,000
Less: cost of sales		
Opening stock	12,000	
Purchases	162,000	
	174,000	
Less: closing stock	?	
		168,000
Gross profit		72,000

Therefore the closing stock value must be £6,000.

INDEX